# POLITICAL PARTIES
# AND THE
# COLLAPSE OF THE
# OLD ORDERS

SUNY series in Political Party Development
Susan J. Tolchin, Editor

# POLITICAL PARTIES AND THE COLLAPSE OF THE OLD ORDERS

JOHN KENNETH WHITE

PHILIP JOHN DAVIES

State University
of New York
Press

Published by
State University of New York Press, Albany

© 1998  State University of New York

Production by Susan Geraghty
Marketing by Nancy Farrell

Printed in the United States of America

For information, address State University of New York
Press, State University Plaza, Albany, N.Y., 12246

**Library of Congress Cataloging-in-Publication Data**

Political parties and the collapse of the old orders / John Kenneth
    White, Philip John Davies, [editors].
        p.     cm. — (SUNY series in political party development)
    Includes bibliographical references and index.
    ISBN 0-7914-4067-2 (alk. paper). — ISBN 0-7914-4068-0 (pbk. :
alk. paper)
    1. Political parties. I. White, John Kenneth, 1952–      .
II. Davies, Philip, 1948–      . III. Series.
JF2051.P575 1998
324.2′09182′2—dc21                                            98-6506
                                                              CIP

10  9  8  7  6  5  4  3  2  1

# CONTENTS

# LIST OF
# TABLES AND FIGURES

## TABLES

## FIGURES

*For*

*Jeannette Brigitte Prevost White*
*Carolyn Wybray Maria Davies*
*Andrew Lucas Blaize Davies*

PREFACE

# Political Parties in an Era of Change

## John Kenneth White and Philip John Davies

A decade ago, toward the end of the 1980s, a group photograph of the leaders of the nations described in this book would feature Ronald Reagan, president of the United States; Margaret Thatcher, prime minister of Great Britain; François Mitterrand, president of France; Bettino Craxi, prime minister of Italy; Brian Mulroney, prime minister of Canada; Robert Hawke, prime minister of Australia; Miguel de la Madrid, president of Mexico; Yitzhak Shamir, prime minister of Israel; Helmut Kohl, chancellor of West Germany; P.W. Botha, president of South Africa; and Mikhail Gorbachev, president of the Soviet Union. A current photograph would show Bill Clinton representing the United States; Tony Blair, Great Britain; Jacques Chirac, France; Romano Prodi, Italy; Jean Chretien, Canada; John Howard, Australia; Ernesto Zedillo, Mexico; Benjamin Netanyahu, Israel; Nelson Mandela, South Africa; Boris Yeltsin, Russia; and Helmut Kohl, Germany. Only the bulky Kohl remains a fixed presence, even though he leads a recently unified Germany.

The new photograph signifies much more than the transfiguration of an old negative. In some cases, the actual names of the countries have changed—most notably the Union of Soviet Socialist Republics has become the Commonwealth of Independent States. Altering a country's formal name is something once thought reserved for the former colonial nations of Africa, as was recently the case when the name Zaire gave way to the Democratic Republic of the Congo, or when communists seized power and proclaimed the new nations to be instruments of democracy (as in the Democratic People's Republic of Korea—i.e., North Korea). A senior cartographer at the U.S. Central Intelligence Agency lamented the altered maps and names changes, saying: "Suddenly, everything we had produced was out of date—hundreds, thousands of maps, all out of date."[1]

In other cases, the leaders in the 1997 photograph hail from countries that have retained their formal names, but represent different political parties than their predecessors. Even so, the change has been dramatic. Some parties that held substantial legislative majorities in 1987 have seen their standing so severely decimated that they have been left to wander in obscurity. The most prominent examples of such political upheavals are in Canada where the Progressive Conservatives went into the 1993 elections with a 154-seat majority in the Canadian parliament and managed to hold onto just two seats afterward. A similar experience recently transpired in Great Britain where the Conservative Party yielded power to New Labour led by Tony Blair. The Conservative defeat was so large that the party was left with just 164 seats in Parliament to the Labor Party's 419 seats. The Labor majority actually *exceeds* the total number of Tory seats. Most stunningly, apartheid in South Africa was ended as whites ceded power in a new constitutional arrangement following the election of that country's first black president, Nelson Mandela, who had spent twenty-eight years in a South African prison.

In nearly every instance, the new leaders can attribute their positions to the end of the Cold War. Without the communist threat, it is unlikely that Bill Clinton would have seized power in the United States. Certainly, the collapse of communism made Boris Yeltsin the man of the hour in Russia. Some of the other nations covered in this book played important roles in the bitter struggle between East and West. Israel was an important beachhead for U.S. interests in the Middle East, as the Soviet Union struggled for a geographic foothold first in Egypt and then in other Mideast nations that remained obdurately opposed to the existence of the Jewish state. Keeping South Africa stable, given its vital natural resources and strategic location, was also deemed vital to American interests. Australia remained an important ally in the Pacific, and that country even sent troops in support of the failed U.S. effort during the Vietnam War. The United States also desired stability in neighboring Canada and Mexico and got it—not only there, but in Western Europe, where communists were kept from seizing power in France and Italy. Of course, keeping Germany from becoming a military threat remained an important objective for both superpowers.

Since the end of the Cold War, a "new world order," once proclaimed by President George Bush following the Persian Gulf War, has finally come to pass. While the shape and dimensions of that new world order have yet to coalesce, several features are evident. One is that postindustrialization continues apace on a global scale. Another involves the creation of the World Wide Web and the instant communication the Internet makes possible among individuals without regard for national boundaries or government intervention (such as opening the mails), thereby obviating the need for intermediaries. A third, and most disturbing, feature is an increase in ethnic, religious, and regional tensions as evidenced in the near breakup of Canada and the battle between the Russians and the dissatisfied citizens of Chechnya. President Clinton acknowledged that victory in the Cold War had brought its own set of new difficulties: "The disintegration of the former Soviet Union eliminated the preeminent threat but exposed many others: an increasingly tangled and dangerous web of international terrorism, crime, and drug trafficking; the aggression of rogue states and vicious ethnic and religious conflicts; the spread of dangerous weapons, including nuclear, biological, and chemical ones; and transnational threats like disease, overpopulation, and environmental degradation."[2]

While the defining characteristics of the post–Cold War era still remain clouded, political leaders are reeling from the collapse of the Berlin Wall in 1989 and the relegation of Soviet-style communism to the ash bin of history two years later. Shortly before his death in 1994, Richard Nixon wrote, "We live in a new world—a world we helped create."[3] But in this "new world" much that was once familiar has disappeared: the old arrangements; the old way of doing things; indeed, the old order itself has collapsed. In Moscow, for example, guardians of Lenin's tomb no longer rely on the Communist Party to pay the bills and have instead turned to a department store located across from Lenin's remains to defray the rent.[4] Meanwhile, in 1995 three hundred Russian troops marched on the plains of Kansas—not as invaders but in a joint training exercise with U.S. soldiers for a peacekeeping mission in strive-torn Bosnia. While the former enemies posed for souvenir snapshots in front of a nattily dressed Russian color guard, Colonel Gennadi M. Averyanov declared: "In the past, we could never imagine that we would one day conduct combined operations on American soil. Every day brings something new."[5]

The fact that nearly every day during the 1990s has brought forth not just something new, but something *extraordinary*, is the primary motivation behind this collection of essays. Specifically, we are interested in knowing more about the altered state of the political parties and their place in polities that are undergoing substantial change in the selected Western and non-Western nations covered in this volume. In each case, the contributors ask an important question: "What does change look like?" Inevitably, the answers vary. In some places, change resembles a shift in the conceptual structure of the Cold War–era parties that are changing in form, if not in name. France, Great Britain, and the United States are interesting examples where the major parties are altering their ideas and their plans for implementing them. In other cases, the collapse of the old institutional orders and their trappings is readily apparent. Russia, South Africa, and Canada fall into this category. Mexico is an instance where the once impregnable Partido Revolucionario Institucional (Institutional Revolutionary Party or PRI) seems on the verge of losing its grasp on the reigns of power. In nearly all of the countries examined, the electoral maps have been redrawn, party structures have been rebuilt, or the mechanisms of the state once controlled by the parties have been replaced. Thus, change continues to be the order of the day. It remains for us not only to pose the question, "What does change look like?" but to attempt to provide an answer.

## NOTES

1. Quoted in Thomas L. Friedman, "Cold War without End," *New York Times Magazine*, August 22, 1993, p. 30.

2. Bill Clinton, *Between Hope and History: Meeting America's Challenges for the 21st Century* (New York: Times Books, 1996), p. 143.

3. Richard Nixon, *Beyond Peace* (New York: Random House, 1994), p. 4.

4. See David Remnick, "America: Love It or Loathe It," *New York Times Magazine*, June 6, 1995.

5. Quoted in James Brooke, "Russians Have Landed in Kansas! But They've Come to Make Peace," *New York Times*, October 27, 1995, p. A-14.

# CHAPTER 1

# The American Experience: Public Skepticism, Economic Dislocation, and Partisan Decay

## John Kenneth White
## and Philip John Davies

Some years ago the novelist Henry James exclaimed, "It's a complex fate being an American."[1] Indeed, ever since its founding the American polity has had almost equal elements of faith and skepticism inbred in its citizens. Faith in the American experiment and the frequent affirmations of its successes are so prevalent that they have become part of the presidential job description. Ronald Reagan, for example, once told a captivated audience: "Think for a moment how special it is to be an American. Can we doubt that only a Divine Providence placed this land, this island of freedom, here as a refuge for all those people in the world who yearn to breathe free?"[2] An 1997, Bill Clinton echoed Reagan by recalling his country's historic commitments to freedom, individualism, and equality of opportunity, and challenged the Republican-controlled Congress to honor these goals: "America is far more than a place. It is an idea, the most powerful idea in the history of nations. And all of us in this chamber, we are now the bearers of that idea, leading a great people into a new world."[3] As political scientist Walter Dean Burnham once observed, the president has become a *"pontifex maximus*, a chief priest of the American civil religion."[4]

But it is not only presidents who act as a Romanesque pontifex maximus. School teachers ritually tell their pupils that they live in a political system inspired by Divine Providence. Their parents agree. A

1

1996 National Opinion Research Center (NORC) poll found large majorities wanting classroom history lessons to include the following themes:

- "With hard work and perseverance, anyone can succeed in America." (83 percent)
- "American democracy is only as strong as the virtue of its citizens." (83 percent)
- "America's contribution is one of expanding freedom for more and more people." (71 percent).
- "From its start, America had a destiny to set an example for other nations." (65 percent)
- "Our nation was founded on Biblical principles." (58 percent)
- "America has a special place in God's plan for history." (50 percent).[5]

These beliefs constitute what Seymour Martin Lipset aptly terms "American exceptionalism," and it sets the United States apart from most other nation states.[6] Lipset's observation that the United States is different has been echoed time and again by foreigners who visit its shores. In 1968, Sacvan Bercovitch, a Canadian national who arrived for an extended stay, was struck by the ideological rigidity he encountered from both ends of the political spectrum:

> My first encounter with American consensus was in the late sixties, when I crossed the border into the United States and found myself inside the myth of America. Not of North America, for the myth stopped short of the Canadian and Mexican borders, but of a country that despite its bewildering mix of race and creed, could believe in something called the True America, and could vest that patent fiction with all the moral and emotional appeal of a religious symbol. . . . Here was the Jewish anarchist Paul Goodman berating the Midwest for abandoning the promise; here, the descendant of American slaves, Martin Luther King, denouncing injustice as a violation of the American way; here, an endless debate about national destiny . . . conservatives scavenging for un-Americans, New Left historians recalling the country to its sacred mission.
>
> Nothing in my Canadian background had prepared me for that spectacle. . . . It gave me something of an anthropologist's sense of wonder at the symbol of the tribe. . . . To a Canadian skeptic, a gentile in God's county . . . [here was] a pluralistic, pragmatic people bound together by an ideological consensus.[7]

The ideological consensus Bercovitch alluded to remains so pervasive that it even influences how the natives speak to one another.

Expressions such as the "American dream" and "the American way of life" (along with the damning phrase "un-American") easily escape the lips, a reflection of the extraordinary self-confidence most Americans have in themselves and their country. According to survey data gathered by the Hudson Institute in 1994, the American dream still lives: 81 percent were "optimistic about [their] personal future"; 74 percent believed that "if you work hard you can be anything you want to be"; 72 percent thought that "we can always find a way to solve our problems and get what we want."[8]

But the same Americans who believe in themselves and want their children to affirm the values they have been taught also retain a healthy skepticism about the power of government. Seventy-four percent thought children should learn that the founders "limited the power of government, so government would not intrude too much into the lives of its citizens."[9] That lesson has always been a prominent chapter in the story of the American founding. But in recent years it has been rewritten to include a critique of government that is deeply cynical and has penetrated virtually all sectors of society. Americans continue to cling to the affirmative notion that their personal futures remain secure (an expression of a private "American dream"), but they have doubts about their government's ability to influence their lives positively. A 1995 survey conducted by Democrat Peter D. Hart, and Republican Robert M. Teeter found 56 percent saying that government does more to hinder the American dream than enhance it. Moreover, in such diverse areas as improving education, dealing with jobs and the economy, reducing crime, protecting the environment, enhancing minority opportunity, promoting culture, improving morals, and strengthening families, the majority wanted these tasks performed by businesses, individuals, or community leaders.[10] By Election Day, 1996, feelings had not changed despite the Clinton victory: 52 percent of voters leaving the polls thought the federal government "was doing too many things better left to businesses and individuals"; only 41 percent wanted a more activist government.[11]

Confidence in government began to slide in the 1960s and continued to do so into the 1970s. Polling by Daniel Yankelovich showed a decline in public trust in government from almost 80 percent in the late 1950s to about 33 percent by 1976.[12] Likewise, Warren E. Miller found that those who were antigovernment cynics nearly quintupled from 11 percent in 1958 to 52 percent twenty years later.[13] During the same period, public conviction that government was wasting money it collected in taxes had grown from 43 percent to 77 percent. Likewise, the proportion believing they could "not trust the government to do the right thing most of the time" rose from 23 percent to 67 percent.[14] In 1979, an alarmed Jimmy Carter proclaimed a "crisis of confidence":

We can see this crisis in the growing doubt about the meaning of our own lives and in the loss of a unity of purpose for our nation. The erosion of our confidence in the future is threatening to destroy the social and the political fabric of America. . . . Our people are losing . . . faith, not only in government itself, but in their ability as citizens to serve as the ultimate rulers and shapers of our democracy. . . . Restoring that faith and that confidence to America is now the most important task we face. It is a true challenge of this generation of Americans.[15]

This catastrophic shift of opinion happened rapidly and steadily—continuing almost unabated in the decades following the Kennedy assassination, Vietnam, Watergate, and the malaise of the Carter years. In 1973, 24 percent expressed "a great deal of confidence" in the Democratic-controlled Congress that was embarking on impeachment proceedings following the Watergate burglary. By 1997, only 11 percent had "a great deal of confidence" in the Republican-controlled Congress following its enactment of the Contract with America. Likewise, the numbers for the executive branch have not been especially impressive. In 1973, 29 percent had "a great deal of confidence" in Richard Nixon's executive branch; by 1997, the figure had fallen to just 12 percent support for Bill Clinton's administration.[16]

Other data also point to the growing doubts the public has in its elite institutions. In 1996, a Gallup survey found that respondents believed the "governing elite" to be "insensitive to the people's concerns" (64 percent), "unconcerned with the common good" (54 percent), and only concerned with the elite's own agenda (69 percent). These and a myriad of other polling data show that during the last quarter century there has been a steady, solid public negativism regarding government. One 1994 survey, for example, found an astounding 74 percent agreed with the statement, "Most public officials are not really interested in the problems of the average man."[17] In 1994, the *Times-Mirror* polling organization described the prominent features of what it called the "new American landscape": "Voters' frustration with the political system continues to grow, as does animosity toward the media. . . . This discontent with Washington that gained momentum in the late 1980s is even greater now than it was in 1992."[18] In effect, a generation of mistrust has been spawned.[19]

One reason for the discontent is the power of television, which has enhanced the citizen's immediacy in experiencing the world as it entices viewers to focus on the problems put before them. Vietnam, the first televised war, is illustrative of television's ability to bring a "virtual reality" into the nation's living rooms as it transforms viewers into cynics. The power of television is especially pronounced in the United States: 81 out of every 100 people own a television set; in the European Union, 44 per 100; Japan, 62 per 100.[20] The creation of the information super-highway on the World Wide Web has a similar potential to enhance the quality of information received and the skepticism that may flow from it.

For these and many other reasons, the electorate's sense of estrangement continues to find expression at the polls. In 1992, Ross Perot received an astounding 19 percent of the popular vote. In the twentieth century among third parties, only Theodore Roosevelt's 1912 showing as the Progressive Party candidate exceeded Perot's 1992 percentage. Perot's support was even more remarkable given that unlike ex-president Roosevelt (and most other important third-party candidates of the twentieth century) Perot never held public office. By 1996, Perot's support had been more than halved to 8 percent. Still, these totals are the best independent/minor party results achieved in two consecutive elections in U.S. history. The dissatisfaction that Perot and his people have with the two-party system is shared by an even larger number of Americans. In 1995, 60 percent told the Gallup Organization that they would like to see a third major party take root.[21] Dissatisfaction with the two parties and its nominees was also evident in the relatively low turnout for the 1996 presidential balloting: just 48.8 percent of those eligible voted.

## THE DECLINE OF THE AMERICAN MIDDLE CLASS

Much of the political cynicism can be attributed to the economic dislocations the middle class experienced following the end of the Cold War. At its zenith, median take-home pay grew at an annual rate of 2 percent in constant U.S. dollars.[22] But with the fall of the Soviet empire, "downsize" became a newly coined verb. Fifteen giant corporations, many once mainstays of the "military-industrial complex," downsized their workforces, resulting in layoffs ranging from 18,000 to 123,000 employees.[23] Clinton's first-term Labor Secretary Robert Reich worried about the impact these layoffs were having on the American psyche:

> All the old bargains, it seems, have been breached. The economic bargain was that if you worked hard and your company prospered, you would share the fruits of success. There was a cultural bargain, too, echoing the same themes of responsibility and its rewards: live by the norms of your community—take care of your family, obey the law, treat your neighbors with respect, love your country—and you'll feel secure in the certainty that everyone else would behave that way.[24]

But one by one the "old bargains" have been torn asunder. A study published by the Economic Policy Institute in 1996 noted that median family income had declined in real terms during the early 1990s.[25] Meanwhile, corporate executives prospered. A survey of seventy- six of the nation's largest corporations found that the total compensation package for chief executives in 1995 (including stock options) rose 31 percent to nearly $5 million, increasing the ratio between the typical worker and executive—once 30-to-1 in the 1960s—to more than 100-to-1, the largest gap in the industrialized world.[26] MIT economist Lester Thurow has observed that industrial giants were reluctant to approve such bonuses after World War II because they were "scared to hell" over communism: "If you had done this twenty-five years ago, the Communists would have been winning elections in France and Italy. The socialist parties would have been doing well in places like Germany and England. And in the United States, the Democrats would have been moving very quickly to the left." Now, says Thurow, "With socialism and communism gone—with the Democrats depending on the same financial sources as the Republicans for political funds—as a capitalist CEO, I don't have anything to worry about."[27]

Corporate downsizing and soaring executive salaries are just two indicators of the economic transformation Western democracies have undergone in the last quarter century. Heavy manufacturing industries have declined, while service and high technology industries have grown. The pace of change has been startling. Those finding their skills out-moded, and their expectations no longer fitting reality, have suffered distress. One example: in November 1995, Bethlehem Steel extinguished its last blast furnace at its Bethlehem, Pennsylvania facility. The mill, which had been making steel since the Civil War, sent its remaining 1,800 workers home. Local 2599 union boss Danny Mills observed: "There was a time when we were unbeatable." But American invincibility had long subsided: of the 31,000 employed in the steel plants during the 1960s, only 1,200 remain. Larry Brandon, a furnace operator, described their fate: "There's nothing here for them anymore. Just a town looking over a graveyard."[28] Vying for the 1996 Republican presidential nomination, Patrick J Buchanan exploited the plight of those manufacturing workers who had lost, or feared losing, their jobs: "We have a government that is frozen in the ice of its own indifference, a government that does not listen anymore to the forgotten men and women who work in the forges and factories and plants and businesses of this country. We have, instead, a government that is too busy taking phone calls from lobbyists for foreign countries and the corporate contributors of the *Fortune 500*.[29]

Given these economic exigencies, it is not terribly surprising that so many Americans are so distrusting of their government. From its inception, H. G. Wells observed that the United States was a middle-class community "and so its essential problems are the problems of a modem individualistic society, stark and clear."[30] Thus, a doubting middle class, sensing its own self-created government's inability to deal with its economic problems, subscribes to Ronald Reagan's adage that "Government is not the solution to our problems. Government is the problem."[31] Replying to a December 1995 poll by Yankelovich Partners for CNN-Time 55 percent agreed that "the federal government has become so large and powerful that it poses a threat to the rights and freedoms of ordinary citizens."[32]

## PARTY DECAY

Just as government officials have suffered from a crisis of confidence, so, too, have political parties. Political parties have historically provoked an ambivalent response from the leaders who are supposed to like them and from the public they are supposed to serve. Many of the founders did not want them, only to see them emerge as a necessary instrument of public power. In his farewell address, George Washington warned of "the baneful effects of the spirit of party," claiming they "distract the public councils and enfeeble the public administration" by their "ill-founded jealousies and false alarms."[33] Washington's view was echoed by his treasury secretary, Alexander Hamilton, who had previously denounced anyone claiming to assert a partisan interest: "Ideas of a contrariety of interests between the Northern and Southern regions of the Union, are in the main as unfounded as they are *mischievous*. . . . Mutual wants constitute one of the strongest links of political connection. . . . Suggestions of an opposite complexion are ever to be deplored, as unfriendly to the steady pursuit of one great common cause, and to the perfect harmony of all parts [emphasis added]."[34] Even Hamilton's erstwhile rival, Thomas Jefferson, eschewed any partisan affiliation upon assuming the presidency: "We are all Republicans, we are all Federalists."[35] Likewise, a contemporary of a leading Virginia farmer, Edward Pendleton, praised him saying: "None of his opinions were drawn from personal views or party prejudices. He never had a connexion with any political party, . . . so that his opinions were the result of his own judgment, and that judgment was rendered upon the best unbiased estimate he could make of the publick good."[36]

The American love affair with nonpartisanship continues. Testifying before the Advisory Commission on Intergovernmental Relations, Colorado Republican Chairman Howard Callaway said, "there has been a strong feeling of independence in the voter, combined with a negative image of party politicians, that makes it fashionable for the average

voter to say, 'I don't vote for the party, I vote for the man or woman.'"
Some, he continued, even make an occasional apology for their own
partisan allegiances.[37] Callaway's observation reaffirms a long-standing
tradition: voters have consistently tempered their support for one party
or another with a suspicion that each may be prone to act excessively on
behalf of its most fervent supporters, but not necessarily on behalf of the
public interest—exactly the sentiments expressed by Washington himself. Thus, in October 1996, only 32 percent expressed their support for
the existing "two-party system of Democrats and Republicans"; 31 percent preferred elections in which "candidates run as individuals without
party labels"; 35 percent called for "the growth of one or more new parties."[38] Absent a third major party, many voters are perfectly happy
splitting their ballots between Democrats and Republicans—adamantly
refusing to place their full confidence in either one. But ticket-splitting
has not always been so commonplace: in 1942, 58 percent said they rou-
tinely voted a straight-party ticket, just 42 percent split their ballots; by
1996, the number of straight-ticket voters had shrunk to 29 percent
while ticket-splitters rose to 71 percent.[39]

The traditional Democratic and Republican duopoly has come
under suspicion along with virtually all other elements of political and
social leadership. When David Broder titled his 1972 book, *The Party's
Over*, he said "the pun was intended, but not the prophecy," adding,
"Our parties, our government will be no more representative than we
make them, by our own commitment and participation."[40] Broder was
onto something—strong evidence for party decline lies in the huge genre
of books describing the decaying partisanship that were published in the
last part of the twentieth century.[41] The party organizations, once
vibrant sources of party life, have suffered. A 1990 World Values survey found just 14 percent of U.S. citizens said they belonged to a political party, and only 5 percent did any unpaid volunteer work for their
party. Yet, even these dismal figures were better than those posted by
other industrial countries. In Canada, membership in political parties
totaled 7 percent; France, 3 percent; (then) West Germany; 8 percent;
Great Britain, 5 percent; Italy, 5 percent; Japan, 2 percent. Similarly,
those doing unpaid party work in Canada equaled 4 percent; France, 2
percent; (then) West Germany, 3 percent; Great Britain, 2 percent; Italy,
3 percent; Japan, 1 percent.[42]

Even the legislative context of political behavior has been altered for
the worse. The Federal Election Campaign Act damaged parties precisely at a time when public opinion of leadership organizations had
fallen to its 1970s lows. Campaign donations were henceforth to be
channeled through candidate campaign organizations, and federal presidential grants were to go to hopefuls and nominees directly, not

through the party organizations. Entrepreneurial campaigning has long been a feature of U.S. elections, but this legal systematization was new, and ignored the long-standing justifications for political parties as necessary intermediaries between voters and governments. Party leadership in Congress was weakened by other reforms enacted at about the same time, and the electoral system was modified to reduce party authority through increased use of primaries. The unintended consequence of this reform was the vast diminution of the decision-making mechanisms housed in the parties' quadrennial national conventions. Activists increasingly put their energy into issue-based advocacy and organizations (the Christian Right for the Republicans and organized labor and women's groups for the Democrats). These groups often targeted government agencies and officeholders directly rather than working though the party as intermediary.

In truth, party leaders had sometimes behaved in authoritarian ways in the past, and reforms intended to increase public accountability were an understandable reaction to such abuses. But the reforms have not increased accountability. Rather than making parties, candidates, and their platforms more accountable, they have managed to disengage the traditional linkages between the party-in-government, party organization, and the party-in-the-electorate, by disrupting the context in which these connections can be made.

In the increasingly entrepreneurial and expensive campaign world of recent years, parties have become less relevant. Certainly, U.S. election laws have generally protected the major parties by making ballot access easier for candidates nominally from the Democratic and Republican parties. But given the dominance of primaries as the selection method of choice, and the growing access to a primary ballot in most states, parties are acting less and less successfully as gatekeepers—even of their own named candidates. One Massachusetts state election official during the 1960s voiced a sentiment privately held by many: "The Republican party is a Hertz car we all rent around election time."[43] Thus, while in name the major parties' grip on government office is almost absolute, in fact their ability to operate cohesively is very limited.

Again, this is part of an historical continuity. Political in-fighting has been commonplace for decades. "I'm not a member of an organized political party," Will Rogers is reputed to have said, "I'm a Democrat." Nonetheless the major political parties were places where major ideological blocs could negotiate, thereby forging an aura of unity however tensely held together. Clinton Rossiter once likened parties to "vast, gaudy, friendly umbrellas under which all Americans whoever and wherever and however minded they may be are invited to stand for the sake of being counted in the next election."[44] By the latter part of the twentieth century, these vast and gaudy umbrellas had become smaller and a lot less friendly. The groups constituting the Democratic and Republican coalitions were increasingly utilitarian in their purposes and decreasingly meaningful in policy terms. Few candidates had strong ties to traditional party outlooks, or had been nurtured through the parties' informal apprenticeship systems, and fewer officeholders were content to follow the lead of their senior colleagues. This brought liveliness and initiative into the political system. But it also contributed to the breakdown of traditional bargaining units within the parties, introducing a more atomized, less predictable, form. If the interest blocs within the parties had on prior occasions reduced administrations to inertia, the emerging fluidity promised less cohesion, frustrating the ability of its nominal leaders to identify bargaining points in the increasingly atomized party atmosphere.

Political parties have been competing for attention and resources—not just with each other, but with candidate and issue organizations. Many activists who were concerned that a growing candidate-orientation was undermining public debate welcomed issue-orientation as a healthy development. Bill Clinton's chief strategist for his 1996 political comeback, Dick Morris, writes that issues, not mood or images, win elections in the 1990s. As Morris told Clinton:

> I think America fell in love with its politicians in the fifties and sixties when we first saw them on TV. Eisenhower was Dad; Kennedy was handsome; Johnson, our uncle; Nixon, the small-town banker. We were innocents. We were newlyweds, and our men could do no wrong. Then came Vietnam, Watergate, lines at gas stations, the bribery scandals of the seventies. Suddenly, our politicians were human beings like us; we became alienated. We got our divorce. We weren't going to be taken in again for a time.
>
> These days, we want to know where a candidate stands—the issues and just the issues. Don't ask us to fall in love; just tell us where you stand, and we'll vote for you. We won't bet our hearts on you, but we'll give you our votes until you screw up.[45]

This reliance on issues, often developed by hired guns like Morris, has done little to improve the two-party system. The political parties' ability to broker and deliver issue-based platforms is undermined by the willingness of candidate organizations and other single-issue advocacy groups to go it alone. Each is responsive to their geographic or ideological constituencies. But without the intermediary of a party organization that can deliver legislative results they are left promising more than they can produce, and repeatedly blame the system for their failures. The unwillingness of candidate and issue organizations to admit the need for compromise takes away the leavening of reality from campaigns. In the welter of individualized, tightly targeted candidate promises and various issue group agendas, the development of integrated policy aims through party mechanisms is lost. Disillusionment increases, and the environment in which organizations such as political parties might be able to reintroduce a negotiated and deliverable public policy is less likely.

All organizations competing for market share attempt to manage the market so as to reduce risk and maximize benefits. Political parties and candidates operating in an entrepreneurial environment are no exception. Before and during the 1996 campaign, various attempts to succeed through top-down management were evident. Within the Republican Party, Newt Gingrich manipulated the 1994 congressional campaign with skill into a referendum on his Contract with America. Although only one voter in eight knew much about the contract, and seven-in-ten had never heard of it, Gingrich's charisma and his energetic public pursuit of the contract's various elements imposed a partisan dynamic on the election results.[46] Some welcomed the return of responsible party government, but unlike the responsible party government envisioned by the American Political Science Association in 1950, this was management in its top-down form rather than the firm piloting of an agenda decided by broad party discussion. [47]

Some candidates have taken a top-down management approach in their relationship with their parties and the electorate by making extensive use of personal wealth that is allowed within the framework of current federal campaign laws. The Iowa caucuses have traditionally been a place where personal appearances and contacts have been most important. Republican multimillionaire candidate Steve Forbes broke with this tradition in 1996, visiting Iowa on far fewer occasions than his rivals, relying instead on an expensive media blitz financed out of his personal funds, which were not subject to federal campaign limits.[48] Forbes was following in the footsteps of another wealthy candidate, Ross Perot, whose independent challenge for the presidency in 1992 was financed almost entirely from personal funds. In 1996, Perot took federal campaign support under the banner of his new personal vehicle, the Reform Party. While Forbes was nominally working within the traditional party system, and Perot was attempting to break its stranglehold, both were challenging the linkages that supposedly exist between the party-in-the-electorate, party organizations, and the party-in-government.

In an increasingly expensive antiparty system, the management of risk by political parties as well as individual candidates often takes the form of heavy financial expenditure. The Clinton reelection effort made skillful use of national party committee channels and campaign funds to conduct a long, targeted, and well-managed media refurbishing of the president's image. In 1996, the Democratic National Committee (DNC) began an extensive series of television advertisements that ran virtually nonstop from July 1995 until Election Day the following November. The DNC spent *$85 million* on these commercials. To give some perspective, the 1992 Clinton and Bush campaigns together spend about $80 million on television advertising during their primary and general election campaigns.[49] In 1996, the Clinton campaign absorbed substantial party resources, but they were used to deliver a message rather than receive one.

The firm control exercised by party officials in 1996 over both national conventions was another example of the determination to impose top-down management. While the Republicans did not manage to control the platform committee, where the Buchananites had their major victories, the party managed the more public, media-visited elements on the convention floor. As for the platform, both Bob Dole and party chair Haley Barbour made it clear that not only had they had not read the document, they were not bound by it. After the Republican convention was characterized as a "four-day press conference," Democratic leaders happily introduced their affair using exactly the same language. The firm management of both conventions had journalists breathless for lack of stories and hostage to the party managers. Viewers switched off in droves, the television audience was 25 percent lower than in 1992.

The party managers professed to welcome 1996-style convention. Former party chairs Frank Fahrenkopf (Republican) and Paul Kirk (Democrat), along with Democratic chair Chris Dodd and the vice president's director of operations Fred Duvall, confirmed their belief that the conventions had naturally evolved to become mere ratifiers with the platform proceedings scripted for television and the delegates acting as an audience of extras.[50] This is likely to lead to shorter conventions designed to showcase the ticket. The diminishment of the party convention began in the 1950s. Since 1952, conventions have not gone beyond a single presidential ballot. Still, even during the turbulent 1960s, they remained important places for choice and debate. But the 1968 Democratic convention proved that the party with the most contentious floor fights would lose the election. Thus, the transformation to a coronation. As one Democratic operative stated, "By the time of the convention it is too late to be discussing differences." In 1996, the differences (including Clinton's controversial signature on a welfare reform bill) were smothered in an air of good feeling. Clinton turned the podium over to paralyzed actor Christopher Reeve and gunshot victim James Brady so that they could tell their dramatic stories of hope and courage. From an electioneering viewpoint, these pictures translate into votes, but the acceleration of the convention to its new form, if successful, leaves both parties

without any national forum where the party-in-the-electorate, in organization, and in government can meet to discuss policy.

Each of these management styles described above has serious flaws.
The Contract with America resulted in far less legislation than
promised, and the ideological fervor with which it was pressed has
faded. Steve Forbes's enormously expensive Iowa campaign put him in
fourth place behind the traditional campaigners. Iowa's caucus-goers
produced a delegation that combined pragmatic support of Bob Dole
with a unanimous commitment to right-to-life and other Buchananite
principles. A message was sent but was not willingly received by the
party management. Ross Perot's personalized challenge, while
immensely successful in third-party terms, still looks quixotic. The huge
1996 Democratic Party investment was only partly successful: a Democratic president was reelected and a Republican Congress was left in
place. Moreover, the party managers' vision of an infinitely repeating
series of carefully choreographed conventions must bow to the reality
of quadrennial intraparty battles for nomination that may not be so
finitely constrained.

There is little likelihood that conditions which would stimulate the
more successful and symbiotic articulation of the connections between
the party-in-the-electorate, party organization, and the party-in-government are likely to return. The political context continues to favor competition between multiple independent forces. The Supreme Court's
1996 decision that party campaign committees can spend independently
on campaigns for both houses of Congress is likely to contribute further
to this atmosphere.[51] In *Colorado Republican Federal Campaign Committee v. Federal Election Commission*, the court maintained, "The
independent expression of a political party's views is 'core' First Amendment activity."[52] The court reaffirmed its view that money is equivalent
to speech. Reactions to the verdict are likely to result in further moves
by activists from both parties toward a highly managed approach supported by the maximum possible spending. If so, each party will fail to
live up to public expectations. But the failure of Democrats and Republicans to meet the already low public expectations is only half the problem. The other half lies in the cynicism that, as noted earlier, is intrinsic
in the American psyche. After visiting the United States in 1842, Charles
Dickens spoke admirably of Americans in his incisive book *American
Notes*. On a journey that carried him from Boston to Virginia, and
Philadelphia to St. Louis, Dickens wrote that Americans were by nature
"frank, brave, cordial, hospitable, and affectionate." But Dickens saw
"one great blemish in the popular mind of America . . . Universal Distrust." Casting himself in the role of the stranger, Dickens described the
"ruin" such distrust created:

"You carry," says the stranger, "this jealously and distrust into every transaction of public life. By repelling worthy men from your legislative assemblies, it has bred up a class of candidates for the suffrage, who, in their every act, disgrace your Institutions and your people's choice. It has rendered you so fickle, and so given to change, that your inconstancy has passed into a proverb; for you no sooner set up an idol firmly, than you are sure to pull it down and dash it into fragments: and this, because directly you reward a benefactor, or a public servant, you distrust him, merely because he *is* rewarded; and immediately apply yourselves to find out, either that you have been too bountiful in your acknowledgments, or he remiss in his deserts. Any man who attains a high place among you, from the President downwards, may date his downfall from that moment; for any printed lie that any notorious villain pens, although it militate directly against the character and conduct of a life, appeals at once to your distrust, and is believed. You will strain at a gnat in the  way of trustfulness and confidence, however fairly won and well deserved; but you will swallow a whole caravan of camels, if they be laden with unworthy doubts and mean suspicions. Is this well, think you, or likely to elevate the character of the governors or the governed, among you?"

The answer is invariably the same: "There's freedom of opinion here, you know. Every man thinks for himself, and we are not to be easily overreached. That's how our people come to be suspicious."[53]

It remains for parties, presidents, and most of all the public to overcome the conundrum that Dickens so aptly described. Only then, will the parties work in the way political scientists think they should.


## NOTES

1. Quoted in William L. Shirer, *Twentieth Century Journey: The Start: 1904–1930* (New York: Bantam Books, 1985 edition), p. 15.

2. Remarks by the-president and first lady in a national television address on drug abuse and prevention, Washington, D.C., September 14, 1986.

3. Bill Clinton, State of the Union Address, Washington, D.C., February 3, 1997.

4. Walter Dean Burnham, "The Reagan Heritage," in Gerald M. Pomper, ed., *The Election of 1988: Reports and Interpretations* (Chatham, New Jersey: Chatham House, 1989), p. 6.

5. National Opinion Research Center, General Social Surveys, 1996 poll. Reported in *The Public Perspective*, February/March 1997, p. 9. Text of question: "In teaching the American story to children, how important is the following theme?"

6. Seymour Martin Lipset, *American Exceptionalism: A Double-Edged Sword* (New York: W. W. Norton, 1996).

7. Ibid., p. 291.

8. Ibid., p. 287.

9. National Opinion Research Center, General Social Surveys, 1996 poll.

10. Hart-Teeter survey, March 16–18, 1995. Text of questions: "Overall, do you think that government programs and policies do more to help or more to hinder your family in trying to achieve the American Dream?" More to help, 31 percent; more to hinder, 56 percent. "Now I'm going to read a list of goals. For each one, please tell me which of the following groups you think has the greatest responsibility for achieving that goal—government, businesses, community leaders, or individuals?" Improving education: government, 44 percent; businesses, 2 percent; community leaders, 25 percent; individuals, 19 percent; all, 8 percent; not sure, 2 percent. Creating more jobs and strengthening the economy: government, 43 percent; businesses, 35 percent; community leaders, 9 percent; individuals, 5 percent; all, 7 percent; not sure, 1 percent. Reducing crime: government, 39 percent; businesses, 1 percent; community leaders, 25 percent; individuals, 22 percent; all, 11 percent; not sure, 2 percent. Reducing air and water pollution: government, 31 percent; business, 20 percent; community leaders, 11 percent; individuals, 27 percent; all, 9 percent; not sure, 2 percent. Improving opportunities for racial and ethnic minorities: government, 22 percent; businesses, 11 percent; community leaders, 22 percent; individuals, 35 percent; all, 7 percent; not sure, 3 percent. Promoting culture through museums and concerts: government, 15 percent; businesses, 11 percent; community leaders, 44 percent; individuals, 19 percent; all, 6 percent; not sure, 5 percent. Improving moral values: government, 5 percent; businesses, 2 percent; community leaders, 14 percent; individuals, 73 percent; all, 5 percent; not sure, 1 percent. Strengthening families: government, 4 percent; businesses, 1 percent; community leaders, 11 percent; individuals, 81 percent; all, 2 percent; not sure, 1 percent.

11. Voter News and Surveys, exit poll, November 5, 1996. Text of question: "Which comes closer to your view: government should do more to solve problems or government is doing too many things better left to businesses and individuals." Do more, 41 percent; do less, 52 percent.

12. Iwan Morgan, "Fiscal Politics and the Constitution in the Carter Era: The Constitutional Convention for a Balanced Budget Amendment Issue," paper delivered at the annual conference of the American Politics Group, January 1997, p. 2. Morgan used data from the *Washington Post*, February 14, 1979, and the *New York Times*, March 5, 1979.

13. Warren E. Miller, "Misreading the Public Pulse," *Public Opinion*, October/November 1979, p. 11.

14. See Morgan, "Fiscal Politics and the Constitution in the Carter Era."

15. Jimmy Carter, Address to the Nation, Washington, D.C., July 15, 1979.

16. National Opinion Research Center, 1973 poll. Text of question: "I am going to name some institutions in this country. As far as the people running these institutions are concerned, would you say you have a great deal of confidence, only some confidence, or hardly any confidence at all in them?" Reported in *The Public Perspective*, February/March 1997, p. 2. The 1997 data are from Louis Harris and Associates, survey, January 9–13, 1997.

17. National Opinion Research Center, General Social Surveys, 1994 poll. Reported in *The Public Perspective*, October/November 1996, p. 19.

18. Quoted in Lipset, *American Exceptionalism*, pp. 283–84.

19. Results quoted in Thomas B. Edsall, "America's Most Hostile," *Washington Post National Weekly Edition* 13.43 (October 28–November 3, 1996): 35.

20. Lipset, *American Exceptionalism*, p. 286.

21. Ibid., p. 283.

22. Cited in Robert Wright, "Who's Really to Blame?" *Time*, November 6, 1995, p. 34.

23. See Louis Uchitelle and N. R. Klienfield, "On the Battlefields of Business, Millions of Casualties," *New York Times*, March 3, 1996, p. A-1.

24. Quoted in E. J. Dionne Jr., *They Only Look Dead: Why Progressives Will Dominate the Next Political Era* (New York: Simon & Schuster, 1996), p. 90.

25. See Lawrence Mishel, Jared Bernstein, and John Schmitt, *The State of Working America: 1996–1997* (Washington, D.C.: Economic Policy Institute, 1996).

26. Louis Uchitelle, "1995 Was Good for Companies and Better for a Lot of CEO's," *New York Times*, March 29, 1996, p. A-1.

27. Randall Richard, "MIT Economist: Hard Times Ahead for Middle Class," *Providence Journal*, March 31, 1996, p. A-1.

28. Associated Press, "Town Built on Steel Industry Resigns Itself to End of Era," *New York Times*, November 19, 1995, p. 27.

29. Buchanan speech reprinted on his home page on the World Wide Web, Spring 1996.

30. Quoted in Lipset, *American Exceptionalism*, p. 31.

31. Ronald Reagan, Inaugural Address, Washington, D.C., January 20, 1981.

32. Reported in "Opinion Outlook," *National Journal*, December 9, 1995, p. 3060.

33 George Washington, Farewell Address, reprinted in Diane Ravitch and Abigail Themstrom, eds., *The Democracy Reader* (New York: Harper Collins, 1992), pp. 137–38.

34. Quoted in John Kenneth White, *The New Politics of Old Values* (Hanover, N.H.: University Press of New England, 1990), pp. 31–32.

35. Thomas Jefferson, Inaugural Address, March 3, 1801.

36. Quoted in Richard Hofstadter, *The Idea of a Party System: The Rise of Legitimate Opposition in the United States, 1780–1840* (Berkeley: University of California Press, 1969), p. 13.

37. See Philip John Davies and Fredric A. Waldstein, *Political Issues in America Today* (Manchester, U.K.: Manchester University Press, 1987), p. 80

38. Reported in "Opinion Outlook," *National Journal*, November 16, 1996, p. 2514.

39. First survey by the Gallup Organization, July 16–21, 1942. Text of question: "Do you usually vote a straight-ticket, that is vote for all the candidates of one party, or do you vote a split-ticket, that is vote for some candidates

of one party and some of the other?" Straight-ticket, 58 percent; split-ticket, 42 percent. Second survey by the Media Studies Center/Roper Center, February 1996. Text of question: "When voting in elections, do you typically vote a straight-ticket—that is for candidates of the same party, or do you typically split your ticket—that is vote for candidates from different parties?" Straight-ticket, 29 percent; split-ticket, 71 percent. Reported in *The Public Perspective*, October/November 1996, p. 48.

40. David S. Broder, *The Party's Over: The Failure of Politics in America* (New York: Harper Colophon Books, 1972), pp. 264–65.

41. See among others Martin P. Wattenberg, *The Decline of Political Parties, 1952–1994* (Cambridge: Harvard University Press 1996) and Martin P. Wattenberg, *The Rise of Candidate-Centered Politics* (Cambridge: Harvard University Press, 1991).

42. See Lipset, *American Exceptionalism*, p. 279.

43. Quoted in John Kenneth White, *The Fractured Electorate: Political Parties and Social Change in Southern New England* (Hanover, N.H.: University Press of New England, 1983), p. 79.

44. Clinton Rossiter, *Parties and Politics in America* (Ithaca, N.Y.: Cornell University Press, 1960), p. 1.

45. Dick Morris, *Behind the Oval Office: Winning the Presidency in the Nineties* (New York: Random House, 1997), p. 47.

46. Polling data cited in Guy Molyneux, "The Big Lie," *Rolling Stone*, December 29, 1994, p. 154.

47. See American Political Science Association, Committee on Political Parties, "Toward a More Responsible Two-Party System," (New York: Rinehart, 1950). For a more extended discussion of the APSA report, see John Kenneth White and Jerome M. Mileur, eds., *Challenges to Party Government* (Carbondale: Southern Illinois University Press, 1992).

48. See Philip John Davies, "The Iowa Caucuses and the U.S. Presidential Election," *Talking Politics* 9.1 (Autumn 1996): 57–63.

49. See Morris, *Behind the Oval Office*, pp. 138–39.

50. Briefings at the Democratic National Convention, Chicago, August 1996.

51. James A. Barnes, "New Rules for the Money Game," *National Journal*, July 6, 1996, p. 1501.

52. *Colorado Republican Federal Campaign Committee and Douglas Jones v. Federal Election Commission* (1996), U.S. Supreme Court Reports, 135, Led, 2nd, 795, p. 805.

53. Charles Dickens, *American Notes and Pictures from Italy* (New York: Oxford University Press, 1957 reprint), p. 245.

# CHAPTER 2

# *The United Kingdom: Change within Continuity*

## Tim Hames

### POLITICAL PARTIES IN THE UNITED KINGDOM

Political parties in the United Kingdom have been confronted by a powerful set of fresh challenges in the last decade. The net result is that one of the two major parties—the Labour Party—has engaged in a comprehensive overhaul of its internal structure. The other major force—the Conservatives—now seems set to undertake a similar exercise. Within the context of British politics, such shifts are extremely significant. However, compared with other countries included in this survey where long-established political parties have vanished and completely new forces replaced them, the British experience might appear rather unspectacular. For almost everything that follows in this chapter will involve the two political parties that have dominated the British landscape since the late 1920s. This is perhaps to reinforce what might be seen as one of the most distinctive features of British public life: quite substantial change operating within the context of broad continuity. That continuity often means that the degree and importance of change in Britain is underestimated.

Those themes can be seen in the last British general election. At one level the results produced on May 1, 1997 were spectacular. The Conservative Party that had held office for eighteen years—a modern record—was dramatically ejected from power. The two-party swing—10.2 percent against the government—easily outperformed any relevant twentieth-century election. Tony Blair and the Labour Party seized an overall parliamentary majority of 179 seats: an outcome that exceeded the achievements of Clement Attlee and Labour in 1945 or Margaret

Thatcher and the Conservatives in 1983. The defeated Tories were left without representation in Scotland, Wales, and most of England's most populated cities.

At another level, continuity can be detected. Three out of four votes were cast for one of the two major parties. That pattern has been established since the reemergence of the Liberal Party and the rise of nationalist sentiment in Scotland and Wales in the early 1970s. Although the Liberal Party doubled its parliamentary caucus in 1997, its share of the national vote actually slipped slightly. The performance of both the Scottish and Welsh nationalists fell below expectations—not least their own. Little more than a decade ago, respected observers of British politics suggested that the Labour Party might be entirely eclipsed as an electoral force. That has obviously not happened. A few commentators are now suggesting a similar fate lies in store for the Conservatives. That notion is unlikely to prove much more prophetic.

The circumstances of the 1997 election were largely shaped by the difficulties faced by the Conservatives in office. However, the modernization of the Labour Party initiated by Neil Kinnock and John Smith but fully implemented by Tony Blair were also important. Without those reforms, Labour's margin of victory would certainly have been smaller and the character of the party in office would surely be different. That process reflected the party's appreciation that there was a fundamental mismatch between its traditional party structure and the society and electorate it faced. This mismatch partly explained its successive failure in four general elections. The Conservatives have now completed a radical reassessment of their own that has also questioned whether the traditional structure of Britain's oldest political party is fit for the challenges of the next century. The new Conservative leader, William Hague, at thirty-seven the youngest figure in his party's long history, has followed Labour's example and initiated root-and-branch reform.

## THE TRADITIONAL BRITISH POLITICAL PARTY MODELS

Although their particular traditions are distinct, until recently the two major political parties in Britain had retained structures that had seen only evolutionary change over the preceding half century if not longer. Comparative analysis is best served by examining the two parties separately.

### The Conservative Party

The Conservatives have always been seen as a top-down political force. The party emerged from the gradual formation of a stable parliamentary caucus in the nineteenth century. What structure then existed was based entirely in Westminster or on the personal resources of Westminster figures. All issues of policy and leadership resided with the caucus. Other matters such as membership or fund-raising were not considered relevant.

That structure changed as the result of an expansion in the electorate—a process that Conservatives usually resisted. The passage of the Second Reform Act (1868), which enfranchised the middle class and indicated that the skilled working class would soon be similarly treated, led Benjamin Disraeli to create a political party beyond Westminster. Within a relatively short period of time, the Conservative Central Office and the National Union of Conservative Associations had been established. Mass membership was encouraged. New organizations such as the Primrose League stressed issues of imperialism and patriotism in an attempt to entice the recently enfranchised. A network of Conservative clubs (essentially outlets for relatively inexpensive alcohol) emerged that had a semidetached relationship with the formal party apparatus.

That model was entrenched by Lord Salisbury during his tenure as party leader (1881–1902) and extended by Stanley Baldwin (1922–37). The basic structure has remained the same throughout this century. Its purpose has always been the broadening of the social base for Conservative support. The effective secret of the Tories during this century has been their success in holding the bulk of the upper- and middle-class vote while still attracting one third or more of working-class ballots. Electoral defeat, especially heavy losses, have invariably seen fresh attempts at expanding membership numbers. This was notably effective in the aftermath of the 1945 Labour landslide. It was also important after the two election defeats of 1974.

The distribution of power between the party at the center and in the country has also been consistent. The structure has been superficially federal but with an extremely strong core. Thus matters of policy and party leadership have been based at Westminster. However, questions of candidate selection and membership recruitment have largely rested with the constituency associations. The solicitation of party finances has historically been divided between the two spheres. Conservative Central Office has predominantly confined itself to seeking small numbers of large donations from very wealthy individuals and sympathetic institutions (usually big business.). Conservative associations have sought large numbers of small donations. Occasionally jurisdictional disputes would arise but these were not usually troublesome.

The most striking example of this distribution of power is the character of the Conservative Party Conference. Except on relatively rare occasions this has not been an explicitly policy-making body. Instead it has served as a four-day political rally largely directed by the party leadership. This allows the center to pursue political themes that it hopes (and usually expects) will be adopted and amplified by the party in the country. Nevertheless, despite its control in this sphere, the central party has had relatively little influence over those areas—candidates and membership— effectively conceded to local associations by Disraeli nearly 130 years ago.

### The Labour Party

The Labour Party has a rather different history. It might be regarded as a bottom-up political force. It emerged from the political quest  of the British trade union movement to increase the parliamentary influence and hence economic standing of their membership. The arrival of mass trade unions representing relatively unskilled workers made the attainment of universal adult suffrage (at least for men) a central objective. Thus in 1900 the Labour Representation Committee was created. The Labour Party's history as an organization is usually dated from that moment.

Labour's traditional structure was not so much decentralized as cross-sectional. The relationship between the trade union movement and the party itself has always been the central issue. Although the two are formally separate, the Constitution of the Labour Party makes clear its dependence on the unions. Before the 1980s an effective bargain operated between the two bodies. The trade unions contributed 90 percent of party funds. They held 90 percent of the votes at the party conference, which (unlike the Conservative example) was regarded as the sovereign policy-making body within the party. Trade unions also dominated the National Executive Committee (NEC), which ran the party and its central operations on a daily basis.

The vast majority of successful parliamentary candidates would be sponsored by an individual trade union. The final choice of such candidates would be made by constituency Labour parties whose officers were usually trade union officials who operated primarily out of loyalty to their own individual trade union. The selection of the party leader, though, rested exclusively with the parliamentary caucus at Westminster.

That balance was altered by a set of constitutional changes instituted by the left wing of the party during the period 1979–81. The principle of mandatory reselection increased the power that constituency Labour parties enjoyed over their Member of Parliament (MP). Until that point Labour followed the Conservatives in generally awarding an MP unlimited tenure except in circumstances of dire personal behavior. This change was supported by those who favored the rise of the constituency party activist: individual members who might or might not be trade unionists but whose primary loyalty was to an ideological agenda rather than a particular trade union. The choice of party leader was removed from Westminster. Instead an electoral college was created. This initially consisted of a 40% share for trade unions, 30% for constituency parties, and only 30% for Labour MPs.

Thus the Labour Party that elected Neil Kinnock to its leadership in 1983 looked much like the organization that had existed sixty years previously. Constituency party activists were somewhat stronger and Members of Parliament rather weaker. But the trade unions remained the bedrock of the party structure. The working class (especially those members of the working class that held trade union membership or lived in public sector housing) remained the bedrock of Labour's support in the electorate. This ensured that the party could not be displaced as a major actor in British politics. Nonetheless, Conservative success at attracting working-class support (and Labour's poor showing outside the working class), limited Labour's effectiveness as an electoral machine. The period 1900–1996 saw only two examples of Labour holding power with a secure parliamentary majority (1945–50, 1966–70).

Academics have often debated whether the seeming differences between the two major parties in Britain mask an essential similarity. Robert McKenzie, writing in the 1950s,[1] argued that Robert Michel's "iron law of oligarchy" applied in both cases. In other words McKenzie believed that Labour also functioned as a top-down party, despite appearances, because this was the only practical option for a modern party organization in a mass democracy. The internal changes of the early 1980s made other observers reject this analysis. The real issue to confront both political parties was whether events were rendering their structures equally obsolete.

## THE CHALLENGE TO TRADITIONAL
## PARTY STRUCTURE IN BRITAIN

To crudely summarize, the two major political party structures in Britain a decade or so ago might be described thus. The Conservatives relied on decentralization but with considerable deference to the center. Their electoral base was drawn evenly (in total numbers of votes not relative proportions) between the upper/middle classes, and the working class (especially the skilled working class). The Labour Party remained dominated by the trade unions, who had themselves been reluctant to undertake substantial internal change. That dominance was partly challenged by a new cadre of constituency party activists. The electoral base of the party remained overwhelmingly concentrated among the working class.

A set of social forces, not in any sense unique to Britain, emerged from the 1970s onwards to challenge these structures. The nature of these forces, their cause, and their precise impact on politics in the United Kingdom are all enormously controversial and contested matters. The discipline of political sociology exists in large part as a forum for these debates. Out of sheer practicality and intellectual cowardice I will not attempt to deconstruct those debates here. Instead, this section will outline the elements that appear to be involved but leave all issues pertaining to their internal features and interrelationship untouched. Their significance in this context is viewed solely through the organizational questions confronting British political parties.

Three broad phenomena can be identified. First, a significant decline in traditional class alignments at the ballot box. This can be measured in at least three ways:

1. The percentage of all voters willing to support an alternative to the two traditional camps has risen. These "third party" backers have increased from an average of 3 percent of the electorate in the 1950s, to 10 percent in the 1960s, and then 25 percent in the 1970s.

2. Opinion polls, local government elections, and parliamentary by-elections have all witnessed a steady rise in voter volatility from the 1960s onwards.

3. The composition of the two main blocs has also altered. While their overall share of the national electorate remained steady (at 42–43%) at four elections between 1979 and 1992, the Conservatives saw support amongst the upper/middle classes decline while backing from the skilled working class increased.

The net impact of all this, while fiercely contested by scholars in the field,[2] has been to reduce the linkage between class and party identification and to make overall party identification weaker. In the 1950s class was a reliable predictor of any individual's party preference on some 70% of occasions. By 1992 it had the same reliability in only 50% of cases. Meanwhile class composition was also changing. The unskilled/semiskilled working class was in relative decline while the middle class and skilled working class claimed a larger share of the population. Both these forces—declining class attachment to politics and a shrinking working class were especially challenging for the Labour Party given its historic reliance on strong class-party loyalty from a working class that was now shrinking.

These forces led British psephologists to look at election contests in a different fashion. Class was downgraded in favor of a more consumerist outlook. Voters were seen as independent entities seeking to maximize their political preferences in the electoral "market." Notions of "retrospective issue voting" and "prospective issue voting" became increasingly fashionable. This shift would have an obvious impact on electoral politics. However, it also suggested that party structure in Britain, which assumed a large and stable pool of automatic sympathizers from which membership and funds could be drawn, would also encounter difficulties in this new environment.

The second trend, which might have been the catalyst for the first, involved a rapidly changing economic structure. This in turn contained several different strands. The first was that while the overall workforce was (across economic cycles) increasing, not least because of the rising proportion of women entering the labor market, the total numbers of unemployed were significantly higher than had been seen in the postwar period. Sharp economic downturns in the early 1980s and early 1990's saw official unemployment (almost certainly an underestimate of the real numbers) peak at 3.4 million and 3.1 million respectively.

Within the world of work substantial change also occurred. The numbers engaged in full-time employment fell as those (willingly) offering themselves for part-time posts increased. The two recessions (but especially that of the 1980s) saw the proportions involved in manufacturing industry slump while the service sector advanced rapidly. This had a regional effect as manufacturing had been historically centered in the North of England, Scotland, and Wales (Labour territory politically), while services were centered in southern England (Conservative country). This same process, when allied with the privatization programs undertaken by the Thatcher and Major administrations, produced a reduction in the public-sector workforce and an increase in private-sector employment. In an allied development, housing patterns also shifted away from the public toward the private sector. In this case the movement was encouraged by the sale of council houses pioneered by Mrs. Thatcher in the early 1980s, which saw 3.5 million people purchase their own municipally owned accommodation.

This radical transformation had an especially powerful impact on the Labour Party. Its structure was based on the trade unions. Yet the total membership of trade unions fell from 12.2 million in 1980 to 7.3 million in 1993. The proportion of all employed persons who were trade union members had slumped from almost half in 1976 to barely a third twenty years later. This decline would have been even more dramatic had not the huge fall in the membership of traditional working-class unions been partly offset by rising numbers from more middle-class occupations based in the public sector.

The final trend related to traditional solidaristic institutions. This is inevitably more difficult to measure than the economic indicators previously cited but is nonetheless important. Well-established bodies—mainstream churches, sectional interests, promotional bodies such as the Royal Society for the Prevention of Cruelty to Animals or the Council for the Protection of Rural England—all struggled to maintain previous membership levels. These difficulties had two apparent sources. First, it proved much more difficult to persuade younger people from groups who had traditionally provided the membership base for such bodies to enlist as their parents had done. Second, a plethora of new alternative institutions mushroomed. These tended to be more specific in their goals, more dynamic in their methods, and more fluid and informal in their internal structures.

In short, large traditional organizations across the spectrum appeared threatened by the combined impact of individualism, antipathy, and fresh alternatives. While statistically it could not be conclusively demonstrated that total voluntary activity was falling (although some would certainly claim that it had) the character of such voluntarism had obviously changed. This had produced a much more diverse and less predictable pattern.

All three trends had consequences for both parties. The Conservatives saw a consistent decline in their membership figures. As such data is collected locally and not centrally, and even then not consistently or accurately, precise evaluation is not possible. Best estimates[3] suggest that total membership exceeded two million in the 1950s. It was still in the region of one million at the outset of the 1980s. It had fallen to around 500,000 by the early 1990s. Since then, matters have stagnated further. By 1997 it was suggested that a generous census would produce 350,000 members. During the recent contest for the post of Conservative leader, one candidate, John Redwood, publicly canvassed a figure of 120,000 members. As membership numbers fell the Conservatives became more reliant on very large financial donations from a small number of contributors. This fueled accusations of corruption or "sleaze" that dogged the party in the last parliament.

Until the changes that will be shortly presented, the Labour Party was similarly afflicted. Exact figures are difficult to obtain. However, reliable estimates[4] suggest that individual membership—which had exceeded one million in the 1950s and still topped 660,000 in 1979—had sunk to barely 260,000 in the run-up to the 1992 general election.

## THE TRANSFORMATION OF THE LABOUR PARTY

Defeat in the 1992 general election was especially bitter for the Labour Party. Unlike the three preceding contests that it had lost, it entered this campaign ahead in the opinion polls and expecting to form at least a minority administration. The formidable figure of Margaret Thatcher had been removed from the political scene by her own parliamentary party. The economy was in a state of advanced recession. After thirteen years in office, the Conservatives appeared intellectually as well as electorally exhausted. Furthermore, Neil Kinnock had engaged in a ruthless reassessment of party policy. Unpopular commitments had been abandoned and the left wing of the party firmly crushed. The preconditions for victory appeared in place.

Despite that, Labour lost and lost badly. Although John Major's parliamentary majority was thin—twenty-one seats—this disguised a triumph in the popular contest. The Conservatives recorded some 14 million votes, the largest ever attained by a British political party. Labour trailed by 2,500,000 votes or just over 7.5 percent of the electorate. Few serious party operatives could now avoid the conclusion that the structure and consequent image of the Labour Party was a serious impediment to its political progress. That structure had not changed despite a society around it that had been thoroughly transformed. The party would need to modernize or atrophy if not die.

That process has largely been the story of Tony Blair's transformation of the Labour Party since he became leader in July 1994. The actions of his two predecessors, Neil Kinnock and John Smith, provided Blair with an invaluable platform. Kinnock, as has been mentioned, had dumped the most contentious policy positions. He had also encouraged party supporters in the advertising and marketing industries to help update presentational methods. John Smith had contributed to the democratization of the party by his promotion of a "one member, one vote" method for the selection of parliamentary candidates. This improved the public image of the party as well as providing an additional incentive for individual membership.

The impact of the Blair prospectus on the traditional structure of the Labour Party can be examined in five key areas:

1. *Membership.* The solicitation of party membership has been centralized, computerized, and personalized by the Labour Party. An appeal has been offered on the basis of the personal standing and policy preferences of the leader rather than support for more collective attitudes. Furthermore, party operatives have deliberately sought to attract younger and more professional members from outside the social cohorts that have historically dominated membership rolls. This high-profile approach succeeded in forcing total individual membership up from under 300,000 at the time Tony Blair became party leader to 500,000 at the general election. When dis-

placement is considered, over half of the current individual membership has been associated with the party for less than three years. Tony Blair has used his membership drive to create what can literally be described as a new political party.

2. *Finance.* The complete dominance of the trade unions over Labour Party funds had been steadily weakened during the 1980s not least because of the financial crisis faced by the trade unions themselves. Michael Pinto-Dushinsky, Britain's foremost authority on these matters, has suggested that as late as 1980 the trade unions supplied 90 percent of all Labour funds. By 1992 that number had fallen to 65 percent. Tony Blair has forced that figure down further and faster. The combination of rising membership dues, additional appeals to those members, and an outreach to wealthy individuals and the business community may well have seen the trade unions percentage of party coffers fall below 50 percent for the first time in the party's history.

3. *Internal power.* The trade unions have seen their political influence fall alongside their financial standing. Their proportion of votes at Labour Party conference was reduced from 90% to 70% and then to 50%. Members of Tony Blair s entourage have intimated that the leader would like to see their role eliminated altogether. The conference itself has become less significant and has moved, at least in part, toward the political rally model long associated with the Conservatives. Tony Blair bypassed conference by submitting the party's draft manifesto to a popular vote of all members. The National Executive Committee has similarly been seized by allies of the Labour leader and has had its importance diminished.

4. *Policy.* Tony Blair completed the policy shift started by his predecessor. In an audacious move he challenged his party to recant its historic attachment to the nationalization of industry embodied in Clause IV of its 1918 Constitution. After a spirited campaign, a special Labour conference confirmed this dramatic change. While the trade union movement was divided on the wisdom of the move, the new constituency party members strongly supported their leader. In numerous other areas, the Labour leadership simply shifted policy with little regard for, or resistance from, other party institutions.

5. *Presentation.* All issues of party message have been comprehensively centralized and professionalized. During the general election, Labour's campaign largely proceeded along a script directed from Millbank Tower—the party's expensive communications center. That in turn required the continuous repetition of a small number of (popular) rather incremental policy promises strongly associated

with Tony Blair personally. Labour's mastery of the modern media contrasted sharply with the performance of the Conservatives. Their lines of authority were often unclear and hence their message was rarely focused and occasionally verged on the chaotic.

These reforms have dramatically altered the structure of the Labour Party. This new model involves the centralization of power within the party organization proper (at the expense of the trade unions) and then the subjugation of that party organization to the office of the leader. A wider membership has been successfully sought not least because it has provided a means by which Labour could be detached from its original sponsors. A plebiscitary model has been created whereby the leader seeks validation of policy positions via an appeal to the whole party membership: a body that largely exists because of its support for the policies and personal qualities of the leader. Once again, the old structure has been marginalized.

This has produced an astonishing transformation in the relative fortunes and characters of the two main parties. For the first time in its history Labour almost certainly exceeds the Conservatives in individual membership. Although the Conservatives outspent Labour during the general election, Labour's finances are in a more robust state than those of their opponents. Even the activist base has altered. The Conservatives now have a hard core of ideologically driven members. That is most obvious on issues pertaining to the European Union. Tony Blair, by contrast, appears to enjoy a loyalty previously only associated with the Conservatives.

The international context of this shift should briefly be sketched. Party structure in the United Kingdom was largely shaped by internal, domestic, characteristics. It is not surprising that issues involving the apparent crisis of the nation-state (interdependency and integration) or changes in the international system (the end of the Cold War) appear to have little impact here. Political parties in office are, of course, profoundly shaped by these developments as the experience of John Major as prime minister vividly shows. Organizational features have not been so affected. The increasing autonomy of the individual as a political creature, rather than transnationalism, was the factor that threatened the Labour Party in the 1980s and to which it has responded with such determination in the 1990s.

One irony should be noted though. The Labour Party has been keen to stress its European sympathies especially when compared with the last Conservative administration. Yet in embarking upon its transformation, it does not appear to have looked to continental Europe for inspiration. Instead the United States, the Clinton administration, and the contemporary Democratic Party have been the real models. The new Labour membership has a similar social profile to that seen among American Democrats. Numerous policy innovations in the United States (Democrat and Republican) have been shamelessly stolen by New Labour. Their presentation techniques were often appropriated from the Clinton campaigns of 1992 and 1996. To some degree Labour in the 1990s has been Americanized as well as modernized.

## CONCLUSIONS

The new model party structure pioneered by the Labour Party under Tony Blair is certainly designed to recognize and then adapt to the challenges that social change in Britain have provided. If it succeeds then political parties in the United Kingdom will not be part of the collapse of old orders that others in this volume have described for different countries. Not for the first time, British political elites will have proved themselves unusually circumspect at survival through adaptation to difficult circumstances. For most of this century it had been the Conservatives who demonstrated such flexibility, continuing to dominate electoral politics under universal adult suffrage much as they had done on a much narrower franchise.

That Conservative flexibility has, in part, been eroded by their eighteen-year period in power. Internal party matters were neglected in favor of the more pressing issues of state. It is likely that they will readdress this balance in opposition. William Hague's campaign for the Conservative leadership was based on the need for substantial internal reform. His proposals borrowed extensively from the Labour experience. In effect he favored recasting the bargain between the center and local associations that has endured for well over a century. The center will have much greater authority over questions of candidate selection and membership solication. In return, party members will be offered the chance to vote in future party leadership elections and will be balloted before the adoption of the next party manifesto. Conservative Central Office was brought directly under the command of the party leader. Presentation will be similarly centralized. Such measures will, William Hague hopes, enable the Conservatives to join Labour as a thoroughly modernized political party.

This chapter will close with some words of caution. The historic differences between the two major parties may make it more difficult for the Conservatives to successfully imitate the Blair model than they presently envisage. Decentralization has long been at the core of the Conservative tradition whereas Labour has enjoyed competing but largely centralized power centers. The Blair model has been about the increasing dominance of one particular power center and its control by the party leader. It seems improbable that a Conservative leader could capture command over party membership and candidates in an equivalent fashion. Time will tell.

Nor has the new Labour model been properly tested to date. It has been developed in opposition by a power-hungry party facing an exceptionally unpopular government. It remains to be seen if Tony Blair can retain present levels (and loyalty) of party membership when his administration begins to lose popularity. Only then will political scientists discover whether party structures have made a successful transformation in Britain or whether further upheavals remain in prospect.

## NOTES

1. Robert McKenzie, *British Political Parties* (London: Heinemann, 1955).

2. For the main competing views, review the vast outputs of Ivor Crewe and Anthony Heath.

3. Membership details in David and Gareth Butler, *British Political Facts 1990–1994* (London: Macmillan, 1994).

4. Ibid.

# CHAPTER 3

# French Political Parties: A State within the State?

## Colette Ysmal

In the introduction to their book *When Parties Fail*, Kay Lawson and Peter Merkl pointed out that "the phenomenon of major party decline, often remarked in the context of the American political system, is becoming increasingly apparent in other political systems as well." All over the world, dominant parties lost the confidence of their electorates and could not prevent single-issue movements or special interest groups assuming partylike status. This trend was generally related to a change in citizens' ties with political parties. The major parties would testify to an *old order* where party affiliation was a sort of emotional and affective bond generally inherited from the family. The process of secularization experienced by Western societies has weakened ascriptive and hereditary ties. Better educated, more focused on individual goals and new values—the so-called postmaterialism[1]—citizens were no longer interested in these party machines where collective goals were emphasized, where democratic principles were not applied, and where new issues were not taken into consideration. In fact, "new" voters more sensitive to "new" issues were dissatisfied with organizations that were slow to address their concerns. Therefore, in the 1970s and the 1980s, the trend was toward the development of new kinds of organizations: environmentalist movements and sometimes ecological parties; and supplementary, communitarian, or antiauthoritarian organizations.[2]

In the late 1980s and in the early 1990s, in many countries, other parties on the extreme right of the political spectrum were challenging the established parties. They represented other ideological orientations (economic liberalism, law and order, and anti-immigrant stands). Their credo was "neoconservatism" but also, as pointed out by Ignazi,[3] a propensity to delegitimize, in more or less euphemized words, the "fundamentals" of liberal democracies. Even if they did not directly contest the parliamentary regimes, as did their counterparts in the 1920s or the 1930s, they emphasized such values as inequality between citizens or races, consequently the dominance of "natural" elites and the supremacy of "natural" communities such as the family and the nation.

In the Lawson and Merkl volume, Frank Wilson stressed the specificity of the French case. Despite successive challenges from a variety of organizations in the 1970s and the early 1980s, the parties "refused to fail."[4] According to him, many factors could explain the vitality of the major parties: the relative youth and modernity of the party system; the significance of the left and right divisions based not only on ideological alignments but on class conflicts; the constraints of institutional rules adopted in 1958; and, finally, a long tradition of political protest, always, however, controlled by parties and governments, that "has developed a response to such challenges from alternative organizations or other potential rebels."

In the late 1980s and the 1990s, the situation appeared to be very different. On the one hand, the party system was seriously shaken both by changes in the electoral fortune of parties that had been the pillars of the previous system and by the emergence of new parties. On the other hand, ideological and class dealignments weakened ties with political parties. Moreover, the inability of major political parties to solve the unemployment problem as well as affairs of illegal financing of political parties, corruption, and, personal enrichment undermined the confidence of French citizens in political parties and in the working of democracy.

## THE PARTY SYSTEM IN THE 1990s

Electoral laws adopted in 1958—a two-ballot majoritarian system—as well as the election of the president of the republic by popular suffrage led to a party system structured around the left and right polarity that has characterized French political life since 1789. Yet constitutional constraints pushed the parties to enter into electoral and political coalitions. All in all, the 1978 general elections made clear a new system: two electoral blocs (left and right) roughly equal in terms of electoral support, each consisting of two main parties also nearly equal at the polls: the Communist Party (Parti communiste français—PCF) with 21.4% of the vote, the Socialist Party (*Parti socialiste*—PS) with 25.1%, the Union for French Democracy (*Union pour la Démocratie française*—UDF) and the Rally for the Republic (*Rassemblement pour la République*—RPR) with respectively 22% and 22.8% of the vote. The four main parties formed the "*quadrille bipolaire*"[5] and this quadripartite structure took together 95 percent of the vote.

In the 1990s the efficiency of institutional constraints was not so evident when new conflicts and cleavages appeared within French society. The party system, as established in the 1970s, was seriously questioned. First there were changes in the electoral fortune of the parties described as the pillars of the previous party system. Second, there was the emergence of new parties. Third, the dissatisfaction of the French people with political parties in general pushed them to vote for minor parties or for candidates without party affiliation.

## The End of the "Quadrille Bipolaire"

The stability and the coherence of the party system, as established at the end of the 1970s, was questioned with Mitterrand's successful bids for the presidency in 1981 and 1988. One can emphasize three elements.

First was the loss of electoral credit for the PCF which gained 15.4% in the 1981 presidential election; 9.6% in the 1986 general election; 6.9% in the 1988 presidential election; and 8.7% in the 1995 election. Even if the party performed generally better in general elections (see table 3.1), thanks to the personal influence of its incumbent deputies or mayors, it was marginalized in terms of electoral support. Those electoral showings were the result of the erratic PCF strategy. In 1972, the Communists joined with the PS in the "Common Program for Government"; but, in 1977, they considered such tactics of "class cooperation" to have been damaging to the party. Therefore, they sabotaged the new agreement and turned back to isolation and strong polemics with the PS. In 1981, having helped to elect Mitterrand, they were obliged to participate in the first Socialist cabinet; but, in 1984, they left the government. The collapse of Communist regimes in Russia as well as in East European countries had ambiguous consequences for PCF's party line and strategy. It did not move, as did its Italian counterpart, toward sociodemocratic positions but rather firmly adhered to the Communist credo. At the same time, it tried to modify the more or less Leninist model of party leadership and to promote the PCF as a "governing party" devoted to representing, in France, "the left of the left." Therefore, relations with the PS remained conflictual since the Communist Party did not want to enter into a new political alliance with the Socialists. Such a strategy did not enable the Communists to increase their share of the vote, however. In the 1997 general election they took some 10 percent of the vote. The PCF entered into the Socialist-led government but conflicts remained strong within the party about participation in the gov-

TABLE 3.1

Results of the General Elections, 1958–1997 (in percent of the vote cast)

| | 1958 | 1962 | 1967 | 1968 | 1973 | 1978 | 1981 | 1986 | 1988 | 1993 | 1997 |
|---|---|---|---|---|---|---|---|---|---|---|---|
| Extreme left | 1.6 | 2.0 | 2.2 | 4.0 | 3.2 | 3.3 | 1.2 | 1.5 | 0.4 | 1.8 | 2.2 |
| Communist Party | 18.9 | 21.9 | 22.5 | 20.0 | 21.4 | 20.6 | 16.3 | 9.7 | 11.2 | 9.1 | 9.9 |
| Socialist Party | 15.5 | 12.4 | – | – | 19.1 | 22.8 | 36.4 | 31.2 | 36.4 | 19.0 | 25.0 |
| FGDS | | | 18.9 | 16.5 | | – | | – | | | |
| *Divers Gauche* | – | – | – | – | 2.1 | 2.2 | 1.5 | 1.2 | 1.2 | 1.1 | 3.7 |
| Radical Party | 9.2 | 7.5 | – | – | 4.1 | – | – | – | – | | |
| MRP | 11.1 | 7.9 | – | – | – | – | – | – | – | | |
| CNIP | 14.2 | 7.3 | – | – | – | – | – | – | – | | |
| *Modérés* | 5.8 | 4.2 | 1.9 | 1.2 | 3.4 | 1.9 | 0.9 | 1.6 | 2.0 | 3.2 | 4.4 |
| Centre Démocrate | – | – | 15.4 | 11.2 | 9.2 | – | – | – | – | | |
| FNRI | – | 2.3 | 5.5 | 8.4 | 7.2 | – | – | – | – | | |
| CDP | – | – | – | – | 3.9 | – | – | – | – | | |
| UDF | – | – | – | – | – | 22.0 | 20.8 | 16.0 | 17.6 | 20.7 | 14.9 |
| Gaullists | 20.6 | 33.7 | 33.0 | 38.0 | 25.9 | 22.8 | 21.2 | 26.9 | 20.9 | 20.2 | 16.5 |
| Extreme right | 2.6 | 0.7 | 0.6 | 0.1 | – | 0.5 | 0.1 | 0.3 | 0.1 | 0.2 | 0.2 |
| National Front | – | – | – | – | 0.5 | 0.3 | 0.2 | 9.8 | 9.7 | 12.7 | 15.2 |
| Ecologists | – | – | – | – | – | 2.0 | 1.1 | 1.2 | 0.4 | 7.8 | 6.4 |
| Others | 0.5 | 0.1 | – | 0.6 | – | 0.3 | 0.3 | 0.6 | 0.1 | 4.2 | 1.6 |

ernment, and it is questionable whether the Communist Party ever really accepted its status as a governing party.

The Communist organization was dramatically weakened: loss of party membership, decline of party activism, internal dissent. More important was the electoral decline because it destabilized the left-wing camp and the party system. The PCF moved from a "major" to a "minor" party. The PS was promoted as not only once again the main party of the left (as it had been in the late 1970s) but as the sole leftist party able to govern and to represent left-wing voters. And, in fact, in 1981, 1986, and 1988, with its leftist-radical allies, it did take respectively, 37.9, 32.4, and 37.6 percent of the vote. The collapse of the party in the 1993 legislative elections (19 percent of the vote) made the place of the PS in the party system dubious. The performance of Lionel Jospin in the 1995 presidential election (23.2 percent) as well as the results of the 1997 general elections (25 percent) was a renewal of the PS electoral influence. The PS was once again able to compete with the RPR and the UDF but it did not recover totally its central place in the party system. Though better than in 1993, the PS's electoral results in 1997 fell short of those achieved in the 1980s. Even in winning the 1997 parliamentary elections, the left-wing camp took only 41 percent of the vote and the PS had to enter into alliances with other parties that did not share all its political positions: leftist radicals (*the Parti radical-socialiste*), the Greens (*Les Verts*), and the Movement for Citizens (*Mouvement des citoyens*) born in 1992 from a split within the PS and defending a strong Euroskeptic line. All in all, these parties took together 4 percent of the vote, increased their representation in the National Assembly and could act as "pressure groups" on the Socialist Party and the government.

The victory of the left did not dramatically modify the balance of forces between left and right, which was characterized in the late 1990s by a return to the dominance of the conservatives. It made, however, more crucial the problem of the RPR-UDF coalition, which could no longer represent only the right-wing camp. Since 1981 and the Socialist victory, the RPR and the UDF have continuously formed electoral and political alliances, giving support to common candidates in the legislative and local elections (but not in the presidential race). Competition for supremacy within the right-wing camp was less important than the necessity of defeating the Socialists.

Consequently, it is not very interesting to deal with the respective electoral support of the RPR and the UDF, which was strictly linked to the preelection bargaining for common candidacies. More important were the results of the RPR and UDF alliance in the late 1990s compared with their performance in the 1960s, the late 1970s, or the 1980s. In the 1978 general election, the RPR and the UDF took together 44.8% of the vote; the figures were 42% in 1981, 42.9% in 1986, 38.5% in 1988, and 40.9% in 1993 (see table 3.1). Thus the RPR and the UDF won fewer votes in 1993 than in 1978 (a period of the left's ascent). In the 1960s and in the early 1970s, the conservatives (Gaullists and centrists) won more than 50 percent of the vote (table 3.1). The 1997 parliamentary elections dramatically strengthened this trend since the presidential coalition gained only 31.4 percent of the vote. In the 1990s, the RPR and the UDF have lost their hegemony over the right-wing camp. This was the consequence of the institutionalization of the National Front (*Front national*—FN) in French political life.

## The Consolidation of the National Front

The FN was not the first extreme-right party to have been formed in France but it was the first to gain so many votes and to succeed in maintaining/increasing its electoral base. Until the 1980s, the extreme-right organizations were "flash" parties appearing and disappearing according to the logic of the various sentiments at work in French society (anti-Semitism, support for fascism, colonial nostalgia). Formed in 1972, the FN gained, in the late 1970s, less than 1 percent of the vote and, in 1981, Jean-Marie Le Pen, its president, was not qualified to run for the presidency.[6] The turning point was the 1984 European elections: Le Pen's list took 11 percent of the vote. This success was confirmed in the 1986, 1988, and 1993 general elections: 9.8% in 1986, 9.7% in 1988, and 12.7% in 1993. In 1997, the FN once again increased its share of the vote (15.2 percent) and, for the first time, scored as high as Le Pen did in the 1988 and 1995 presidential elections (respectively, 14.6 and 15.3 percent of the electorate).

Many factors explained the FN's sudden emergence in the 1980s.[7] First, proportional representation for the European elections, as well as for the 1986 legislative elections, allowed the party to gain seats both in the European Parliament (EP) and the National Assembly (AN) and thus to be legitimized.[8] Second, the takeover of the left in 1981 led to a radicalization of strong anti-Communist or anti-Socialist voters, who moved from the RPR and the UDF to a more extremist vote. In the 1980s, more than 75 percent of the FN voters were previous RPR/UDF supporters. Third, and probably most important, the electorate moved from leftist political positions in the 1970s to "neoconservative" positions (economic liberalism, individualism, law and order) in the 1980s. Unlike the RPR and the UDF, which were both concerned by such a change in ideology, the FN adopted a specific political line. It chose to make immigrants scapegoats for all the so-called French disorders: unemployment, crime and violence and loss of French "national identity" (due to the massive presence of non-Catholic people).

The FN thus made immigration a very important issue to which the other parties had to react in following, generally, the FN problematics. As a result, the party gained legitimacy and increased its share of the vote. In the 1990s, the FN benefited also from the inability of the governing parties (PS, RPR, UDF) to solve the unemployment problem and from the involvement of those parties in either illegal financing of their activities or individual acts of corruption. Dissatisfaction with those parties increased and the FN used a populist, anti-elitist appeal that grew more credible as the governing parties failed. In the 1995 presidential election, the FN gained new voters coming from the RPR and the UDF but mainly from the left.[9]

In terms of party system, one can conclude that the FN contributed, in the 1980s and the 1990s, to the RPR and UDF's loss of hegemony over the right-wing camp. In the 1990s, it also interfered with a possible electoral recovery by the Socialist Party and, therefore, with its ability to recover its pivotal position in the party system.

*The Ecologists as a "Pressure Group"*

The environmental issue has never been very important in France. In 1974, René Dumont, a presidential candidate, was the first to put issues linked to the use of natural resources on the political agenda and to attempt to demonstrate that the developed countries' model of development had had terrible costs in terms of the environment. He gained, however, only 1.3 percent of the vote. Many ecologist groups proliferated in the late 1970s, finding it unnecessary to launch a centralized and organized party. Candidates to European or presidential elections took 4.5 percent of the vote in the 1979 European elections and 3.9 percent in the 1981 presidential election.

In 1984, the Greens, the Ecological Party (*Verts, Parti écologiste*) was formed but did not change the ecologists' poor electoral support: 3.9 percent in the 1984 European elections, and 3.8 percent in the 1988 presidential election. In the 1989 European elections, the Greens suddenly increased their share of the vote to 10.6 percent. Such a success inspired the creation in 1990 of a second ecologist party labeled Ecological Generation (*Génération Ecologie—GE*) by Brice Lalonde, a former leader of one of the most important ecological groupings in the 1970s (*Les amis de la Terre*, Friends of the Earth) but also a member, in the same years, of the Unified Socialist Party (*Parti socialiste unifié-PSU*) and, in the 1980s, an ally of the Socialists. In the 1992 regional elections, GE took 7.1 percent of the vote (7.5 percent went to the Greens). Due to the electoral law, the two parties entered into an alliance for the 1993 general election and took together 7.8 percent of the vote.

Interpreted as an electoral defeat by both parties, this created a crisis in the ecological organizations. The Greens and GE returned to political and strategical autonomy. The GE, which had been little more than Lalonde's party and a vehicle for securing his personal political influence, was devastated as many of its activists and elected officials left. The Greens, shaken by many splits, were weakened: in the 1995 presidential election, they gained only 3.4 percent of the vote. Therefore, in the 1997 general election they entered into an alliance with the Socialist Party and they gained eight seats in the National Assembly. In 1997, other ecologist groups ran not to secure seats in the National Assembly but to reinforce the influence of the ecologist network that took 6.6 percent of the votes. The ecologists are in 1997 more diverse than in the early 1990s and the most established parties (the Greens and GE) are weaker. However, due to their common electoral outcome as well as to the presence of the Greens in parliament and government, they occupy now an important place in the political system. New developments in governmental policies on the environment or on land use showed that they could act as effective pressure groups.

From this description of the parties' fortune in the late 1990s, one can emphasize two points. First is the fragmentation of the party system. Even if one pays attention only to those parties that are really organized at the national level, intervene more or less continuously into the political debate, and gain a substantial number of votes, the institutionalization of the National Front and the sudden appearance of the ecologists destabilized the party system. In the late 1970s, it was structured around four "major" parties quite equal in terms of electoral and political influence; in 1993, three major parties (PS, UDF, and RPR) and four minor parties (PCF, FN, the Greens, and GE) coexisted. Such an evolution was linked to an extreme electoral volatility, voters shifting from the left to the right and vice versa but also moving, within each camp, from one party to another. As a result, governmental majorities were never secured, as proved by the quick changes in governments' composition (leftist in 1981, rightist in 1986, leftist in 1988, rightist in 1993, and leftist in 1997) and the periods of divided government (*cohabitation*).

Second, at the same time, the ability of the three main pillars of the party system or the "governing parties" to gain extensive electoral support dramatically decreased: they took together 78% of the vote cast in the 1981 general elections, 75% in 1988, but only 60% in 1993 and 58% in 1997. Even the presidential election is no longer an exception: in 1995 the three leading presidential candidates (Jospin, Balladur, and Chirac) won 62% of the vote (compared to 75 and 70% for their counterparts in 1981 and 1988 presidential elections).

## PARTIES AND THE ELECTORATE IN THE 1990s

The evolution of the French party system led to a decline of the major parties and a failure in their ability to control the electoral process. One can object that the three largest parties are quite hegemonic on the second ballot and the only parties able to gain numerous seats in the national parliament as well as the presidency. However, they can no longer be said to represent the entire electorate or to establish their governments in accordance with a *national* (as opposed to a *governing*) majority. Therefore, dissatisfaction with political parties is likely to increase. If such a trend can be observed in France, it has to be interpreted cautiously. The hypothesis of a general crisis of major parties and of the emergence of a new order fits well with countries where the old order was characterized by the importance of political parties recognized as the main organizers of political life. Paraphrasing Epstein,[10] one can say that "political parties in the French mold" present some typical features inherited from history. These traits are very important to note in order to describe and understand how parties work in France in the 1990s and how important the changes were in the status of French parties among the electorate. An increasing skepticism characterizes present relations between voters and parties rather than a dramatic move from loyalty to criticism.

### The Historical Context

If we turn our attention to the historical context, three points appear crucial.

1. Political parties, themselves, as institutions, have never been recognized as a decisive factor in the process of a participatory democracy. Historically speaking, both the left and the right, for different reasons, contested the role of political parties. The development of a well-established left and strongly organized parties linked to trade unions was made impossible by all the forces (unions, revolutionary groups, and voters) that thought that parties could not be an efficient channel for revolutionary change of society. As far as rightist leaders were concerned, they considered the existence of political parties as an element for dividing a naturally unified French society according to more or less false political conflicts.[11] Therefore, political parties had, in France, no particular legal status.[12] When for the first time they were officially recognized as political actors, they acquired a limited role since, according to Article 4 of the Constitution of the Fifth Republic (1958), they are described as "participating in the making up of the vote" that is simply granted the opportunity to play a role in the electoral arena.

As a consequence, French political parties have always been very weak in terms of membership, internal party organization, and ability to organize or control civil society. They have also been unable to really participate in the formation of governments. Under the Third and the Fourth Republics, the role of the "government party" was little more than bargaining among party leaders within the parliament, with only weak control by party organizations. When coalitions in government changed, parties were not asked to give formal approval. The direct power of appointment of ministers by parties was reduced under the Fifth Republic. Prime ministers and ministers were generally members and sometimes leaders of political parties. However, this transfer of party personnel into government was decided by the president and his prime minister in the case of united government, the prime minister alone in the case of a divided government. The specific role of parties in appointments could vary from being a bargaining power with the president (and the prime minister) to an almost complete exclusion from the appointment process.

2. It has been always difficult, in France, to know what "party" means exactly and to determine the identity of all those groups that participated in political life and especially in elections. First, the historical rejection of parties led many organizations to avoid the term in their official names. They preferred to be known as Alliance, Union, Center, Rally, or Movement. Second, "new" parties appeared generally solely as a change in name never linked to a change in party organization or in party positions within the political system. New labels would just emphasize to the public that they have a new image or a new ability to shape the political life.[13] Third, "parties" have proliferated in recent years. According to the Ministry of Home Affairs, fifty-five parties, groups, and movements had candidates in the 1993 general election. In 1994, forty-five "parties" qualified for state aid to political parties.[14] Of course, many of these organizations were limited in terms of territorial presence and political appeal. Many of them sprung up only at the whim of a single person and disappeared just after the election. Therefore, French people had difficulty in identifying parties and, moreover, in aligning themselves with a specific party.

3. As quoted in Converse and Dupeux's "Politicization of the Electorate in France and the United States," "reported levels of party loyalty were remarkably limited among French voters, relative to other countries in which this phenomenon has been investigated."[15] When asked what parties they generally felt close to, a substantial number of French voters cited a variety of items such as political leaders, labor unions, or general positions on the left-right spectrum. More noteworthy was the extraordinary frequency with which French people interviewed in opin-

ion polls indicated that they felt close to no party at all. In the 1950s and in the early 1960s, less than 60 percent of the electorate reported some generally preferred party of identification against 75–90 percent in other countries such as United States, Canada, Great Britain, Germany, or Sweden.[16]

### An Increasing Skepticism

These traditional features make it difficult to document the thesis of party decline in France according to the most relevant criteria provided by the literature on the topic: membership size, voters' party affiliation, links between party affiliation and vote, confidence in parties in general or as efficient channels of representation for the citizenry. This is not to say that nothing changed in the recent years. However, the situation must be described in terms of increasing skepticism rather than in terms of dramatic loss of confidence in parties.

A first sign of this evolution is membership size. The traditional weakness of French parties was confirmed in the 1990s. Though there is a lack of creditable longitudinal data, estimates suggest that, in 1995, some 555,000 people were members of a political party. The trend indicates a decline of party membership since the figures were 875,000 in 1982 and 626,000 in 1986 and 1992. In fact, in the late 1990s, membership size was back to the level it had been in the late 1960s.[17] However, the most striking finding was that the overall stability (compared to the 1960s) or the membership decline (compared to the early 1980s) was the result of contrasting single-party trends. Of the most important parties in the party system since 1958, the Gaullist party—under its different labels—and the organizations united in 1978 under the banner of the Union Démocratie française (UDF) maintained relatively stable, low membership levels. Leftist parties displayed opposite trends. From the 1960s–80s the Communist Party was the only well-organized French party, with some 500,000 members; in the late 1990s, they were less than 200,000. The evolution of the Socialist Party was different. Membership growth was pronounced in the 1970s since 70,000 people belonged to the party in 1971 (rebirth of the PS at the Epinay Congress) while 200,000 did so in 1981. In the 1990s, the twilight of the PS membership was also evident: there were only 100,000 members in 1995–96.

One could argue that the crisis of both the Communist and the Socialist parties testified to the crisis of the mass-party model. As catchall parties, the RPR and the UDF, which were not so interested in the development of their membership in quantitative terms, would have been less concerned with a decline in membership. Such an hypothesis is not totally confirmed if one looks more closely at the trends. The decline of leftist parties' membership was consistently linked to institutional and political reasons. First, in a system where parties are not very efficient in determining policies, it is less interesting to join an organization that is in government since members and even party leaders have no input; second, members' dissatisfaction with policies and strategies led to a decrease in membership. Not so different was the case of the RPR, which had a relative increase in membership in the 1980s but lost members in the 1990s when it was back in power.

If we move from members to voters and consider party identification measures commonly used to assess party strength, no clear pattern emerges. The reorganization of the party system in the 1970s did not really change the level of party identification among the French electorate.[18] In 1978, when the party system was the most structured and simple, more than a third of the voters declared that they "did not at all feel close to a party" or did not answer the question. As shown by table 3.2, the trend was to an increase of those who identified with no party in the late 1980s and the early 1990s (40% in 1991 and 41% in 1992). However, these figures concerned nonelectoral periods. In the wake of an election, political mobilization led to a remobilization of the electorate: in 1993 and 1995, only 33 and 32 percent of those interviewed identified themselves with no party. One can, however, note a general fading of party affiliation. First, people responding that that were "very close" to a political party declined strongly in the 1980s and the 1990s from 13% in 1978 to 4 or 5%; second, more people chose items that signify a relative lack of concern: in 1978, only 21% "felt not very close to a party"; they were 34% in 1995.

The evolution in party identification was, however, less striking than the loss of credibility suffered by political parties. In 1978, voters were confident in the ability of political parties (or at least of their own party) to solve "the problems that France would have to face in the next months or the next years."[19] As shown in tables 3.3 and 3.4, the situa-

TABLE 3.2
Evolution of Party Identification, 1978–1995 (in percent)

|                | 1978 | 1988 | 1991 | 1992 | 1993 | 1994 | 1995 |
|----------------|------|------|------|------|------|------|------|
| Very close     | 13   | 9    | 5    | 4    | 5    | 5    | 4    |
| Quite close    | 33   | 33   | 25   | 24   | 27   | 27   | 30   |
| Not very close | 21   | 23   | 29   | 31   | 34   | 30   | 34   |
| Not at all close | 29 | 33   | 39   | 38   | 30   | 33   | 29   |
| No answer      | 4    | 3    | 1    | 3    | 3    | 5    | 3    |

Source: SOFRES opinion polls

tion appeared very different in the late 1990s. When asked to say, at the eve of the 1997 general elections, whether certain parties "had proposals to improve the economic and social situation," French people were extremely dubious. If the two extreme parties (the Communists and the National Front) received a low rate of positive answers, mainstream parties and notably the PS, the UDF, and the RPR were not really better off.

TABLE 3.3
Ability of Political Parties to Face French Problems in 1997 (in percent)

|  | *Yes* | *No* | *No Answer* |
|---|---|---|---|
| Communist Party | 18 | 74 | 8 |
|  | (71) | (25) | (3) |
| Socialist Party | 35 | 58 | 7 |
|  | (61) | (36) | (3) |
| Greens | 28 | 66 | 6 |
|  | (65) | (35) | (–) |
| UDF | 29 | 62 | 9 |
|  | (63) | (30) | (7) |
| RPR | 33 | 59 | 8 |
|  | (71) | (26) | (3) |
| National Front | 14 | 80 | 6 |
|  | (70) | (20) | (10) |

Source: BVA Opinion polls 14 and 15 March 1997. Figures in parenthesis concern people who declared to be a sympathizer of the party.

TABLE 3.4
Ability of Political Parties to Solve the
Most Important Issues in 1997 (in percent)

| *Hierarchy of the Issues* | *Leftist Parties* | *Rightist Parties* | *None* |
|---|---|---|---|
| 1. Fighting unemployment | 28 | 33 | 39 |
| 2. Securing the welfare of the people | 48 | 48 | 28 |
| 3. Promoting economic growth | 24 | 45 | 31 |
| 4. Solving the problems of young people | 37 | 25 | 38 |
| 5. Fighting political corruption | 28 | 23 | 49 |
| 6. Fighting violence and insecurity | 18 | 43 | 39 |
| 7. Fighting social inequalities | 54 | 19 | 27 |
| 8. Fighting illicit immigration | 18 | 54 | 28 |

Source: CSA opinion polls May 9 and 10, 1997.

On the other hand, table 3.3 indicates that party loyalty did not totally determine how voters appreciated a party's performance. A quarter to a third of party sympathizers thought that the party they felt close to was unable to improve the French economy. Such a skepticism did not disappear during the electoral campaign (table 3.4). For the eight issues having highest priority on the political agenda, more than a quarter of those interviewed thought that either the leftist nor the rightist parties would be the best at "dealing with them efficiently."

In conclusion, political parties appeared to be more and more incompetent and inefficient and therefore more and more distant from voters' demands and preoccupations. In opinion polls, citizens were asked to say whether parties are qualified to face the problems that France is confronted with; their answers were that parties are not capable of dealing with the country's problems and that they think they have not benefited from policies initiated by the parties, especially when they were in government. The gap between voters, parties, and political leaders—the "political class"—increased in the late 1980s and the 1990s. In November 1996, only 37% of those interviewed thought that "political leaders pay very much attention to [the voters'] daily problems"; down from 53% in the late 1970s and 45% in the early 1980s (table 3.5). In the same way, but over a shorter period of time, fewer citizens felt themselves to be "well represented by a political party": 39% in 1989 and 27% in 1996 (see tables 3.5 and 3.6).

## CHANGE IN PARTY ROLE AND FUNCTIONS

This inability of parties to represent citizens refers to changes in the role of parties as agencies of linkage between citizen and state. With Lawson, one can argue that "creating linkages is itself an extremely important function of politics . . . and that the political party is the one agency that can claim to have as its very raison d'être the creation of an entire linkage chain, a chain of connections that runs from the voters through the candidates and the electoral process to the officials in government."[20] In practice, political parties never assume these functions totally or very well. As is well known, even parties that have strong grassroots organization and manage to engage the voters in political life did not succeed in organizing a democratic infrastructure.[21] As previously noted, French parties were historically too weak to give the voters real opportunities, via party members, to shape party programs, choose candidates, and hold elected representatives responsible for the party program. However, in recent years, French parties have tended to become more independent from the voters, less focused on performing the function of linkage with the society (even a little mythical), and more preoccupied with their own interests.

TABLE 3.5
Parties and Attention to Voters' Demands (in percent)

| | 1977 | 1979 | 1983 | 1985 | 1990 | 1991 | 1992 | 1993 | 1994 | 1995 | 1996 |
|---|---|---|---|---|---|---|---|---|---|---|---|
| Yes | 53 | 48 | 45 | 38 | 33 | 29 | 35 | 42 | 36 | 39 | 37 |
| No | 42 | 47 | 51 | 58 | 65 | 69 | 64 | 56 | 63 | 59 | 62 |
| N.A. | 5 | 5 | 4 | 4 | 2 | 2 | 1 | 2 | 1 | 2 | 2 |

Source: SOFRES opinion polls.

TABLE 3.6
Representation by a Political Party (in percent)

| | 1989 | 1990 | 1991 | 1992 | 1993 | 1994 | 1995 | 1996 |
|---|---|---|---|---|---|---|---|---|
| Yes | 39 | 31 | 20 | 23 | 28 | 25 | 29 | 27 |
| No | 50 | 60 | 73 | 70 | 65 | 70 | 65 | 67 |
| N.A. | 11 | 9 | 7 | 7 | 7 | 5 | 6 | 6 |

Source: SOFRES opinion polls.

## Parties as a Pure Arena for Power Seeking

The first point I wish to make concerns party organization and the place of the members and activists in shaping party activities and manifestos and in nominating party leadership. As stressed by Katz and Mair, "members still matter" but members were, more and more, valuable merely to assess the strength of the organization vis-à-vis the other parties.[22] Due to state or private financing, members were no longer a channel for fund-raising; at the same time party members had fewer opportunities to provide labor for campaigning and the diffusion of the party programs. On the one hand, placarding party posters was in the hands of private firms that established market relations with all the parties having recourse to them. On the other hand, party leaders used television channels rather than members and activists when they wanted to inform the voters about important decisions. In 1979, the leader of the Communist Party announced on television that the party would abandon the dictatorship of proletariat, a cornerstone of Communist doctrine. This change had never been discussed within the party and was learned by the members via the television. . . . In the same way, candidates for the presidency made their decisions public in special programs organized by television at their request. If this method is quite normal for UDF and RPR candidates (Giscard d'Estaing in 1974 and 1981; Barre in 1988; Chirac in 1981, 1988, and 1995; Balladur in 1995) since parties have no statutory role in nominating candidates to the presidency, it constituted an important change in rules for the Socialists who are theoretically entitled to nominate their candidates to any election.

The power of members and activists was also dramatically limited in shaping party programs or at least in discussing party manifestos. As to the UDF and the RPR, the evolution led to increasing authoritarian practices and allowed party leaders, in the 1980s and the 1990s, to publish the party program before conferences discussed party proposals. The problem was, however, more acute in the Socialist case. Due to both Mitterrand's personal skills and access to government in 1981, the PS was more or less deprived of any power in the 1980s and the early 1990s. Changes in economic and social policies in 1982–83—when the PS (partially) withdrew its program of nationalization, of development of the welfare state, and moved to more mainstream pro-market policies—were decided by the president and the government. Members and activists as well as the parliamentary party had to attempt to understand a new course never really explained or theorized. Party conferences in these years were particularly morose since delegates were dissatisfied with both their party organization and its political orientations. These years were also a period of strong conflicts within the party.[23]

All in all, dissatisfaction with the place granted to members and activists increased in the late 1980s. Surveys conducted by SOFRES among delegates at party conferences in 1990 showed that 65 percent of the PS delegates, and 56 and 51 percent of their RPR and UDF counterparts, thought that "the party did not work well" and that the trend was toward a decline of their role. Middle-level elites emphasized, in fact, true changes in their ability to link voters and state, to participate in the shaping up of citizens' political orientations and party loyalties. Political parties became, more and more, electoral machines at the disposal of leaders fighting mainly to control party internal power and, via this control, to secure their positions as potential presidential candidates.

The decreasing function of the great parties in the "representative-democratic" process is surely not a French characteristic. The evolution took, however, a particular form due to the influence of the presidential election on party organization. In the 1970s, major parties or parties that wanted to secure a role in French political life had to become large organizations, to turn to voters rather than members, and to organize their electoral appeal round a quite unquestionable leader able to run for the presidency. Generally these leaders "created" their parties, as Giscard d'Estaing did the Federation of Independent Republicans (*Fédération des Républicains indépendants*, 1966), Mitterrand and the Socialist Party (1971), and Chirac the RPR (1976). As such, they chose their entourage but their position as founding fathers allowed them to do so with consensual approval. The situation became different when, for different reasons, either succession was opened or "natural leaders" were contested. The general tendency was to turn the party into an arena where potential presidential candidates and their teams gave high priority to a single issue: how to eliminate other contenders. Party leaders achieved this "task" in different ways according to particular traditions and internal rules. In the RPR, the power of nominations at national and local levels allowed the president and the general secretary nominated by the former to secure their control over the party and to marginalize their opponents. This was the case in the 1990s when Chirac and Juppé succeeded in limiting the influence of Pasqua and Séguin among party members and in eliminating them from the executive bodies.[24] The electoral defeat of the RPR and of Chirac in the 1997 general election gave a new opportunity to Pasqua and Séguin, along with their new Balladurian allies, to take over the RPR. However, if members, activists, and officeholders, shocked by the defeat, agreed with this takeover, they were also afraid that Séguin's arrival sounded less like a renewal of the party than a new instrumentalization of the RPR as a base for Séguin's presidential goals. In the UDF, co-optation offered opportunities to leaders to gain control over the party with the support of some important officeholders more interested in securing the influence of the party—vis-à-vis other parties entering into the coalition and vis-à-vis the RPR—than in promoting party policies.

In the 1990s, in terms of program, there were no real differences between *Force Démocrate* (Democratic Force, new name of the Christian Democrat Center of Social Democrats, *Centre des Démocrates So ciaux-CDS*) and the Republican party. However Bayrou and Léotard had a strong interest in maintaining two parties and in emphasizing two political lines in order to make clear that they would run for the presidency and to organize their respective parties as natural reservoirs of committed backers. Within the PS in the late 1980s and the early 1990s presidential teams were organized along factional lines constitutive of the party since 1971. Two changes were, however, striking. In the 1970s factions represented different views about party strategies and policies. Under Mitterrand's leadership, the "dominant coalition"[25] was more or less unified around some common principles and policies. In the late 1980s and the early 1990s, factions were simply organized around a man who attempted to promote himself as the party leader who would be the best candidate for the presidency. As a consequence, factions could no longer be described in terms of political or ideological choice. The Fabius, Jospin, or Mauroy factions shared common political views but no common loyalty to the potential presidential candidate. It was also impossible to design a stable "dominant coalition."[26] Even if Jospin attempted to limit the power of factions, it is not clear that he quite succeeded.[27] For the first time since 1981 a Socialist government was not composed on a strict balance between party factions. However, those not represented in government took the control of the parliamentary party and prepared their comeback.

In conclusion, because they were devoted to nominating and supporting the candidate for the next presidential election, parties became more cut off from citizens. They made more credible the idea of a "political class" focused on its own interests and indifferent to voters' demands and expectations. The presidentialization of political parties in France made more questionable, among other things, the participation of party members in the party activity and consequently the parties' ability to act as an effective link between voters and state.

### The Occupation of the State

If party leaders and subleaders (in the case of parties divided into factions) occupy internal party positions for their own benefit, one can add that they also use public resources for the benefit of their parties. New forms of patronage that had appeared in the 1960s and the 1970s dramatically developed in the 1980s and the 1990s. The long tradition of the public sector in France and its expansion in 1981 with nationalizations initiated by the Socialists as well as decentralization (which began in 1982–83) increased the number of positions to be filled in agencies, in companies controlled by the government, and in national or local bureaucracies.

Few parties resisted the temptation to colonize society since, with the notable exception of the Greens, they had at least power in towns, departments, and regions. Mayors (in large cities) and presidents of departmental and regional councils increased their personal staffs with diverse councillors, assistants, and experts. At the same time, they created numerous large "technical" agencies in diverse areas (town planning, housing, campaigning, and so on). Last but not least, they encouraged the forming of associations strongly linked to the party and financed according to their loyalty. Theoretically founded in order to modernize and rationalize local policies and to improve relations between politicians and voters, all these agencies and associations gave opportunities to the parties to reward party members and sometimes friends and family. Sawicki emphasized the multiplication of positions the PS had to offer in the 1970–80s and suggested that many party activists joined the party to gain access to these positions.[28] The most striking example was Chirac, who, deprived of national governmental resources, used the city hall of Paris as a substitute. As suggested by

Haegel, Chirac, as mayor, "became the head of a staff of 40,000 civil servants which, from a financial and administrative but also from a symbolic point of view, was able to rival the state administration."[29] Moreover, the city hall and all the public services linked to it became a "shelter" for Chirac's entourage and aides who moved naturally from the government to city hall, from the RPR to the Parisian administration, and vice versa. If we consider, in Paris, the collapse of the left in the late 1980s and the early 1990s, one can understand that the RPR colonized Paris without any check and to its benefit included illegal financing of the party, corruption, and privileges for its members and leaders.

The case of Paris is but the most known and sophisticated example but it is not isolated. One can, however, note that the RPR reproduced and also developed at the local level mechanisms through which the Gaullist party had ensured its power at the national level in the past. Nevertheless, the Socialist Party, once in power, followed the same path. As far as the high administration was concerned, a spoils system, which led to changes in personnel according to political affiliation, was enforced. Direct nominations by the president and the prime minister increased. Judges, prefects, rectors of educational districts, chairmen of the most prestigious administrative bodies as well as high-level managers of nationalized firms were chosen in the weekly cabinet meeting. If their competence was not questionable, it is true that competence plus loyalty gave better chances to get high positions in the state apparatus.

Even privatizations or more freedom granted to state agencies did not really change the situation. In 1986, the first privatizations initiated by Chirac and Balladur had nothing to do with free-market rules. The president and the prime minister chose who would be entitled to participate in privatization and to enter into the enterprises' capital (the so-called *noyaux durs* or "hard core") in order not only to keep control over important parts of the French economy but also to secure positions to RPR "friends," frequently financial contributors to the party.[30] One might add that the public broadcasting system has always been a means for ensuring party power. As the former French president Georges Pompidou said, "it is the voice of France," that is, the voice for parties in power. All in all, the managers of the television stations as well as people responsible for the news were in the hands of the government and the parties. Reforms initiated by Mitterrand (free radio and private television channels; creation of an independent body to guarantee the freedom of television and radio) did not really alter the relations between parties in government and the broadcasting public sector. The "independent" body in charge of appointing the "independent" managers always put "the right men in key positions," that is, candidates backed by the government and parties in power.

CONCLUSION

Patronage has always been a function of political parties. One can, however, note how modern forms of patronage differ from traditional clientelism, which established unequal relations between parties and the voters. The clientelistic linkage required exchanges between individuals: a vote against some benefit for the voter. The colonization of the state, as implemented today by political parties, made the parties more anonymous and more cut off from the voters. They became a "state within the state" and therefore completely unable to link citizen and state. Dissatisfaction with them increased.

French parties are not so different from other parties in Europe.[31] As suggested by Katz and Mair, they tended to become "cartel" parties.[32] However, this change in party organization, role, and functions was made possible by two French particularities: the traditional lack of influence of parties in the political life and the increasing presidentialization of politics. Regarding relations between parties and the electorate, the same can be said. In a country where parties have always been criticized, where they have never had a recognized status, they were the perfect scapegoats for a French malaise that concerns not only the organization and role of political parties but more generally how democracy works in France.

As they were the pillars of the party system and of the regime, the major parties (PS, UDF, and RPR) were particularly questioned. Their failure had, however, contrasting consequences. The ecologists did not succeed in mobilizing a large part of the electorate and in making attractive their particular concerns: defense of the environment and new forms of democratic participation. Their electoral success in the early 1990s was based less on these concerns than on voters' dissatisfaction with the Socialist Party. On the contrary, the inability of political leaders to seek other goals than power over their own organization and the colonization of the state paves the way for the National Front and its populist appeal against the established parties named, in Le Pen's words, "the Gang of Four." All in all, change in parties' roles and functions altered not only the party system but also the general environment for democratic political life in France.

NOTES

1. Ronald Inglehart, *The Silent Revolution* (Princeton, N.J.: Princeton University Press, 1977).

2. Kay Lawson and Peter Merkl, *When Parties Fail* (Princeton, N.J.: Princeton University Press, 1988), pp. 5–10.

3. Piero Ignazi, *L'estrema destra in Europa* (Bologna: Il Mulino, 1994) and "The Intellectual Basis of Right-Wing Antipartyism," *European Journal of Political Research* 29: 279–96.

4. Frank L. Wilson, "When Parties Refuse to Fail: The Case of France," in Lawson and Merkl, *When Parties Fail.*

5. Colette Ysmal, *Les partis politiques sous la Vème République* (Paris: Domat/Montchrestien, 1989) and Colette Ysmal, "The Evolution of the French Party System," in *The Organization of Southern European Parties*, ed. Piero Ignazi and Colette Ysmal (Westport, Conn.: Greenwood Press, 1997).

6. Every candidate for the presidency must be supported by at least five hundred local and/or national office workers in at least thirty departments.

7. Piero Ignazi, "Un Nouvel Acteur Politique," in *Le Front National à De'couvert*, ed. Nonna Mayer and Pascal Perrineau (Paris: Presses des Science Politiques, 1989).

8. In 1985, Mitterrand decided to move from the majoritarian system adopted in 1958 to proportional representation. The NF gained thirty-five seats. The majoritarian system was reintroduced in 1986 by the victorious right-wing coalition. The FN took one seat in 1988, none in 1993, and one in 1997.

9. Pascal Perrineau (ed.), *L'engagement politique. Déclin ou mutation?* (Paris: Presses de Sciences politiques, 1994).

10. Leon Epstein, *Political Parties in the American Mold* (Madison: University of Wisconsin Press, 1986).

11. The most well-known example is General de Gaulle who fought the Fourth Republic as the "regime of parties," founded a party mamed Rally of the French People in order to indicate that the party had a vocation to unify French people without giving attention to political affiliation, social class, or religion. However, under the Third Republic some right-wing leaders developed the same orientations. Under the Fifth Republic, the Gaullist tradition was used by Raymond Barre and, partially, by the RPR.

12. Like any other association, according to the law, they have just to declare to the police (generally in Paris) their name and the place of their headquarters.

13. Ysmal, *Les Parties Politiques* and Ysmal, "Evolution of the French Party System."

14. They are qualified whether they get seats in the National Assembly and the Senate and/or they had candidates in general elections in at least seventy electoral districts.

15. Philip E. Converse and Georges Dupeux, "Politicization of the Electorate in France and the United States," *Public Opinion Quarterly* 26: 1–23.

16. Philip E. Converse and Roy Pierce, *Political Representation in France* (Cambridge, Mass.: The Belknap Press of Harvard University Press, 1986).

17. Colette Ysmal, "Transformations du militantisme et déclin des partis," *L'engagement politique. Déclin ou mutation?* ed. Pascal Perrineau (Paris: Presses de Sciences Politiques, 1994). "The Evolution of the French Party System," in *The Organization of Southern European Parties*, ed. Piero Ignazi and Colette Ysmal (Westport, Conn.: Greenwood Press, 1997).

18. Converse and Dupeux, "Politicization of the Electorate"; Converse and Pierce, *Political Representation in France.*

19. Jacques Capdevielle, Elisabeth Dupoirier, Gérard Grunberg, Etienne Schweisguth, and Colette Ysmal, *France de gauche, vote à droite* (Paris: Presses de Sciences politiques, 1981).

20. Lawson and Merkl, *When Parties Fail*, pp. 15–16.

21. Roberto Michels, *Les partis politiques* (Paris: Flammarion, 1971, orig. pub. 1914).

22. Richard Katz and Peter Mair, *How Parties Organize: Change and Adaptation in Party Organizations in Western Democracies* (London: Sage, 1994).

23. Frédéric Sawicki, "The French Socialist Party 1971–1993: From a Party of Activists to a Party of Government," in Ignazi and Ysmal, *Organization of Southern European Parties*.

24. In 1990, and for the first time in the RPR history, two motions concerning party program and strategy were proposed to the delegates at the party conference. The Pasqua and Séguin motion was supported by 35 percent of the delegates.

25. Angelo Panebianco, *Modelli di partito* (Bologna: Il Mulino, 1982).

26. Sawicki, "French Socialist Party."

27. The PS first secretary, previously appointed by the executive committee, is directly elected by the members since 1995. In the same way, the candidate to the presidency is nominated by the members.

28. Sawicki, "French Socialist Party."

29. Florence Haegel, "The Rally for the Republic: Conflict and Change," in Ignazi and Ysmal, *Organization of Southern European Parties*.

30. As revealed by investigations of illegal fund-raising by the party, corruption, and sometimes personal enrichment.

31. Piero Ignazi and Colette Ysmal, *The Organization of Southern European Parties* (Westport, Conn.: Greenwood Press, 1997).

32. Richard Katz and Peter Mair, "Changing Models of Party Organization and Party Democracy: The Emergence of the Cartel Party," *Party Politics* 1 (1995): 5–28.

# CHAPTER 4

# Whither the Old Order?
## The Collapse of the GDR and the
## "New" German Party System

## Charlie Jeffery and Charles Lees

This chapter is naturally concerned with the collapse of one "old order," in the form of the German Democratic Republic, that was absorbed into an expanded Federal Republic of Germany in 1990. The core question it addresses, though, is the extent to which the pre-unification—that is, West German—party system of the Federal Republic has proved capable of rising to the challenge of integrating the expanded electorate of the united Germany. In this as in other areas, opinion remains divided as to whether the Federal Republic has emerged relatively unscathed from the "system shock" implicit in a unification process that essentially extended established western structures eastwards. There are certainly many signs that suggest that the "old order" of western party politics has been placed under growing strain by the challenges of post-unification east-west integration since 1990.

A much-used metaphor for this challenge is provided by the phrase *die Mauer im Kopf*, the "wall in the head," that supposedly separates westerner from easterner in united Germany. This ironic analogy to the physical walls that used to divide the West and East German states has both historical and contemporary "brickwork." On a general level, forty-one years of separate development within two ideologically opposed states has imbued easterners and westerners with differing sets of political and social values. This historically based cleavage between east and west has subsequently been sharpened since 1990 as a result of some of the practical problems thrown up by unification.

Eastern Germans have become increasingly disillusioned by the collapse and subsequent stagnation of their economy since 1990, especially when compared with the generally far higher levels of prosperity in the west. They have also had to confront demoralizing revelations of widespread complicity in the activities of the former GDR's internal intelligence service (the *Stasi*) and the—in part related and similarly demoralizing—need to "import" untainted and experienced westerners to shape and build up public services in the east. In the west, on the other hand, there has been a growing disaffection with the material burdens imposed by the cost of financing social security and economic reconstruction in the east. This dissatisfaction became more profound in the early to mid-1990s, as the wider international recession slowed down the western economy. These differences in experience and perspective produced a sense of distance and tension between easterners and westerners.

Political parties have played a key role in West European democracies in helping to accommodate such differences of background and interest in society. Parties typically emerged in Western Europe as representatives of the interests of particular social groups or collections of groups (for example, class/occupation-based groups, groups based on religious affiliation or regional identity, and so on). By pressing in electoral competition with other party/group interests for their group interests to be met by the institutions of state, parties secured for themselves the continued support and loyalty of those groups. This means of providing stable and reliable channels for the expression of different, competing group interests and the incorporation of at least some of those interests in government policy has led parties to play an important role in bridging and managing social divisions.

The aim of this chapter is to examine the extent to which political parties are capable of performing this bridging role in the context of unified Germany. This question is given a fascinating slant since the party system of unified Germany is essentially that of the old West German Federal Republic. The question remains whether a party system that emerged out of the differences of interest in West German society can bridge the differences of interest that now exist between the western and eastern German electorates. Further nuance is added to the question by the fact that even in the west prior to unification the party system was subject to processes of change and disequilibrium. A brief overview of pre-unification developments therefore provides the initial context against which the post-unification party system(s) should be assessed.

## THE PRE-UNIFICATION PARTY SYSTEM UNDER STRAIN

Prior to the 1983 Bundestag election, the West German party system enjoyed an unusual degree of stability, characterized by the electoral co-supremacy of the two large *Volksparteien* ("people's parties"), the German Democratic Union (CDU)/German Social Union (CSU) and the Social Democratic Party (SPD), and the key "balancing" or "king-making" role played by the small liberal Free Democratic Party (FDP). From 1969 onwards the CDU/CSU and SPD were each able consistently to attract over 40 percent of the vote. The vote-winning capacity of both *Volksparteien* was based on their capacity to project a moderated ideological profile appealing across broad sections of the electorate. However, neither party was able to broaden out its electoral base sufficiently to win an absolute majority over the course of this period. This invested the third party in the *Bundestag*, the FDP, with a key role. With just a modest share of the vote (6–10%), the FDP was the linchpin of a stable "two-and-a-half" party system, which meant it was (normally) indispensable in the construction of any parliamentary majority.

From the early 1980s, however, the patterns of instability and volatility that had begun to rock party systems elsewhere in Western Europe in the 1970s[1] also became apparent in the FRG. The primary indicator of change was the breakthrough of "New Left" politics, in the form of the Greens, as a parliamentary force after 1983. The emergence of the Greens, mainly at the expense of the SPD, seemed to presage a shift away from centrism and toward a form of more polarized party competition. The inroads made by the Greens into the SPD vote were sufficient in both 1983 and 1987 to rule out an SPD-FDP coalition. This destroyed the hitherto pivotal, linchpin position of the FDP, leaving it committed to a continuation of the coalition formed in 1982 with the Christian Democrats. A rudimentary two-bloc party system[2] emerged, polarized between SPD and Greens on the left and CDU/CSU and FDP on the right. This polarization was enhanced in the late 1980s with the emergence of the far right at the subnational level, leading some elements of the CDU/CSU themselves to shift away from the political center and peddle a more conservative and nationalist message in the hope of warding off the far right electoral challenge.[3]

The increasing disequilibrium within the two-and-a-half party system was also a corollary of what Elmar Wiesendahl coined the "modernization trap,"[4] a blurring of party identity and direction inherent in the vote-chasing rationale of the *Volkspartei* model, which disillusioned those supporters still attached to the parties' original or presumed ideological thrust. The process of alienation was known in Germany as *Parteienverdrossenheit*, a growing sense of popular disillusionment with the party system.[5] Such alienation was accelerated by the nature of the established parties' organizational structures, which were typically complex and highly bureaucratized and failed to offer genuine opportunities for new groups of new ideas to shape or modify the parties' established direction. The established parties wielded a form of *Machtmonopol*, a monopoly of power in the hands of an insulated, self-selecting politician caste widely perceived as remote from the electorate and motivated by self-interest.[6] The corollary of this *Machtmonopol* was for some critics the *Entmündigung des Volkes*, a loss of public "voice" in politics[7] and a consequent dealignment of the ties that had been built up between parties and voters in the previous decades of the Federal Republic.

## FACTORING IN THE EAST

Although these were *West* German phenomena, the process and manifestations of dealignment help to put the questions placed for the FRG party system by unification into perspective. Unification presented a unique challenge—the integration of a postcommunist electorate—to a party system already under growing strain.

The East German electorate was the product forty-five years of one-party communist rule, and before that four years of Soviet occupation and the twelve years of the Third Reich. It lacked the usual paraphernalia that help structure voting behavior in liberal democracies, most of all the regular rhythm of competitive elections, but also the party organizations and traditions, buttressed by ties to intermediary organizations like trade unions and churches, which in the west had shaped voter-party alignments. Thus, when the western parties began to organize in the east, they were in many ways entering uncharted waters. It was not clear if this would herald a relatively painless integration of the eastern electorate into the existing party system or, as a worst case scenario, if it would prove to be a transplant of norms and structures that would be rejected by an essentially alien body politic.

In strategic terms, the CDU's proven ability to absorb and integrate a wide spectrum of center-right actors[8] left it well placed to move into the political vacuum left in the GDR during the period of regime collapse in 1989–90. Additionally, in a tactical sense, the CDU—and Chancellor Kohl in particular—showed an unexpected capacity to seize upon events in the GDR as a welcome respite from several years of political decline in the Federal Republic. Within a month of the opening-up of the inter-German border, Kohl had entered the fray with his ten-point program for unification. Kohl subsequently was instrumental in the creation of the "Alliance for Germany," consisting of the East German CDU, the German Social Union (the DSU, backed by the Bavarian CSU), and Democratic Awakening (DA, the conservative wing of the East German dissident movement), which was to fight the East German parliamentary (Volkskammer) election of March 1990 on a united platform.[9]

In similar processes, the East and West German Social Democrats had established extensive interparty cooperation by mid-December 1989, whilst the liberal FDP helped set up the League of Free Democrats in February 1990. The exception was provided by the Greens, whose ambivalence toward the process of German unification inhibited the process of integration with their counterparts in the East. The eastern and western Greens did not formally merge until 1993, with the formation of Alliance '90/the Greens, incorporating some of the citizen movements that had spearheaded initial opposition to the GDR regime in 1989.

The only significant indigenous eastern competitor to these western-influenced party formations was the Party of Democratic Socialism (PDS), the newly minted successor to the Socialist Unity Party (SED), the former ruling party of the GDR. Although the PDS possessed a formidable resource base, in terms of money and know-how, the orthodoxy at the time held that the PDS was fatally tainted by its association with the old order. This assumption has since proven unduly optimistic.[10]

With only a few weeks to the Volkskammer elections, the SPD proceeded to shoot itself in the foot. In the early months of the process of regime collapse, the SPD's stance on unification was quite bullish. With Willy Brandt setting the tone, the SPD proposed a speedy unification and the end of the rights of the Four Powers in Berlin and the two states. However, within the East German wing of the party, sentiment was more in favor of a slow process of unification. Over time, this latter view asserted itself with a consequent loss in electoral support. The SPD's failure to hold on to its early opinion poll lead was aggravated by the decision by Kohl, in February 1990, to reject the interim GDR government's request for DM 15 million in aid. Bonn made it very clear that the Federal Republic was not willing to underwrite what it saw as an illegitimate regime in East Berlin. Although this appeared reasonable in itself, many East Germans read more into the decision than just a rejection of the rump Communist regime. Implicitly, it seemed to indicate that there would be *"no money until there is a government to Bonn's liking."* Whatever the truth of the matter, it is clear that Kohl's decision coincided with a significant increase in support for Alliance for Germany.[11]

## THE LAST GDR ELECTIONS

The Volkskammer elections of March 18, 1990 were the first, and last, free nationwide elections to be held in the German Democratic Republic. They were also the first opportunity for the western parties to test the political waters in the uncharted waters of the east.

Prior to March 1990, the last free election held throughout the GDR's territory had been in November 1932. In the intervening years of Nazi dictatorship, Soviet occupation, and Communist rule, any firm voter-party ties existing in eastern Germany prior to 1932 had withered away. In this sense the March 1990 election was a *Stunde Null*, a "new beginning," in which voter-party relationships were essentially non-aligned. In the absence of established party alignments, East German voters displayed an unusual sensitivity to political issues in the months before the March election. This sensitivity was magnified by the acute sense of disorientation and uncertainty that dominated GDR politics amid the disintegration of the Communist regime and the subsequent emergence and intensification of calls for unification with West Germany. In addition East German voters were faced, after more than forty years of single-party domination, with the problem of choosing from the wide range of parties standing for election, each of which was attempting, not always successfully, to keep pace with events. This fluid and rather chaotic interaction between issues, voters, and parties manifested itself in an extreme volatility of voting intentions in the run-up to what was, ultimately, probably the most open and unpredictable ballot in German electoral history.

A total of twenty-three parties, several of which were united in electoral alliances, stood for election. Only five of these parties and party alliances had a sufficient nationwide profile to suggest a realistic chance of significant electoral support: the PDS; the Alliance '90 of citizens' initiatives, notably New Forum, which had played a prominent role in anti-Communist opposition in 1989; the East German SPD, formed in October 1989; the Christian Democratic Alliance for Germany; and the League of Free Democrats. The election results are set out in table 4.1.

The poor performance of the Alliance '90 may seem surprising given the prominent role its component groups had played in mobilizing anti-Communist protest in the autumn of 1989. However, support for such groups in that period reflected far more a broad identification with their anti-Communist opposition stance than any specific, positive popular commitment to their program of participatory democratic reform. Never much more than a focal point of opposition to the SED-regime, Alliance '90 became increasingly irrelevant for most East Germans as soon as debate in the GDR had moved beyond how to get rid of the Communists and become preoccupied with the question of unification. In the end, the only "indigenous" East German party that proved capable of maintaining a significant popular presence was, on the strength of its continuing support within the ex-Communist "establishment," the PDS.

TABLE 4.1
Elections to the Volkskammer, March 1990

|  | % |
| --- | --- |
| German Democratic Union (CDU) | 40.8 |
| German Social Union (DSU) | 6.3 |
| Democratic Awakening | 0.9 |
| *Total: Alliance for Germany* | 48.0 |
| Social Democratic Party (SPD) | 21.9 |
| Free Democratic Union | 5.3 |
| Greens/Women's List | 2.0 |
| Alliance '90 | 2.9 |
| Party for Democratic Socialism (PDS) | 16.4 |
| Farmers' Party (DBP) | 2.2 |
| National Democratic Party (NDPD) | 0.4 |
| Others | 0.8 |

Note: Electorate: 12.4 million; turnout: 93.2 percent.
Source: Smith et al. (eds.), *Developments in German Politics* (London: Macmillan, 1992), p. 86.

The unification issue ultimately dominated the *Volkskammer* election campaign. Some 48% of East Germans were in favor of unification in November 1989, rising to 76% in February 1990, and 91% by election day. The questions confronting the East German electorate therefore revolved less and less around whether or not to pursue national unity, and increasingly around how, when, and by whom it might best be brought about. In such a situation the western-sponsored parties had an inherent advantage: they could point to the aid their western partners could offer in bringing the desire for unity to fruition.

Up to February 1990, the SPD appeared best able put forward the most plausible answers to the questions posed by unification. It had the pedigree of being one of the first forces to call for national unity at the end of 1989. Subsequently, it developed a clear conception of how the GDR might be incorporated into the West German economic and political order in a gradual, medium-term process that would provide a measure of protection for GDR citizens against social and economic dislocation. However, popular opinion swung decisively away from the SPD and toward the Alliance for Germany from late February onwards.

The vulnerability of the SPD's lead had three main sources. First, it had won its advantage in part by default; it was the only party that had, at that time, developed a clear line on unification. Others, notably the Alliance for Germany, would follow. Second, poll findings suggested that voting intentions were as yet by no means firmly established. Less than 50 percent of professed SPD supporters had made a firm voting decision by February 1990. Most voters were apparently reserving for themselves the option of switching their party allegiance before election day. The third source of the SPD's vulnerability lay in Bonn, or perhaps more precisely, in Saarbrücken: the power base of chancellor-candidate Oskar Lafontaine. Lafontaine's apparent lack of enthusiasm for unification implicitly weakened the East German SPD's claim to possess a reliable and effective partner in the west. It also contrasted starkly to the unequivocal support given by prominent West German Christian Democrats, in particular Chancellor Kohl, to the Alliance for Germany following its formation on February 5, 1990.

Despite the lateness of its formal entry into the election campaign, the Alliance for Germany was therefore able to rely on the unambiguous support of its western partners. Crucially, those partners were also in government in the west and able to swing the full political and economic weight of the Federal Republic behind the Alliance's campaign message of rapid unification. They also committed themselves quickly to the rapid introduction of the deutsche mark (DM) in the east. This commitment was motivated by two factors. First, it might serve to stem the continuing flow of migrants from east to west. Second, in a more positive sense, it was thought that it would provide a kind of therapeutic "shock therapy" to the East German economy. The thinking was that, within the framework of monetary stability provided by the DM, currency union would shake out inefficiency and create the foundations for a prosperous future free market order.

The Alliance was also adjudged to possess significantly more competence than the SPD in managing the problems of transition. This can be attributed above all to the impact created by Helmut Kohl in his addresses to Alliance rallies in the final stages of the campaign. Playing on his capacity as leader of the West German government to "deliver the goods," Kohl evoked an upbeat and optimistic vision of unification by offering protection for East German savings and pensions and promising currency union under highly generous terms. The dramatic swing to the Alliance, which was emphatically confirmed in the final election results, was therefore a vote for the future and an investment in the presumed capacity of the Christian Democrats to deliver future prosperity more effectively and more quickly than its competitors. The scale and speed of the pro-Alliance swing testifies to the extreme volatility of voting intentions in an electorate that lacked established party alignments and was overwhelmingly oriented around current political issues.

Following its belated creation just six weeks before the election, the Alliance succeeded in projecting a platform sufficiently attuned to the aspirations of the East Germans to "mop up," even at the last minute, previously undecided voters. The SPD, pledged to a slower pace of unification and hampered by the apparent ambivalence of its western partner, was the major loser. It was unable to retain the high, but never firmly committed, levels of support it had attracted in February 1990.

The pattern of nonaligned issue-orientation is confirmed by the relative insignificance of group-based patterns of voting behavior in March 1990. Beyond an affinity of the relatively small proportion of voters with a religious affiliation to the Alliance for Germany and of the formerly privileged groups of the Communist regime with the PDS, there existed no clear-cut party alignments based on a sense of collective group identity. In the bulk of the electorate, issue-based voting predominated. This was seen most obviously in the "inverted" profile of the manual worker electorate, a majority of which voted for the future prosperity promised by the Alliance rather than the "natural" representative of manual worker interests, the SPD.

## VOTERS AND PARTIES IN UNIFIED GERMANY

If the extreme issue-orientation within the East German electorate raised doubts about the ability of the parties to retain their vote shares in subsequent elections, the results of the first *Bundestag* election in unified Germany in December 1990 might be seen as something of an anticlimax. The results represented a triumph of the "core" parties of the former West Germany, the CDU/CSU, SPD, and FDP. As table 4.2 demonstrates, they succeeded in mopping up over 75% of the East German vote in 1990 while maintaining their hold on over 90% of the western electorate.

This triumph of the "core" West German parties was, however, interpreted rather divergently in the literature. Gordon Smith, the doyen of German party system studies in the United Kingdom saw it as a telling testament to the integrative capacities of the core parties and, by implication, to an enduring stability of a party system robust enough in its core to accommodate even the upheavals of unification.[12] Smith's commentary is certainly true to the extent that the western parties were able collectively to gather another nine million or so votes in the east and retain their core position into the 1990s. It was, however, countered by an alternative view, represented amongst others by Stephen Padgett, who insisted that the triumph of the core parties rested on extremely shaky foundations, to the extent that he predicted a new era of unpre-

TABLE 4.2
Elections to the Bundestag, December 1990

|  | West % | East % | Germany % | Seats |
|---|---|---|---|---|
| Turnout | 78.6 | 74.7 | 77.8 | |
| CDU | 35.5 | 41.8 | 36.7 | 268 |
| CSU | 8.8 | — | 7.1 | 51 |
| *Total* | *44.3* | | *43.8* | |
| SPD | 35.7 | 24.3 | 33.5 | 239 |
| FDP | 10.6 | 12.9 | 11.0 | 79 |
| Greens (West) | 4.8 | — | 3.9 | 0 |
| Bündnis 90/Greens (East) | — | 6.0 | 1.2 | 8 |
| PDS | 0.3 | 11.1 | 2.4 | 17 |
| Republicans | 2.3 | 1.3 | 2.1 | 0 |
| NPD | 0.3 | 0.0 | 0.3 | 0 |
| DSU | — | 1.0 | 0.2 | 0 |

Source: Smith et al., *Developments in German Politics*, p. 88.


dictable change in German electoral politics, a "*Wende ohne Ende.*"[13] This reflects widely held doubts in the ability of the core parties to maintain a reliable and enduring basis of support across the new united Germany in future elections. To do this, they would not only have to shore up their position in an increasingly disillusioned and capricious western electorate, but also to begin to root themselves in an eastern electorate that, buffeted by the dislocation of post-Communist transformation, has priorities and concerns widely divergent to those in the west.

The latter part of the challenge is an uncommonly difficult one. There exists a rather different social base for electoral politics in the new *Länder*. Despite the processes of dealignment noted above, social background does still provide at least some predictable electoral cues in the west. The most significant of these—the alignment of manual workers to the SPD and of practicing Christians, especially Catholics, to the CDU/CSU—have proved to be of either less relevance, or even of irrelevance in the east. Although the Christian vote has fallen disproportionately to the CDU in the east since 1990, in absolute terms it is of little significance. Following decades of state hostility to organized religion in the GDR, 67% of East Germans (compared to just 19% of West Germans) lacked any religious affiliation according to an official survey in 1992.[14] Moreover, initial expectations[15] that the SPD would be able to draw on its "traditional" strength among the manual workers of the east (as it had done in the interwar Weimar years) proved to be overoptimistic. In fact, the CDU won over 48% of the manual worker vote in the east in 1990, compared to the SPD's 24.7%. Moreover, despite losses among this group—probably the hardest hit by the problems of transformation—the CDU still held a lead of 40.6% to 35.1% over the SPD in the 1994 election.[16] The prevalence of secularism and the "inverted social profile"[17] of class voting compounded the problems facing the western parties in generating a stable, cross-German electoral profile. They have not risen to that challenge effectively.

In fact, seven years after unification, a sense of alienation vis-à-vis the established parties is the prevalent mood in the new *Länder*. Evidence has accumulated since unification that when the western party system "colonized" the east, it took with it the sense of *Parteienverdrossenheit* that had accumulated in the west in the 1980s. Survey evidence shows that the level of confidence and "trust" in political parties had fallen to an unprecedented level in the early to mid-1990s.[18] This reflected in part an extraordinary proliferation of "sleaze" scandals that led the then German president, the widely respected Richard von Weizsäcker, to make a blistering attack on the irresponsibility of the parties in their exercise of power.[19] More broadly, though, it reflected the failure of the CDU/CSU-FDP government and the SPD opposition to offer any real, nationwide sense of direction in political life. Neither has succeeded in carrying out a genuine programmatic or strategic renewal since unification, nor have they succeeded in establishing dynamic eastern party organizations capable of securing genuine East German input into strategic programming. Beyond the tokenistic appointments of prominent East Germans to senior party positions, like Wolfgang Theirs in the SPD and Angela Merkel in the CDU, the overriding picture is one of continued organizational ossification and the unresponsive *Machtmonopol* that characterized party organization in the Federal Republic before 1989.

In addition, the established parties are widely perceived to have failed to deliver in policy terms in both east and west. The record of economic management since 1990 has been at best undistinguished, dogged by a failure to foresee serious problems and a slowness of reaction when the scale of the problems did emerge. Debates in other policy fields—for example, the abortion and asylum issues, and the question of German army contributions to NATO or UN missions—have tended to drag on for months, even years, without effective resolution, compounding an impression of stagnation and immobilism. This policy stagnation undermined public confidence nationwide in both the CDU/CSU-FDP government and the SPD opposition, which has been firmly bound into the government process via its Bundesrat majority and *Vermittlungsauschusspolitik*. Accordingly, public assessment of the "*Leistung*" (general performance) of both government and opposition had fallen to its lowest ever point, according to one regular poll, by 1993.[20]

## EMERGING FROM THE OLD ORDER

These various factors—"sleaze," lack of political direction, organizational and policy stagnation—were reflected in a growing sense of voter detachment from CDU/CSU, FDP, and SPD. This was clearly illustrated in the run of *Land* elections held between the 1990 and 1994 Bundestag elections. A number of broad trends are worth noting. The first is the evidently growing weakness in most of the *Länder* of voter attachments to CDU/CSU or SPD. Second, the FDP has become deeply unpopular, failing to cross the 5 percent hurdle in a long series of *Land* elections in 1992–94 (a trend only partly reversed since 1994). Third, parties outside the core western "establishment" have increasingly benefited from these developments. The most notable example has been the Greens, for whom the *Länder* have provided a basis from which to launch an impressive recovery from the disappointing Bundestag result in 1990. However, in the early 1990s, the *Länder* also provided fertile electoral ground for the parties of the far right, which made significant inroads into both the SPD and, especially, the CDU vote. More significantly, the post-Communist PDS, capitalizing on disillusionment with the perceived incapacity of the other parties to address the concerns of the east, have made substantial advances in the *Länder*, creating an electoral momentum that was to lead it, unexpectedly, to retain Bundestag representation in the 1994 election. Fourth, the weakness of the establishment parties and the success of noncore parties together complicated problems of coalition formation in the *Länder*, forcing the reconsideration of traditional patterns of coalition-building. *Länder* coalitions that cut across Bundestag coalition alignments (CDU-SPD grand coalitions and SPD-FDP coalitions) have become commonplace, as have "red-green" coalitions of SPD and Greens, the latter at times supplemented by unusual variations: "traffic light" coalitions of SPD, Greens, and FDP in Brandenburg in 1990–94 and Bremen in 1991–95; and a red-green minority coalition "tolerated" by the PDS in Saxony-Anhalt in 1994. On one occasion (Baden-Württemberg, 1992) a "black-green" coalition of CDU and the Greens was even briefly discussed.[21] Finally, and more broadly, the outlines of a party system bifurcated by the former east-west border began to emerge, with a four-party system in the west (CDU/CSU, SPD, Greens, and a much weakened FDP) and, given the wholesale failure of the FDP and the parliamentary representation of the Greens in only one eastern *Land* parliament, a three-party system in the east (CDU, SPD, and PDS).

These features of the *Länder* elections of 1990–94 collectively suggest that the weak post-unification condition of voter-party alignments—characterized by continuing dealignment in the west and a wholesale lack of stable alignments in the east—had not changed significantly by the time of the 1994 Bundestag election. However, the actual pattern of the 1994 election gave a different impression (table 4.3), returning as it did the same CDU/CSU-FDP government and the same group of opposition parties.

However, a number of comments need to be made that qualify this superficial image of stability. The first point is that the FDP's weakness after 1990 raised severe doubts about whether it would clear the 5 percent hurdle and re-enter the Bundestag. Although it did so quite comfortably in the end—albeit only with the "loaned," tactical votes of CDU/CSU supporters—the prospect of FDP failure launched intense debates about coalition possibilities without the FDP. These debates drew on the experiences of *Länder* elections and coalition formation after 1990, with some foreseeing a grand coalition of CDU/CSU and SPD, and others a "red-green" coalition of SPD and Greens, possibly

TABLE 4.3
Elections to the Bundestag, December 1994

|  | West % | East % | Germany % | Seats |
|---|---|---|---|---|
| Turnout | 80.6 | 72.9 | 79.0 | |
| CDU | 33.2 | 38.5 | 34.2 | 244 |
| CSU | 8.8 | — | 7.3 | 50 |
| *Total* | *42.0* | | *41.5* | |
| SPD | 37.5 | 31.5 | 36.4 | 252 |
| FDP | 7.7 | 3.5 | 6.9 | 47 |
| Bündnis 90/Greens | 7.9 | 4.3 | 7.3 | 49 |
| PDS | 1.0 | 19.8 | 4.4 | 30 |
| Others | 3.9 | 2.4 | 3.5 | 0 |

Source: S. Green, "All Change? The German Party System and the Aftermath of Superwahljahr," Institute for German Studies Working Paper No. IGS95/5.

dependent on the support of the PDS, which was (unexpectedly) set to reenter the Bundestag. These debates were in the end academic. That they were conducted at all, though, indicates that a new, open, and rather unpredictable mode of party competition has emerged in the new Germany. This was the closest fought election in the FRG since 1949, and the closest ever that a sitting government has come to being voted out of office. It pointed to a potential for governmental turnover unprecedented in a political system used to long periods of coalition government. Moreover, as table 4.3 shows, the east-west pattern of results confirms the tendency to a bifurcation of the party system with just two genuinely national parties—the CDU/CSU and SPD—and three parties with a limited, regionally based electoral potential—the Greens and FDP in the west, and the PDS in the east. This tendency to bifurcation has the potential severely to complicate the dynamics of coalition-formation in the future. The question posed by Bürklin and Roth[22] before the 1994 election may prove to be a prescient one for observers of the German party system: "Are we standing at the end of an era of stable party-political majorities and therefore of workable [majority] governments?" In other words, whither the old order?

## NOTES

1. Cf. P. Mair, "The Problem of Party System Change," *Journal of Theoretical Politics* 1 (1989): 261–62.

2. S. Padgett, "The New German Electorate," in *Parties and Party Systems in the New Germany*, ed. S. Padgett (Aldershot, U.K.: Dartmouth/Association for the Study of German Politics, 1993), pp. 127–30.

3. C. Clemens, "Helmut Kohl's CDU and German Unification: The Price of Success," *German Politics and Society* 22 (1991).

4. E. Wiesendahl, "Der Marsch aus den Institutionen," *Aus Politik und Zeitgeschichte* b21 (1990).

5. Cf. C. Jeffery and S. Green, "The Sense of Malaise in Germany," *Parliamentary Affairs* 48 (1995).

6. What Erwin and Ute Scheuch (1992) memorably describe as an unpalatable combination of "cliques, cabals and careers."

7. E.g., H. H. von Arnim, "Entmündigen die Parteien das Volk? Parteienherrschaft und Volkssouveränität," *Aus Politik und Zeitgeschichte* b21 (1990).

8. Since 1949 the CDU/CSU has mobilized the center/right majority in the Federal Republic by reaching across class/confessional cleavages to a broad electoral base, commanding the largest share of the electorate for all but four years since the war. German Christian Democracy cannot simply be likened to conservatism, having as it does a distinct Christian-Democratic "mix." First, it shares with its European sister parties a broad commitment to such "Christian" values as basic human rights, the individual, and the family.

Second, it supports the liberal conception of democracy. Finally, it espouses an integrative function—both nationally (through the *Volkspartei* principle) and internationally (especially through European integration). The emphasis on combining social justice (in the tradition of Catholic teaching) with support for the market has given it considerable appeal, despite the increasing secularization of society.

9. This move was significant because, up until then, Kohl had been wary of the CDU's East German sister party. The main reason for this was the perception that the East German CDU was tainted by its role as a "bloc" party under the old regime. However, Kohl was concerned by a string of opinion polls that indicated that the SPD was set for a comfortable victory at the first free Volkskammer elections planned for March. This would not only damage the cause of center-right politics in the GDR, but would impact badly upon the CDU's campaign for the Bundestag elections that December. As a result, Kohl decided that the GDR electorate had to be given the opportunity to vote for a credible center-right party that would mount a serious challenge to the SPD. Given this requirement, misgivings about the efficacy of the East German CDU were to be ignored.

10. Nevertheless, the PDS still attracts opprobrium. Labels such as "ex-Stasi," the "Eastern League," the "nostalgic association," or even "Red Polished Fascists" have been used to attack the party. Ironically, this has apparently helped the PDS as much as hindered it. The success of the PDS in entering the Bundestag following the October 1994 elections was evidence that the party had consolidated its status as the "eastern" party of protest. Moreover, the continued social dislocation in the new *Länder* means that the PDS's position is secure for the time being. Cf. Lees, "Bringing the PDS into the Coalition Equation," *German Politics* 4.1 (1995).

11. D. Conradt, "The Christian Democrats in 1990: Saved by Unification?" in *The New Germany Votes*, ed. R. Dalton (Oxford: Berg, 1993), p. 65.

12. G. Smith, "Dimensions of Change in the German Party System," in *Parties and Party Systems in the New Germany*, ed. S. Padgett (Aldershot, U.K.: Dartmouth/Association for the Study of German Politics, 1993).

13. Padgett, "The New German Electorate."

14. W. Gibowski, "Germany's General Election in 1994: Who Voted for Whom?" in *Germany's New Politics*, ed. D. P. Conradt, G. R. Kleinfeld, G. K. Romoser, and C. Søe (Tempe, Ariz.: German Studies Review, 1995), pp. 105–8.

15. A. J. McAdams, "Towards a New Germany? Problems of Unification," *Government and Opposition* 25 (1990): 305.

16. Gibowski, "Germany's General Election," p. 108.

17. Padgett, "The New German Electorate," p. 39.

18. Cf. Jeffrey and Green, "Sense of Malaise."

19. R. von Weizsäcker, *Richard von Weizsäcker im Gespräch mit Gunter Hofmann and Werner Perger* (Frankfurt/Main: von Eichorn, 1992).

20. D. Roth, "Das Bild der Parteien in der Öffentlichkeit," *Politische Studien* 44 (1993): 62.

21. C. Lees, "Bringing the PDS into the Coalition Equation," *German Politics* 4.1 (1995) and "Paradise Postponed: An Assessment of Ten Years of Gov-

ernmental Participation by the Green Party in Germany," in *Ecological Modernisation*, ed. S. Young (London: Routledge, 1998).

22. W. Bürklin and D. Roth, "Das Superwahljahr 1994. Deutschland am Ende einer Ära stabilen Wahlverhaltens?" in *Das Superwahljahr 1994. Deutschland vor unkalkulierbaren Regierungsmöglichkeiten?* ed. W. Bürklin and D. Roth (Cologne: Bund-Verlag, 1994), p. 26.

CHAPTER 5

# Italy:
# The Demise of the
# Post-War Partyocracy

## Nick Carter

Since unification in 1870, Italy's political order has experienced three periods of collapse: 1919–25, 1943–46, and 1989–1994. The last of these, which saw the end of Christian Democratic political hegemony, the destruction or fragmentation of all the main postwar political parties, the rise of new political forces, and major electoral reform (though as yet no fundamental structural reforms) is the subject of this essay. These most recent events have encouraged talk of an end to the First Italian Republic (established in 1946) and the birth of a Second Republic. The purpose of this paper is to illustrate and to explain the changes in this most recent period of old order collapse, to assess the extent and significance of those changes, and to suggest possible future developments.

### THE NATURE OF THE OLD ORDER, 1946–89

Despite chronic government instability since the war (on average more than one government per year), the most striking characteristic of the Italian political system in 1989 was how little it had altered since the first postwar elections, which were held in 1948 under the new republican constitution. As Martin Clark notes, "Italian politics was, superficially, complex; but underlying it there was stability, even monotony."[1]

Table 5.1 shows the joint electoral dominance of the Christian Democrats (DC) and the Italian Communist party (PCI), and the remarkable stability of voting patterns, from 1948 until 1987. As a combined percentage of valid votes cast, the DC and PCI consistently polled

TABLE 5.1
Percentage Share of Valid Votes Cast in Elections to the
Chamber of Deputies for the Main Postwar Parties, 1948–87

|      | 1948 | 1953 | 1958 | 1963 | 1968 | 1972 | 1976 | 1979 | 1983 | 1987 |
|------|------|------|------|------|------|------|------|------|------|------|
| DC   | 48.5 | 40.1 | 42.4 | 38.3 | 39.1 | 38.7 | 38.7 | 38.3 | 32.9 | 34.3 |
| PCI  |      | 22.6 | 22.7 | 25.3 | 26.9 | 27.1 | 34.4 | 30.4 | 29.9 | 26.6 |
| PF   | 31.0 |      |      |      |      |      |      |      |      |      |
| PSI  |      | 12.7 | 14.2 | 13.8 |      | 9.6  | 9.6  | 9.8  | 11.4 | 14.3 |
| PSU  |      |      |      |      | 14.5 |      |      |      |      |      |
| PSDI | 7.1  | 4.5  | 4.6  | 6.1  |      | 5.1  | 3.4  | 3.8  | 4.1  | 3.0  |
| PRI  | 2.5  | 1.6  | 1.4  | 1.4  | 2.0  | 2.9  | 3.1  | 3.0  | 5.1  | 3.7  |
| PLI  | 3.8  | 3.0  | 3.5  | 7.0  | 5.8  | 3.9  | 1.3  | 1.9  | 2.9  | 2.1  |
| MSI  | 2.0  | 5.8  | 4.8  | 5.1  | 4.4  | 8.7  | 6.1  | 5.3  | 6.8  | 5.9  |

Note: DC: Christian Democrats, PF: Popular Front (PCI and PSI), PCI: Communists, PSI: Socialists, PSU: Unified Socialists (PSI and PSDI), PSDI: Social Democrats, PRI: Republicans, PLI: Liberals, MSI: Italian Social Movement.

Source: P. Ginsberg, *A History of Contemporary Italy* (Harmondsworth, U.K.: Penguin, 1990), p. 442.

more than 60%. The DC/PCI vote, however, was not split evenly between the two parties: the DC only once received *less* than 34% of the vote (1983); the PCI only once won *more* than 34% of the vote (1976). The PCI never closed within three percentage points of the DC in national elections.

With the exception of 1948, though, the DC could never translate its electoral domination into a parliamentary majority—a consequence of Italy's electoral system (a very pure form of proportional representation). Nonetheless, the DC was never out of power between 1948 and 1993. Rather, it dominated a succession of coalition governments made up of parties drawn from the center and center-left of Italian politics: the Liberals (PLI), the Republican Party (PRI), the Social Democrats (PSDI), and the Socialist Party (PSI). Even in 1948, with a majority of seats, the DC chose to govern at the head of a coalition.

The basic purpose of these coalitions was simple: to deprive the Communist PCI of the opportunity to govern. Italy was on the front line of Cold War politics after 1948. The DC and its coalition partners, backed by the United States, the Vatican, and, indeed, by the majority of Italians, were charged with the task of "defending democracy" in Italy (and Western Europe) by keeping the Italian Communist Party (and, by extension, the Soviet) threat at bay. Always second to the DC in terms of votes and seats, the PCI's only chance for power in Italy was to make alliances with other parties in order to construct a parliamentary majority against the DC. The center party bloc, especially when joined by the PSI, the PCI's most likely—or least unlikely—political partner, rendered this impossible. Postwar Italy, therefore, was a "special democracy": a blocked political system where, to many, the main opposition party was not seen as a legitimate alternative to the existing government, and hence where there could be no alternation in government. Consequently, it was the same parties, and the same people, who made up the succession of short-lived administrations.

## The Impact of "Blocked Democracy"

Since power was assured to the DC and its coalition partners, the prime concern of the ruling *partitocrazia* (partyocracy) became the division of spoils within and between parties. Clientelist networks developed, via a burgeoning public and semipublic sector—the *sottogoverno*—for the mutual benefit of the party and its constituency. By a formal mechanism called *lottizzazione* (literally, "division into lots"), management of, and employment in, the *sottogoverno* was divided between the partyocracy in accordance with their political power. This meant that the DC enjoyed the major (but by no means all the) spoils of office. Jobs within the individual party fiefdoms in the public sector were also subject to *lottizzazione*, reflecting the relative strengths of party factions. Italy's public sector economy became a by-word for inefficiency and corruption.[2]

## Public Attitudes toward the Italian State

Historically, the Italian state had always suffered from a lack of popular legitimacy. This situation persisted after the creation of the Republic, stemming from the obvious shortcomings of the Italian political system: a lack of transparency (government coalitions were always made behind closed doors), lack of accountability, lack of mobility, ineffective, inefficient, and corrupt government. Morlino has pointed out that in Italy levels of "moderate and deep dissatisfaction" with the democratic process "have always been much higher than in other countries."[3] He also notes that these levels "grew significantly" at the end of the 1980s, mainly because of economic crisis. Not until the 1990s, however, did such discontent clearly express itself in electoral terms. Instead, the majority of Italians, to borrow from Indro Montanelli's famous phrase, continued to "hold their noses" and vote for the DC and the other traditional parties of government, rather than risk the alternative: the PCI. Besides, millions of Italians were implicated, to a lesser or greater degree, in the system of patronage and *clientelismo* operated by the partyocracy. To claim—as

Morlino has—that "all the conditions for [political] change existed" by the late 1980s is to ignore the fact that nobody in the late 1980s could— or did—anticipate fundamental change in the foreseeable future. Ginsborg described the 1980s as "a period of great political continuities." Leonardi and Wertman forecast that the DC's "unparalleled record among parties in Western democracies of remaining in power for the entire post war period is very likely to be extended well beyond the late 1980s."[4]

*Signs of Change*

The Italian political system was not, however, wholly immune to change. In the 1970s, economic depression, a number of major corruption scandals involving the DC (although nothing like on the scale of the 1990s), and the public warring between DC factions led to "the draining of that massive reservoir of public esteem that the DC had acquired during the 1950s and 1960s as the guarantor of Italian democracy and the godfather of the Italian economic miracle." The increasingly popular view of the DC was of "a divided, dishonest, not very modern party."[5] Increasing secularization and the "crisis of Catholic subculture" linked to the economic miracle and the social transformation of Italy from the late 1950s (modernization, consumerism, individualism, urbanization) also weakened the DC's traditional support base. As a consequence, the DC's election fortunes became more dependent on the anti-Communist vote, less on the pro-Catholic vote. This was not a problem, as long as there remained a Communist threat. In the 1980s, however, the PCI appeared increasingly benign. First, its slow electoral advance (1948–76) had been abruptly reversed in 1979 and its share of the vote continued to fall in the 1980s (consumerism and individualism were also enemies of the PCI). Second, the PCI since the 1960s had clearly moved further and further away from the Soviet orbit and ever closer to "bourgeois democracy." Third, the collapse of the 1970s "historic compromise" with the DC (whereby the PCI had agreed not to oppose the DC government)—which cost the PCI both moderate and left-wing support—and the reentry into government of the PSI (see below) left the PCI marooned and impotent in parliament. The PCI offered neither a real alternative to parliamentary democracy nor a realizable "democratic alternative" to the DC.

The DC's relatively poor electoral showing in the 1980s (in comparison with previous decades) can partly be attributed to the declining value of the anti-Communist card. A small percentage of DC voters felt "released" to vote for other, "cleaner" center parties (the case in 1983), or for regionalist, issue, or protest parties (in 1987). The DC also found it impossible to embrace fashionable "modern" right-wing free-market ideology, and thus could not appeal to a new constituency. "Modernizing" talk alarmed its traditional electorate. More to the point, the DC was symbiotically tied to the state-run economy and bureaucracy. For the DC to have "rolled back the frontiers of the state," would have been equivalent, "to the self-amputation of both legs."[6]

In contrast to the two major parties, the PSI—which in the 1970s had appeared to be in decline—experienced an electoral revival in the 1980s. Its electoral growth coincided with the dumping of socialist baggage and the embracing of modernizing rhetoric (though this was only rhetoric) under the leadership of the highly ambitious Bettino Craxi. Elected as party secretary in 1976, Craxi sought not only to make the PSI a permanent party of government but also to challenge the DC's domination of government. Craxi achieved one of his main goals in 1983 when, after parliamentary elections that saw the DC's vote fall by over 5 percent (the result of the DC's first and last experiment with neo-conservative ideas), he became the first Socialist (and only the second non-DC) prime minister in the Republic's history, even though the PSI had won just 11.4 percent of the vote. Craxi's arrival as a political force intensified competition within the partyocracy, especially between the DC and PSI. Although Craxi was prime minister, and although the DC required the PSI if it was to secure a working parliamentary majority, the DC clearly was not prepared to relinquish its central role to a junior partner who, after all, could not do without DC support. The DC-PSI alliance remained intact for the rest of the decade, but, it was

> not a political alliance based on mutual trust, parity, or programmatic accord. It is, rather, riven by suspicion, by personal rivalry, by an eternal jockeying for position. It makes any strategic planning next to impossible, wastes an extraordinary amount of time and energy and leads inexorably to weak rather than strong government.[7]

The hostility and competition between the two parties also spilled-over into the *sottogoverno* world of party control of the public sector, inevitably increasing the size, cost, inefficiency—and corruption—inherent in the state-run economy. The financial consequences of this would become all too apparent in the 1990s. The inability of the two main governing parties to govern effectively would be ruthlessly exposed. It was to prove a fatal embrace.

## THE COLLAPSE OF THE OLD ORDER, 1989–94

The confluence of a variety of factors accounts for the spectacular unraveling of the postwar party political order between 1989 and 1994:

the collapse of the Communist bloc and the end of the Cold War in 1989, economic recession and financial crisis in the early 1990s, the *Mani pulite* ("Clean Hands") investigations into political corruption launched in 1992, the successful referendum campaign for electoral reform.

### The Collapse of the Communist Bloc and the End of the Cold War

**The dissolution of the PCI.** While the PCI had been already treading a reformist path for at least the previous two decades, it was the collapse of Communism in Eastern Europe that brought its journey to an end. "The disintegration of the USSR . . . was also the definitive answer to the old internal debate on 'real socialism': the communist alternative had been made bankrupt."[8] Five days after the fall of the Berlin Wall, Achille Ochetto, the leader of the PCI, declared his intention to dissolve the party. The PCI's traumatic rebirth (1989–91) as a social democratic party (Partito democratico della sinistra [PDS]—without the hammer and sickle and the old PCI's "hard-left" element (which left to form the Communist Refoundation [RC] Party)—was at first welcomed by the leaders of the governing parties. It seemed that the collapse of Italian Communism—and the subsequent fragmentation of the left—meant their political hegemony was secured.[9] In fact, the opposite was true. The dissolution of the PCI "unblocked" the party system.[10] With the Communist "threat" gone, so too had the underlying reason for many moderate Italian voters to "hold their noses" and vote for the DC and its coalition partners. Instead, they now had the opportunity to register their discontent with the traditional governing parties via the ballot box—not by voting for the new PDS (still not trusted[11]) but by voting for the "new" center, or center-right alternatives that were opposed to the old parties and were in favor of fundamental political or economic change. The most spectacular (but by no means the only[12]) example of this electoral phenomenon in the early 1990s was the Lega Nord (Northern League).

**The Leghe and the Lega Nord.** The first Leghe appeared in northern Italy at the end of the 1970s. Essentially linguistic-cultural organizations, these small and disparate autonomist bodies were very much in the tradition of existing Italian autonomist groups, possessive of local traditions and hostile to non-natives. Their electoral appeal in the early 1980s was negligible: the Liga Veneta's 4.2 percent share of the Veneto vote in the 1983 national elections was by far the best regional performance of any Leghe. The 1987 elections, however, saw the Leghe make minor advances across the north, taking around 4% of the total vote for

Piedmont, Lombardy, and the Veneto, and 8% of the vote in some provinces.

The 1987 elections also marked the emergence of the Lega Lombarda under the leadership of Umberto Bossi. The Lega Lombarda, which won 3% of the regional vote in 1987, improved upon this two years later when it received 8.1% of the regional vote in the European parliamentary elections of 1989, making it by far the strongest of the northern leagues. Significantly, the Lega Lombarda's improved electoral performance coincided with the playing down of ethnoregionalism and the playing up of a distinct "northern" economic identity. According to Bossi, the successful northern economy was based upon a common "entrepreneurial" culture of honest hard work and individual initiative. This he contrasted with the inefficient and corrupt "statist" culture of national government and of the southern economy. Bossi's political objective was to "free" the north from government "run by thieves and mafiosi" by creating three macroregions of Italy: north, center, and south. His economic policy was drawn from the new right: privatization, deregulation, free market competition—the opposite to that of the partyocracy.[13]

The Lega Lombarda's real electoral breakthrough did not come, however, until 1990—*after* the collapse of the Soviet bloc and *after* Ochetto's decision to dissolve the PCI. In regional elections of that year, the Lega Lombarda won 18.9% of the vote in Lombardy. This included spectacular advances in some provinces: in Valenza Po, for example, the Lega's vote rose from 2% to 23.5%. Advances were made mainly at the expense of the DC and PSI.[14] The gains were repeated in local elections held in November 1991. In these the Lega Lombarda (under the banner of the Lega Nord—a federation of the northern Leghe created in 1990, and under the control of Bossi) claimed the major electoral scalp of Brescia from the DC with 24.4% of the vote. Local success was eventually translated into national success in the April 1992 parliamentary elections. The Lega Nord won 8.7% of the national vote (in 1987 the combined Leghe vote accounted for only 0.5% of the national vote). In the Veneto, a traditional DC area, one in four people voted for the Lega. In Lombardy—including Milan, "the PSI's historic stronghold—not to mention Craxi's personal fiefdom"—the Lega took more than one fifth of the vote.[15]

For the governing parties, the 1992 elections represented a severe (though not yet mortal) blow. The DC remained the largest party in the new parliament, but it's share of the vote had fallen below 30% for the first time since the war. The PSI vote fell for the first time since 1976. The four parties (DC, PSI, PLI, PSDI) that made up the new government were those that had made up the previous administration, but they failed to win a majority of the votes cast.

*Economic Crisis*

The "unblocking" of Italian democracy was only one part of a complex "structural crisis" afflicting the Italian political elite in the early 1990s.[16] Another: the Italian political system was simply running out of money.[17] A wholly ineffective tax system, a clientelist welfare state (unemployment and sickness benefits fraud in return for votes or other "favors"), and the financial burden of an increasingly corrupt and inefficient public sector industry had seen the national debt rise from 71.99% of GDP in 1983 to 100.50% in 1990—by which time Italy's national debt constituted one third of the debt of the whole European Community. Not only this, but the Maastricht treaty committed Italy to a level of economic efficiency (if she was to meet EMU entry criteria) that was impossible to realize without fundamental change in the way the party system operated (the need for governability via institutional reform) and how parties ran the economy (the need for an efficient and much reduced public sector). The sense of economic and financial crisis in Italy was heightened by the international recession of the early 1990s and rising domestic inflation and unemployment. The difficulty for the governing parties, however, was that their power derived from the existing political system and from their control over the public sector economy. To tackle either issue would expose their own position. To fail to address either issue would risk further electoral drift.

*Tangentopoli*

Suffering from bitter inter- and intraparty disputes on the questions whether to reform, how to reform and how much to reform, widely blamed for the political and economic difficulties confronting Italy, and roundly criticized for their inability to respond to these difficulties (not least by the president of the Republic, Francesco Cossiga[18]), the beleaguered governing parties soon found themselves under attack from another, unexpected, source: the Italian judiciary. In February 1992, what began as a local investigation by Milan magistrates into illicit political-business links, quickly snowballed into a nationwide judicial assault on political corruption. The *Mani pulite* ("clean hands") investigations led by the Milan pool of magistrates, and the resulting *tangentopoli* scandals (*tangente*: bribe or "kick-back"; *tangentopoli*: "kickback city"—a term first applied to Milan) engulfed Italian politics and public administration. By the end of 1992 nearly 100 parliamentary deputies had received an *avviso di garanzia* (official notification that they were under investigation). During 1993 that figure rose to more than 300. This decapitated the governing parties. Craxi, after receiving his fourth *avvisi*, resigned as secretary of the PSI. Craxi's deputy, Claudio Martelli, also found himself under investigation (and, like Craxi, was later convicted). Amongst the DC hierarchy, Giulio Andreotti, six times prime minister of Italy, was accused (amongst other things) of collusion with the Mafia. Arnaldo Forlani and Ciriaco De Mita (both former DC party secretaries) were investigated on suspicion of receiving stolen property, fraud, and extortion. Giorgio La Malfa, Renato Altissimo, and Carlo Vizzini, the respective party secretaries of the PRI, PLI, and PSDI, all received *avvisi* and resigned within five weeks of one another in the spring of 1993. This list is by no means exhaustive. By the end of 1993, and in addition to the national political figures drawn into the *tangentopoli* scandals, hundreds of local administrators, nearly all of whom were tied to the governing parties, had also been charged or arrested, or were under investigation. Magistrates estimated that the total money paid in *tangenti* amounted to £70 billion, over two-thirds of Italy's public debt.[19]

The *Mani pulite* investigations were both the product and the catalyst of the crisis of the Italian political elite. Prior to 1992 investigations into political corruption had usually been swiftly suppressed by the governing parties, who kept a tight rein on the judiciary. In this context, the rise of the Lega at the same time as the "clean hands" investigations were beginning in Milan is particularly significant. The successes of the Lega, in 1990–92, broke the PSI stranglehold on Milan and gave the magistrates vital space to work in.[20] The PSI in Milan—which was the focus of the initial *Mani pulite* investigations—was faced with allegations of corruption at the same time as its local political power was ebbing away. Indeed, one can speculate that the decline in the political fortunes of the PSI in Lombardy (and the north generally) in the local elections of 1990 actually encouraged business to question the value of continuing to pay *tangenti* (or *tangenti* on the scale they were being asked to pay) to a party whose hold on local power seemed to be increasingly insecure. (It was a complaint to the authorities by a businessman regarding *tangenti* paid to a PSI official that opened the way to the first *Mani pulite* investigation in Milan).

It can also be argued that for the *Mani pulite* investigations to have taken off as they did required the coincidence of the PSI (as the initial focus of the investigations) and Milan (as the center of those investigations). The PSI's startling rise under Craxi to the heart of national government in the 1980s had enabled the party to indulge in corruption on a massive scale. "As with socialist parties in other southern European countries, rather than use its new power to reinvent the political system, it used the political system to maximise its own advantages."[21] Milan, as Craxi's personal power base, was particularly exploited. But the PSI— and Milan—represented the soft underbelly of the party establishment.

Given that the PSI's rise to political prominence was a relatively recent one, its corrupt relationship with (predominantly northern) private business was less well established and therefore less stable than was, for example, that between the DC and (predominantly southern) state-reliant business in which the ties of loyalty in the corrupt exchange were older and stronger (enforced if necessary by criminal organizations). The PSI's approach to corruption was more businesslike than that of the DC, where the nature of corruption was more personal. Craxi, for example, employed a set of "auditors"—and sometimes even intervened himself—to check the accuracy of PSI representatives' declarations on levels of bribes received, and to acquire information on firms not yet "donating" to the party.[22] Power within the PSI resided, ultimately, with Craxi, whose own power base was Milan, unlike in the DC where the power structure was less linear and hence the location of power more diffuse. Would a southern businessman have been so ready to break his corrupt pact with a DC official? Would an investigation into this allegation of corruption have moved so quickly (if at all) from the local to the national level? Probably not. In the first *Mani pulite* case in Milan, however, it was a PSI official who was "betrayed" by a businessman. In turn he implicated other PSI officials in Milan—including Craxi's son, the secretary of the Milan PSI. The link then between the local and national political leadership of the PSI was a relatively easy one to make. And once the web of corruption involving the PSI began to unravel, it drew in the DC and the other parties of government, because these shared amongst themselves the major source of corruption, the *sottogoverno*.

## Electoral Reform

As the full scale of corruption was revealed to an ever more outraged Italian public, the old parties found themselves on an inexorable path to political oblivion. One of the ironies of the last months of the old political elite was that it was this same discredited elite in 1993 that was obliged as a consequence of a popular referendum[23] to introduce electoral reform designed to end their hegemony.

Reform of the electoral system had long been muted as a possible solution to the defects of the Italian democratic process but since the 1950s (when the DC had tried and ultimately failed to alter the electoral rules in their favor) the issue had never "breached the boundaries of minority passions."[24] This changed in the early 1990s. The momentum for electoral reform was provided by Mario Segni, a pro-reform Christian Democrat deputy. Frustrated by the failure of his and the other ruling parties to tackle the issue of institutional reform, Segni sought to impose change through the use of referendum. Segni's first target was multipreference voting in the electoral system for the Chamber of Deputies.[25] With support from other pro-reform Catholics, and from a majority in the PDS, Segni secured (albeit with some difficulty) the prerequisite 500,000 signatures for a referendum to be held. The referendum itself, in June 1991, attracted a 62.5% turnout and 95.6% support. This was the first time that a referendum had obtained the support of a majority of all eligible voters (57.1%). It was the clearest sign yet of popular dissatisfaction with, and public distancing from, the old order: the DC leadership had refused to back the referendum; Bettino Craxi had advised the Italian electorate to ignore it altogether and instead "go to the seaside" (for a referendum vote to be valid it requires at least a 50% turnout). A single preference voting system was introduced for the 1992 elections.

The success of the 1991 referendum moved the issue of electoral reform from the margins to the center of political debate in Italy. Even the governing parties began to discuss seriously the question and in 1992 a bicameral commission was set up to look at possible options. However, no agreement was reached, and consequently no reform introduced. Segni, now the popular champion of reform (though, until March 1993, still formally a member of the DC), responded by launching a new referendum campaign, this time targeting the electoral laws for the Senate. The "Segni referendum" on Senate reform took place in April 1993. A "Yes" vote was never in doubt. After fourteen months of *tangentopoli* revelations, the referendum was not about the respective merits of different voting systems but an opportunity for the Italian electorate to deliver a damning judgment on the political class. A vote against the existing electoral system represented a vote against the existing political order. The level of the turnout and the size of victory were, however, remarkable. Seventy-seven percent of the electorate voted, of which 82.7% voted for reform—equivalent to 60.4% of all eligible voters. Seven other referenda held the same day—the majority of which were aimed in one way or another against the powers of the parties—produced similarly overwhelming majorities. This amounted to a massive vote of no-confidence in the old parties. The governing DC-PSI-PSDI-PLI coalition, headed by Giuliano Amato, collapsed. Amato talked of the "death of a regime." His replacement was Carlo Azeglio Ciampi, the governor of the Bank of Italy, and the first nonpartisan prime minister in the history of the republic. Heading a caretaker government made up largely of nonpartisan technocrats, Ciampi was given the task of ensuring that new electoral laws for the Senate were in place prior to the holding of a general election. Because of the scale of the referendum "Yes" vote, and the fact that, since the government was equally responsible to the Senate and the Chamber of Deputies, it made sense to have similar electoral procedures for both, reform of the electoral laws for the lower house also became necessary. New electoral laws for both houses were agreed to by Parliament in August 1993. The speed with which new legislation was ultimately agreed to was partly because much of the preliminary debate had already taken place (through the bicameral commission) and partly because new national elections could not be much delayed after the old parties suffered crushing losses in the municipal elections of June 1993.

## A SECOND REPUBLIC? 1994–1996

### 1994 Elections

**Parties and alliances.** By the time of the March 1994 general election, the first to be held under the new electoral laws (a complex mixture of first-past-the-post and proportional representation[26]) the destruction of the old parties was virtually complete. Figure 5.1 shows the fragmentation of the old political parties. In March 1994, there was no Christian Democrat party. The DC formally dissolved itself in January 1994, renaming itself the Popular Party (PPI) and hoping to (continue to) occupy the middle ground of Italian politics. Right-wing Christian Democrats opted out of the new party and formed the Christian Democratic Centre Party. By then the DC had already lost its left wing (who formed the Christian Socialist Party). It had also lost Mario Segni. Having reached the conclusion that it was "hopeless to attempt to reform . . . [the DC] from the inside," Segni left the party in March of 1993. He launched the Segni Pact at the end of 1993.

As regards the PSI, though it still existed, it was in a relaunched and much reduced form. Craxi's successor, Giorgio Benvenuto, had resigned the leadership after only a few months and, with his supporters, had left the party to form Socialist Renewal. In January 1994, Craxi loyalists also left the PSI to form the (right-wing) Democratic Socialist Federation.

In March 1994, the PRI, PLI, and PSDI did not present independent party lists. Given the collapse and fragmentation of the traditional parties of government, and the much trumpeted (if little understood[27]) new electoral laws, the 1994 elections appeared to offer the genuine prospect of a new era in Italian politics—a "Second Republic." The novelty of the 1994 elections was further enhanced by two significant developments in the weeks leading up to the vote. First, a major new political player appeared on the scene: Forza Italia, a "virtual party" created in January 1994 by the Milanese entrepreneur Silvio Berlusconi. Second, Italian voters found

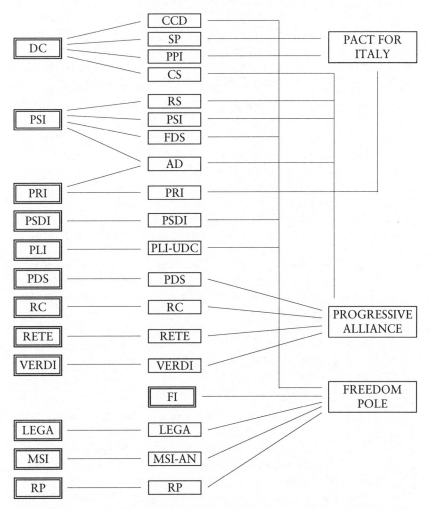

FIGURE 5.1
The Fragmentation of the Italian Political Parties, 1992–1994,
and the Electoral Alliances of 1994

Note: DC: Christian Democrats, CCD: Christian Democratic Centre, SP: Segni
Pact, PPI: Popular Party, CS: Christian Socialists, PSI: Socialists, RS: Socialist
Renewal, FDS: Democratic Socialist Federation, AD: Democratic Alliance, PRI:
Republicans, PSDI: Social Democrats, PLI: Liberals, UDC: Union of the Demo-
cratic Centre, PDS: Democratic Party of the Left, RC: Communist Refounda-
tion, FI: Forza Italia, MSI: Italian Social Movement, AN: National Alliance, RP:
Pannella Radicals.

themselves being asked to vote not just for a party candidate (via the PR party list component for election to the Chamber of Deputies) but also for a candidate representing one of three broad electoral alliances: the center-right Freedom Pole, the center Pact for Italy, and the center-left Progressive Alliance (see figure 5.1). These were cobbled together in January and February 1994 for the purpose of fighting the single-member seats. Such alliances were necessary partly because of the "meltdown of the old party constellation," more so because of the dangers inherent in splitting the vote when operating under first-past-the-post rules.[28]

**Forza Italia and the Freedom Pole.** The neoconservative Forza Italia (Go Italy!) was Berlusconi's response to left-wing victories in local elections of December 1993, and the evident reluctance of the existing center-right parties to work with one another in order to defeat the left. Berlusconi's intention was twofold: (1) to create a party that would attract that large constituency of center-right voters who found the federalist Lega too northern, and the neofascist Italian Social Movement–National Alliance (MSI-AN) too southern (and too right-wing), and who had no intention of voting for one of the center incarnations of the old order; and (2) to weld the disparate center-right and right-wing parties into an electoral alliance. Berlusconi managed to achieve both objectives. Making full use of his near monopoly of commercial television, Berlusconi sold Forza Italia to the Italian public as a national party of the center-right. In so doing, he was able to convince the regionally entrenched Lega Nord and MSI-AN that an alliance with Forza Italia was in both their interests. The resulting Freedom Pole was effectively two alliances in one: Forza Italia worked with the Lega in the north and the MSI-AN in the south. The southern alliance, although formally part of the Freedom Pole, was known as the "Alliance for Good Government."

**The Progressive Alliance and the Pact for Italy.** Like the Freedom Pole, the Progressive Alliance, headed by the PDS and consisting of parties drawn from the center, center-left, and left of Italian politics, was very much an electoral marriage of convenience. The same could be also said of the center Pact for Italy. Although essentially a "neo-DC"[29] alliance, it was somewhat ironic that the Pact for Italy should bring the PPI and the Segni Pact together, considering the damage Segni had done to the PPI's predecessor, the DC. Both, however, now needed the other. Segni, after a brief involvement with the center-left Democratic Alliance and a disastrous flirtation with the Lega, had run out of potential allies. The PPI had never had any.

**The Results.** On a number of levels, the election results of 1994 can be seen as the final blow to the old order in Italy. The Catholic center, represented by the Pact for Italy, won only 46 (7.3%) of the seats in the Chamber of Deputies and 31 of the 315 seats in the Senate. The PSI meanwhile won only 2.2% of the vote. The victorious alliance—the Freedom Pole—seemed defiantly "new": an alliance between one brand-new political "firm-party"[30] (Forza Italia, with 21.1% of the vote), one recently established anti-partyocracy party-movement (the Lega Nord, with 8.4% of the vote), and one "traditional" party uncontaminated by *tangentopoli* simply because until now it had always been a marginal and marginalized political force (the MSI-AN, with 13.5% of the vote). Adding to the picture of renewal, the new parliament was made up of a largely virgin political class. The majority of incoming deputies— 71.3%—had no previous parliamentary experience (cf. 42.9% in 1992, 28.2% in 1987). A third of deputies claimed to have no previous experience in party or electoral politics. Only 12% of deputies had experience of three or more parliaments (i.e., had been elected in or before 1987). In the Senate, nearly two out of every three senators were new to parliament. The social-economic composition of the new parliament was also significantly different: 44% of deputies came from the private sector (cf. 34.6% in 1992, 25.7% in 1987). Clearly, "in addition to, an in partial substitution of the traditional lawyers or civil servants, private [economic] interests" had "decided to enter the political arena directly."[31]

The Berlusconi government that followed the election was, however, in many respects very similar to the old governments of the "First Republic." First, it took nearly two weeks of hard bargaining between the alliance partners before Berlusconi could announce his cabinet. The process of government formation, therefore, was hardly a more transparent process than previously. Second, the government was unable to govern because of infighting between the erstwhile coalition partners. Bossi was particularly combative having seen the Lega's support squeezed in the March election by Forza Italia. Third, Berlusconi— despite his carefully cultivated image as a political outsider—was very much tied to the old regime, in particular to Craxi and the PSI. Like Craxi, Berlusconi's power base was Milan. His rise to tycoon status coincided with Craxi's rise to political preeminence. In 1990, Craxi was best man when Berlusconi married for the second time. Rumors concerning the precise nature of Berlusconi's relations with Craxi and of his involvement in Masonic conspiracy abounded in the months prior to the election. As the election result showed, however, many Italians were not dissuaded from voting for Berlusconi or his party.

When investigations into Berlusconi's Fininvest holding company intensified after March 1994, Berlusconi reacted in a manner reminiscent of Craxi and the now defunct "old" parties of government. Key magistrates were moved from their posts, inspectors from the Ministry of Justice were sent to look for irregularities in the *Mani pulite* investigations, and a government decree was signed limiting the use of preventive custody (one of the most powerful weapons in the magistrates' armory). The decree was hastily retracted after a public protest and the threat from the Lega to withdraw from government. Berlusconi was eventually served with an *avviso di garanzia* by the Milan magistrates in November 1994. Berlusconi's government collapsed the following month after Bossi finally withdrew the Lega's support. Berlusconi was succeeded as prime minister by Lamberto Dini, at the head of another technocrat government, this time (unlike the Ciampi administration) peopled entirely by nonparliamentary deputies.

The new parliament also showed signs of continuity with the old order. The reformed electoral system did not reduce the number of parliamentary parties—something that had been one of the main objectives of the reform lobby. The new Italian parliament also saw little evidence of a reduction in the disparity between male and female representatives—though both Senate and Chamber electoral laws contained commitments to increasing female representation. In addition, the new parliament continued to reflect the traditional "regionally differentiated political classes."[32] The left remained dominant in the center, the MSI-AN's success was based on an increased vote in what were their historic areas of support in the south, Forza Italia did well in the old DC areas of northern and southern Italy (particularly Sicily), and the Lega remained confined to its strongholds in the northeast. Lastly, and perhaps most importantly, the desired bipolarization of Italian politics had not occurred. In short, the "fundamental dynamics of Italian politics . . . changed far less than advocates of electoral reform hoped."[33]

## CONCLUSIONS

Events post-Berlusconi have continued to disappoint those impatient to see changes to the "fundamental dynamics of Italian politics." The party system has become increasingly complicated. In 1995, the PPI split in two, becoming the PPI (center-left) and the Christian Democratic Union (center-right). The absorption of the MSI within the AN (January 1995) resulted in MSI die-hards leaving the party to establish the Fiamma Tricolore. The Lega's parliamentary group split after Bossi took the Lega out of the Freedom Pole. Reflecting the increasingly fragmented nature of Italian party politics, the electoral alliances for the April 1996 parliamentary elections were considerably different from those of 1994. On the center-left, the Progressive Alliance gave way to the Ulivo (Olive

Tree) coalition. Led by Romano Prodi, an ex–Christian Democrat, the Ulivo consisted of the PDS (now under Massimo D'Alema), the "European Left" (left-wing groups close to the PDS, including the United Communists, an offshoot from Communist Refoundation), the "Popolari" (center parties including the "For Prodi" group, PPI, the South Tyrol People's Party, and the Democratic Union, an alliance of ex–PLI, PSI, and PRI members), the "Dini list" (including Lamberto Dini's own Italian Renewal Party, the remnants of the PSI [now called the SI—Italian Socialists], the leftovers of the Segni Pact, and the new Italian Democratic Movement), and the Greens. Although Communist Refoundation was not formally part of the Ulivo coalition (it had been part of the Progressive Alliance in 1994) mutually beneficial stand-down arrangements were agreed upon prior to the election. On the center-right, the Freedom Pole still existed, minus the Lega, but plus the new CDU. The center ground was claimed by the Lega, which stood alone. As in 1994, alliances had little to do with political compatibility, and there was very little discussion of party programs during the campaign. Though the Ulivo won—the first time a left-wing government had been elected in Italy's history—the victory "owed more to a combination . . . of the electoral system and a change in the configuration of parties (compared to 1994) than . . . changes in voting propensities."[34] Despite this first "alternation" in government, governability has remained a problem, given the galaxy of interests represented by the Ulivo, and its reliance upon RC support for a majority in the Chamber of Deputies.

More seriously, as commentators have been quick to point out, there has been as yet no constitutional reform and very little reform of the public sector.[35] Until such changes take place, it is "entirely improper to speak of a 'Second Republic.'"[36] At present (March 1997) it is difficult to see a way out of this situation. A bicameral commission is discussing the possibility of constitutional reform, but agreement seems very unlikely given the extreme diversity of opinions amongst the main parties. The Lega's position is particularly uncompromising: Bossi demands the recognition by Parliament of a "Republic of Padania"—an independent state consisting of all Italy to the north of the River Po. This is quite clearly unacceptable to the Ulivo (which nevertheless is prepared to accept regional devolution) and the pro-unity Freedom Pole. There is also considerable disagreement between the Ulivo and the Freedom Pole (and even within the Ulivo coalition) on the issue whether to adopt a presidential or semi-presidential form of government (the Freedom Pole's preferences) or to increase the powers of the prime minister (broadly favored by the Ulivo). Given such differences, Prime Minister Prodi's post-election call for cross-party consensus on the issue of reform appears at best naive, at worst "a pretext to do nothing."[37]

Regarding the parties, it seems likely that further changes will happen—in alliance terms (if 1994–96 is any guide), and also in party terms. Forza Italia, despite its electoral strength, would appear especially vulnerable to spectacular collapse: it lacks any organizational structure and is wholly reliant on Berlusconi—who may still yet fall foul of the law, and who will have to fight to maintain control of his extensive media empire that has played such a vital part in his electoral success so far. It also remains to be seen if business interests involved in Forza Italia stay in politics or return to business. Less transient may be the Lega Nord. Written off after the 1994 elections and its subsequent internal problems, the Lega in 1996 took its largest ever share of the vote (10.1%) at a time when, despite standing as the party of the center, its program was at its most radical (overtly secessionist), and after an electoral campaign with virtually no television publicity. The Lega obtained the largest percentage of the vote of any party in Lombardy, it won the most seats in the Veneto, and took more seats than the Ulivo in Venezia-Giulia. If, as has been suggested, the Lega's election success owed much to a fiscal protest[38]—Italy has one of the highest tax thresholds in Europe—then the increases in taxation proposed by the Prodi government in an attempt to meet the EMU convergence criteria can only strengthen Bossi's hand. As Bossi has already pointed out, the "Republic of Padania" could meet all the convergence criteria without such sacrifices. Bossi also has quite clearly learned his lesson from the 1994 alliance: the Lega's strength is its uniqueness—separatism as a political objective must be reflected in an "outsider" stance when it comes to national party politics. The Lega also has strong local organization. Bossi could still find his much publicized "Republic of Padania" backfires on him— frightening moderate voters away from the movement, but Mannheimer's prediction that "Bossi will get stronger"[39] appears well-founded. As for the PDS and the AN, these perhaps are the best equipped for political longevity. Both have well-established party organizations that, although no guarantee of political survival—let alone success—must be better than having no organization at all (the Forza Italia example). Moreover, the PDS's continuing shift rightwards, and the AN's apparent shift away from the extreme right toward the center ground of Italian politics,[40] may help widen their electoral appeal by attracting voters until now skeptical of the social-cum-liberal democratic rhetoric of the former and of the democratic credentials of the latter.

Perhaps it has always been unreasonable to expect the transition from the "old order" to the "new order" in Italy to be a particularly rapid one. The 1989–94 old order collapse is different from those of 1919–25 and 1943–46. In both of these earlier examples the existing political systems collapsed in the wake of war. In the first instance, the transition from "old" to "new" was relatively swift because it involved the brutal suffocation of democracy by Fascism. In the second instance, the transition from old to new was even quicker as a consequence of the Nazi and allied occupations of Italy in 1943–45, which totally destroyed the indigenous Fascist regime. In contrast, the collapse of the old order in Italy, 1989–94, has not involved the breakdown of the democratic order, nor the complete collapse of the existing political system. The maintenance of democracy in many ways precludes the speedy resolution of Italy's current period of transition. Consequently, Italy may in fact see "a chronic situation for a long time to come."[41]

## NOTES

1. Martin Clark, *Modern Italy 1871–1995* (London: Longman, 1996), p. 333.

2. The debilitating influence of the partyocracy over the public sector is illustrated by the fact that between 1977 and 1992, 600,000 new posts were created in the state administration. Of these only 250,000 were allocated after interviews or tests. The *Guardian*, April 3, 1992.

3. Leonardo Morlino, "Crisis of Parties and Change of Party System in Italy," *Party Politics* 2.1 (1996): 9.

4. Ibid., p. 25; Paul Ginsborg, *A History of Contemporary Italy* (Harmondsworth, U.K.: Penguin, 1990), p. 418; Roberto Leonardi and Douglas Wertman, *Italian Christian Democracy* (London: Macmillan, 1989), p. 245.

5. Ibid., pp. 185–86.

6. Donald Sassoon, "The 1987 Elections and the PCI," in *Italian Politics: A Review*, ed. Roberto Leonardi and Piergiorgio Corbetta (London: Pinter Publishers, 1989), 3:143.

7. Ginsborg, *History of Contemporary Italy*, p. 419.

8. Morlino, "Crisis of Parties," p. 7.

9. Paul Ginsborg, "Explaining Italy's Crisis," in *The New Italian Republic*, ed. Stephen Gundle and Simon Parker (London: Routledge, 1996), p. 19.

10. Martin J. Bull, "The Great Failure? The Democratic Party of the Left in Italy's Transition," in *The New Italian Republic*, ed. Gundle and Parker, p. 159.

11. The PDS won 16.1% of the vote in the 1992 parliamentary elections—a drop of over 10% when compared with the PCI's 26.6% of the vote in 1987. The PDS and RC together only managed 21.7% of the vote in 1992.

12. For example, La Rete. An anti-Mafia, anticorruption movement, La Rete was formally established in 1991 under the leadership of Leoluca Orlando, the popular ex-DC mayor of Palermo. After an encouraging performance in Sicily's regional elections of June 1991 (7.8% of the vote) La Rete won 1.9% of the national vote in April 1992. Though this figure appears modest, La Rete ran

candidates in only two-thirds of the constituencies. More to the point, La Rete had extraordinary success in Sicily, especially Palermo, where it took 24.5% of the vote. As John Foot notes, this "seriously threatened the DC's traditional hegemony in Sicily." John M. Foot, "The 'Left Opposition' and the Crisis: Rifondazione Communista and La Rete," in *The New Republic*, ed. Gundle and Parker, p. 181.

13. Luca Ricolfi, "La Lega," in *La politica italiana: dizionario critico 1945–1995*, ed. Gianfranco Pasquino (Rome and Bari: Editori Laterza, 1995), pp. 261–64.

14. Ilvo Diamanti, "The Northern League: From Regional Party to Party of Government," in *The New Italian Republic*, ed. Gundle and Parker, p. 115.

15. Mark Donovan, "The Referendum and the Transformation of the Party System," *Modern Italy* 1.1 (Autumn 1995): 63.

16. Ginsborg, "Explaining Italy's Crisis," p. 27.

17. Donald Sassoon, "Tangentopoli or the Democratization of Corruption: Considerations on the End of Italy's First Republic," *Journal of Modern Italian Studies* 1.1 (Fall 1995): 134.

18. Calling general elections for April 1992, Cossiga said Italy needed "a government that could govern, a parliament that could legislate, [and] an administrative machinery that could actually administer."

19. Hilary Partridge, "Can the Leopard Change Its Spots? Sleaze in Italy," *Parliamentary Affairs* 48.4 (October 1995): 721.

20. Ginsborg, "Explaining Italy's Crisis," p. 30.

21. Ibid., p. 24.

22. David Moss, "Patronage Revisited: The Dynamics of Information and Reputation," *Journal of Modern Italian Studies* 1.1 (Fall 1995): 64 and n. 11.

23. The right of Italians to challenge most legislation by popular referendum was enshrined in the constitution of the Republic. It was only in 1970, however, that the mechanisms for holding referendum were put in place. A referendum cannot be used to introduce legislation.

24. Diego Gambetta and Steven Warner, "The Rhetoric of Reform Revealed (Or: If You Bite the Ballot It May Bite Back)," *Journal of Modern Italian Studies* 1.3 (Summer 1996): 358.

25. Under the electoral rules for the lower house, voters chose a party (the list vote) and then could vote for up to three or four candidates on the party's list (the preference vote). Segni and his supporters argued that such a system promoted internal struggle within parties and encouraged the spread of patronage and corruption. David Hine, *Governing Italy* (Oxford: Oxford University Press, 1993), pp. 88 and 318, n. 11.

26. The new electoral systems operate as follows: In the Chamber of Deputies 75% of seats are allocated using a first-past-the-post system, where electors vote for a single candidate in their *collegio* (local voting district). the remaining 25% of seats are allocated on a proportional basis: electors cast a second vote for a party list in their *ciroscrizione* (the electoral region). PR seats are allocated at the national level using the Hare method of calculation. To qualify for PR allocated seats a party must win 4% of the national vote. In the Senate, in common with the electoral laws for the Chamber of Deputies, 75% of seats

are allocated using a first-past-the-post system, where electors vote for a single candidate in their *collegio*. Electors, however, do not cast a second vote for the 25% of seats allocated on a proportional basis. Instead, the votes for all the candidates who stood in the single-member (i.e., first-past-the-post) constituencies are compiled at the *circoscrizione* level to give a total vote for each party (party alliance). The PR seats are then divided between the parties according to the D'Hondt method of calculation. In both instances, those parties/alliances that are successful in the single-member constituencies are deducted votes at the PR stage.

27. Gianfranco Pasquino, one of Italy's foremost political scientists, described the new electoral system as "worse than the Irish and the Greek laws, and I have mentioned the two most complicated laws that I am familiar with." Richard Katz, "The 1993 Parliamentary Electoral Reform," in *Italian Politics: Ending the First Republic*, ed. Carol Mershon and Gianfranco Pasquino (Boulder, Colo.: Westview Press, 1995), 9:110.

28. Martin J. Bull and James L. Newell, "Italy Changes Course? The 1994 Elections and the Victory of the Right," *Parliamentary Affairs* 48.1 (January 1995): 79.

29. Ibid., p. 79.

30. Morlino, "Crisis of Parties," p. 16. Jörg Seisselberg offers an alternative, but equally valid, description of Forza Italia: a "Media-Mediated Personality-Party." Jörg Seisselberg, "Forza Italia: A Media-Mediated Personality-Party," *West European Politics* 19.4 (October 1996).

31. Morlino, "Crisis of Parties," p. 18. In addition to Morlino, for analysis of the 1994 parliament, see Richard Katz and Piero Ignazi (eds.), introduction to *Italian Politics: The Year of the Tycoon*, vol. 10 (Boulder, Colo.: Westview Press, 1996), p. 22.

32. Richard Katz, "Electoral Reform and the Transformation of Party Politics in Italy," *Party Politics* 2.1 (1996): 38.

33. Ibid., p. 52.

34. Martin J. Bull and James L. Newell, "The April 1996 Italian General Election: The Left on Top or on Tap?" *Parliamentary Affairs* 49.4 (October 1996): 642.

35. Mario Caciagli and David I. Kertzer, *Italian Politics: The Stalled Transition*, vol. 11 (Boulder, Colo.: Westview Press, 1996).

36. Katz and Ignazi, *Italian Politics*, 10:34.

37. Giovanni Sartori, quoted in *Panorama*, May 2, 1996: Sartori argues that the only solution is the establishment of a constituent assembly —which the Ulivo reject.

38. Valeria Gandus, "Quei due Poli li abbiamo fatti arrosto," *Panorama*, May 2, 1996.

39. Renato Mannheimer, quoted in the *Observer*, September 15, 1996.

40. This is not to say that the AN has disowned its Fascist roots. Ignazi argues that despite cosmetic changes, the AN "remains largely embedded in its original political culture." Piero Ignazi, "The Transformation of the MSI into the AN," *West European Politics* 19.4 (October 1996): 709.

41. Luigi Bobbio, quoted in the *Observer*, September 15, 1996.

# BIBLIOGRAPHY

Bull, Martin J. and James L. Newell. "Italy Changes Course? The 1994 Elections and the Victory of the Right." *Parliamentary Affairs* 48.1 (January 1995): 72–99.

——. "The April 1996 Italian General Election: The Left on Top or on Tap?" *Parliamentary Affairs* 49.4 (October 1996): 616–47.

Caciagli, Mario and David I. Kertzer. *Italian Politics: The Stalled Transition*, vol. 11. Boulder, Colo.: Westview Press, 1996.

Clark, Martin. *Modern Italy 1871–1995*, 2nd edition. London: Longman, 1996.

Donovan, Mark. "The Referendum and the Transformation of the Party System." *Modern Italy* 1.1 (Autumn 1995).

——. "A Turning Point That Turned? The April 1996 General Election in Italy." *West European Politics* 19.4 (October 1996).

Gambetta, Diego and Steven Warner. "The Rhetoric of Reform Revealed (Or: If You Bite the Ballot It May Bite Back)." *Journal of Modern Italian Studies* 1.3 (Summer 1996): 357–77.

Gilbert, Mark. *The Italian Revolution: The End of Politics Italian Style?* Boulder, Colo.: Westview Press, 1995.

Ginsborg, Paul. *A History of Contemporary Italy*. Harmondsworth, U.K.: Penguin, 1990.

Gundle, Stephen and Simon Parker (eds.). *The New Italian Republic*. London: Routledge, 1996.

Hine, David. *Governing Italy*. Oxford: Oxford University Press, 1993.

Ignazi, Piero. "Italy." *European Journal of Political Research* 28.3–4 (December 1995).

——. "The Transformation of the MSI into the AN." *West European Politics* 19.4 (October 1996).

——. *I partiti italiani*. Bologna: Il Mulino, 1997.

Katz, Richard. "Electoral Reform and the Transformation of Party Politics in Italy." *Party Politics* 2.1 (1996): 31–35.

Katz, Richard and Piero Ignazi (eds.). *Italian Politics: The Year of the Tycoon*, vol. 10. Boulder, Colo.: Westview Press, 1996.

Leonardi, Roberto and Piergiorgio Corbetta (eds.). *Italian Politics: A Review*, vol. 3. London: Pinter Publishers, 1989.

Leonardi, Robert and Douglas Wertman. *Italian Christian Democracy*. London: Macmillan, 1989.

Morlino, Leonardo. "Crisis of Parties and Change of Party System in Italy." *Party Politics* 2.1 (1996): 5–30.

Morlino, Leonardo and Marco Tarchi. "The Dissatisfied Society: The Roots of Political Change in Italy." *European Journal of Political Research* 30.1 (July 1996).

Mershon, Carol and Gianfranco Pasquino (eds.). *Italian Politics: Ending the First Republic*, vol. 9. Boulder, Colo.: Westview Press, 1995.

Partridge, Hilary. "Can the Leopard Change Its Spots? Sleaze in Italy." *Parliamentary Affairs* 48.4 (October 1995).

Pasquino, Gianfranco (ed.). *La politica italiana: dizionario critico 1945–1995*. Rome and Bari: Editori Laterza, 1995.

Richards, Charles. *The New Italians*. Harmondsworth, U.K.: Penguin, 1995.

Sassoon, Donald. "Tangentopoli or the Democratization of Corruption: Considerations on the End of Italy's First Republic." *Journal of Modern Italian Studies* 1.1 (Fall 1995).

Scoppola, Pietro. "The Italian Christian Democrats and the Political Crisis." *Modern Italy* 1.1 (Autumn 1995).

Seisselberg, Jörg. "Forza Italia: A Media-Mediated Personality-Party." *West European Politics* 19.4 (October 1996).

Waters, Sarah. "'Tangentopoli' and the emergence of a new political order in Italy." *West European Politics* 17.1 (January 1994).

# CHAPTER 6

# Canadian Political Parties: Contemporary Changes

## Arthur L. Johnson

From its formation as a federal British Dominion on July 1, 1867, until the election of October 1993, Canada had two major parties, the Liberals and the Conservatives. There was no essential difference between the two, although the Liberals in the twentieth century, under William Lyon Mackenzie King, leaned a bit in the direction of labor, the Conservatives (Tories for short) more in the direction of business. As in the United States, there was a Progressive Party in the early 1920s, an attempt to bring farmers and labor together. This was dead by 1925, its program co-opted by the Liberals. The Great Depression led to the formation of two new parties on the left and the right: the social-democratic Cooperative Commonwealth Federation (CCF) and the right-wing Social Credit Party of Bible Bill Aberhart, a prairie radio preacher. These parties managed to garner a few opposition seats every election but never captured the national Parliament although they occasionally held the balance in minority governments. Their strength was in the West.

Canada emerged from World War II with four national parties. The original Liberals and Conservatives (rechristened Progressive-Conservative during the war) remained the mainstream parties until 1993. Despite their names they do not correspond to Democrats and Republicans in the United States. They have not had the identifiably different constituencies of the American parties at least since the Great Depression. It was the Conservatives who tried, under R. B. Bennett, to bring a "New Deal" to Canada, and the Liberals who stood pat. The Liberals, however, did finally usher in the guarantor state in the form of social insurance and family allowances and medical care. Canadians do not declare party affiliations when they register to vote and are less likely than Americans to identify with parties.

The CCF set out to be Canada's labor party with a socialist agenda. Leaders renamed it the New Democratic Party (NDP) in 1961. Social Credit's original program, a sort of share-the-wealth scheme reminiscent of Huey Long's, was never implemented and the party came to be a right-wing organization, mainly rural. After the war it broke into two with Réal Caouette's Ralliement Creditiste going its own way as a Quebec provincial party with a few seats in Parliament from a rural, conservative constituency. It has since faded from view.

Canadian provincial parties are independent in most ways from the federal ones. This is especially true of Quebec, where in the twentieth century the Liberal Party has been independent to a large degree of the the federal Liberals. Quebec emerged from World War II under Maurice Duplessis and his Union Nationale (UN), a strictly provincial party. Strongly conservative or strongly radical Quebeckers have aligned themselves generally with provincial parties with a nationalist, even separatist, message. Duplessis's UN was socially conservative, verging on fascism in the 1930s. It was allied with the Roman Catholic hierarchy and with American and Anglo-Canadian business interests. Duplessis and his successors sought a federal relationship that would give Quebec a special status as an equal partner with the rest of Canada. René Lévesque's Parti Québecois (PQ) began in 1969 with a socialist form of separatism that grew out of the Quebec Liberal Party's Quiet Revolution of the early 60s.

The PQ and the NDP have abandoned doctrinaire socialism for a milder version of welfare statism and pragmatic accommodation with business although the labor unions have been generally their faithful constituents over the years. Both the PQ in Quebec and the NDP in Ontario have enraged labor leaders in recent years with cutbacks and retrenchments of social programs. But these parties are still for them "the only game in town."

## ELECTION 1993

The election of October 1993 broke a longstanding pattern with the nearly complete demise of the Progressive Conservatives, led by Kim Campbell, prime minister at the time. This election gave the Liberals under Jean Chrétien a solid majority with 178 seats and divided the opposition between two regional parties: the Bloc Québecois, committed to Quebec separatism and the Reform Party of Preston Manning with its largely western constituency. Bizarre as it may seem, the official opposition, by dint of a two-seat lead over the Reformers (54-52), was a party committed to breaking up the confederation. The Conservative Party, which had won the greatest election landslide in Canadian history in 1984, was reduced to two seats and lost its official party status. How did it come to this? Campbell's recent book, *Time and Chance*, admits she made a mistake in not resigning from the Mulroney cabinet when she became a candidate for the party leadership. Mulroney apparently dominated her. She blames the campaign team of Allan Gregg and John Tory for a backfiring-ad that made fun of Chrétien's speech defect. Mulroney was aloof during the election campaign, indeed portrayed himself later as a bystander to the 1993 election.[1]

Hugh Segal's book, *No Surrender: Reflections of a Happy Warrior in the Tory Crusade*,[2] criticizes PC internecine strife, sees Joe Clark's leadership as disastrous and views the choice of Campbell to succeed Mulroney as a mistake.[3]

The rapid fall of the Tories has left Canada with only one truly national party and even this must be qualified, given the almost complete absence of Liberal seats west of Ontario and Chrétien's unpopularity in Quebec and Atlantic Canada. In the light of this there is really no party that speaks for Canadians across the national map. The Liberals at least articulate a national vision, albeit a vision that is increasingly threatened.

There is no single explanation for this momentous election result. One factor is the endurance of regional identities. The intense regionalism of Canadians can be understood only by a careful look at Canadian geography. Territorially the second largest nation on earth, in demographic terms Canada is a narrow strip 3,000 miles long, mostly just north of the American border. This strip's inhabitants are divided into five distinct communities: Atlantic Canada, Quebec, Ontario, the prairie provinces, and British Columbia, with a small population up north in the Yukon and Northwest Territories. Culture and language set off Quebec from Anglo Canada, but Laurentian Canada and the other communities are set off by formidable geographic barriers conquered only by the railways in the 1880s. Each of these communities is much older than the federation. Regional loyalties are older and deeper. The proximity of the United States has, in economics, sharpened the divisions, but in a political sense has been a factor for unity. The federation itself was a response to the threat of American absorption and it was pinned together by the Canadian Pacific Railway, which alone prevented its western communities from being stations on American branch lines. Even as the sentimental tie to Britain has waned since World War II Canadian nationalists continue to identify themselves vociferously as non-American, a thing on which most Canadians agree. They know what they are not although they do not agree on what they are.

## FREE TRADE AND MEECH LAKE

Canada's two major historic concerns have been its relationship to the United States and the internal duality of Quebec and Anglo Canada. In nine years Brian Mulroney's Conservatives made momentous policy decisions in both areas and, in so doing, alienated large chunks of their constituency.

The first of these initiatives was free trade with the United States. This meant abandoning the protectionism that had stood since 1878, the "National Policy" of the government of Tory, John A. Macdonald, Canada's first prime minister. Mulroney decided the only solution for Canadian producers was access to the huge American market. This carried a price: the end of protection for Canadian industries. The unions and many other Canadians feared this would mean an exodus of producing companies, particularly the American branch plants as they consolidated facilities in the United States (or in Mexico under NAFTA, which followed hard upon). The intellectuals accused Mulroney of turning Canada into an American colony. The campaigns of 1988 were fought on this issue between Mulroney's Conservatives, Liberals under John Turner (another "blue suit"), and the mildly socialist New Democratic Party under Ed Broadbent, a spirited tryer.

Ironically the positions of the major parties had reversed on the question. A free-trade deal with the United States brought down the Liberal government of Sir Wilfred Laurier in 1911. The Conservatives then held tight to Macdonald's high tariffs, a policy that incidentally promoted American branch plants within the walls. Liberal prime minister Mackenzie King flirted with free trade in 1948 and then backed away. Now the Liberals under Turner led the charge against free trade and accused Mulroney of selling out to the Americans. It didn't work this time, but Mulroney's lead slipped badly from the landslide of 1984.

The turnout on election day, November 21, 1988, was 75% of the electorate. The Conservatives got 43% of the vote and a comfortable majority with 169 seats, down from 211 out of 282 seats. The Liberals climbed to 83 seats, but got only 12 in Quebec and six west of Ontario. The New Democrats' 44 seats were nearly all from the West. Conservatives were strongest in Quebec and Alberta and still fairly strong in Ontario.[4] Quebeckers favored the Free Trade Agreement more heartily than the other provinces. Parti Québecois leaders believed free trade with the United States would free them from "economic blackmail" by other provinces. Mulroney courted the Parti Québecois and Quebec Liberals, bringing nationalists like Lucien Bouchard into the federal government.

Another reason for his popularity in Quebec, apart from being a "favorite son," the fluently bilingual "boy from Baie Comeau," was the Meech Lake Agreement. In 1982 the Trudeau Liberal government had patriated the Canadian constitution, incorporating a Charter of Rights and a Canadian amending formula. Canada was legally independent with the Statute of Westminster in 1931 but since the provinces had never agreed to an amending formula for the constitution this continued to be done by the British Parliament at the request of the Canadian government, usually with unanimous consent of the provinces. Trudeau set out to correct this with a Canadian amending formula. He obtained the assent of nine premiers but not René Lévesque, who was angry at the loss of a Quebec veto. Mulroney, after his 1984 election, hoped to repair the damage and bring Quebec into line by a concession that would presumably give the coup de grace to Quebec separatism. As Mulroney saw it: "The danger with 1981–1982 was that, unlike in 1867, Quebec was no longer a willing partner in the agreement on confederation."[5] Leaving Quebec out would give the sovereignists the argument that "We never consented to this new constitution, therefore we have the right to leave."

By 1985 the Quebec provincial Liberals had won, bringing the nine-year reign of the separatist Parti Québecois to a close. Separatism appeared to be waning and the time seemed ripe for a federal gesture to Quebec. In the spring of 1987 Mulroney called the provincial premiers together at the resort in the Gatineau Hills of Quebec called Meech Lake. The accord struck there called for the recognition of Quebec as a "distinct society" within Canada. Moreover, it would decentralize Canada in important ways, giving every province a veto over constitutional amendments (shades of the American Articles of Confederation), the right to determine its own immigration policy and the right to opt out of shared-cost social programs so long as their own programs met national norms.[6]

The accord was duly launched with the expectation that it would sail smoothly by all the provincial legislatures by the constitutionally mandated sunset date of June 23, 1990. It ran into stormy water and enemy fire and sank just short of safe harbor. The most potent salvo was from former prime minister Pierre Trudeau. Reviled in Quebec, Trudeau still commanded respect in Anglo Canada and remained an eminence grise for the federal Liberals. He sailed out of his Montreal law office to broadside Meech in the press as a dangerous weakening of federal power, a truckling to "blackmailers" who would never be satisfied short of an independent Quebec. Jean Chrétien, Turner's successor as leader of the Liberal Party, seconded the attack. Women's groups saw nothing for, them in Meech. The "First Nations," as the Indians and Innuit were styling themselves, saw nothing in it for them either. Western provinces wanted constitutional reform that would give them an equal voice in the Senate. Constitutional experts attacked it for ambiguity. The Bourassa government in Quebec, with regrettable timing, decided to ban English on outdoor signs, causing a backlash in English Canada. Ultimately, Newfoundland and Manitoba failed to ratify by the sunset date and the accord died.

The defeat of Meech Lake was the first of two major rejections of the political elites. The accord was brokered by national and provincial leaders in the time-honored tradition of "executive federalism." Many Canadians were offended at this process and demanded broader participation in constitutional decisions.[7] But this may be an oversimplification. The defeat of Meech was more than a rejection of elites. It was due also to a feeling in Anglo Canada, especially the West, that Meech was appeasement of an insatiable Quebec nationalism.

Separatism rose again in Quebec where many saw the sinking of Meech as a rejection by Anglo Canada, never mind that seven provinces besides Quebec had approved it. A month before the death of Meech, Lucien Bouchard resigned from Mulroney's cabinet and talked a number of other Quebec ministers and MPs into forming a new federal party called the Bloc Québécois and calling for sovereignty for Quebec. Bouchard blamed changes in the Meech accord suggested by Frank McKenna, premier of New Brunswick, for his last minute resignation even before the Meech sunset, but there are indications even before this that he was moving back to his Quebec nationalist position.[8] Quebec premier Bourassa, ever bending with the political winds, appointed a commission that toured the province sampling opinion and then called for a provincial plebiscite on Quebec's future to be held not later than October 26, 1992, barring some new offer acceptable to the province. The ball was in Mulroney's court. The seemingly extreme reaction by Quebeckers needs some explanation.

The Constitution of 1982, passed without Quebec's approval, changed the basis of Canadian federalism. From its beginnings, Canada has protected the corporate rights of certain groups and has not been built on Lockean ideas of individual rights. The Quebec Act of 1774, shortly after the British conquest, guaranteed the French language, French civil law, and the Roman Catholic Church in Quebec, in short it recognized Quebec as a *distinct society*. The Constitutional Act of 1792 continued to distinguish by setting aside Upper Canada (Ontario) with English law, for American Loyalists and Lower Canada (Quebec) with French institutions, for the original French culture. Lord Durham, heading a royal commission to investigate troubles in Canada in 1838, wrote that he found "Two nations warring in the bosom of a single state."

Even when, at Durham's suggestion, the British Parliament combined the two Canadas in a single province in 1841, Canada East, as Quebec was named, retained its own civil law and distinctness. Critical for French Quebeckers has been this concept of two nations. In their view the federation of 1867, which began Canada as we know it, was a pact between the two nations. The process of amending that constitution, called the British North America Act of 1867, customarily accorded Quebec a veto, in view of its obviously distinctive character and needs. What Trudeau and company did in the patriation of 1982 was to make Canada legally one nation with two languages, something quite different. Louis Balthazar, Quebecker and political scientist, claimed that most Quebeckers do not want to *separate* from Canada. They want a new deal in which Quebec is an equal partner, something English Canada seems reluctant to concede, to put it mildly. Meech Lake was an attempt to correct this, to *restore* not only Quebec's veto but the historic recognition of Quebec as a nation within the federation, and not just another province. Most French Quebeckers supported the Meech Lake Agreement. When it was rejected they lost hope for the restoration within the federation as it exists and turned to sovereignty as the only way to compel a negotiation of the deal.[9]

## THE CHARLOTTETOWN ACCORD

It was apparent that Ottawa would have to try again. This time, unlike the closed-door sessions at Meech Lake, everything would be done in daylight and Canadians would be widely consulted. Every interest group had its say and the result, after two years of discussions, called by one source "two years of navel-gazing, collective psychotherapy and angst-fests," was the Charlottetown Accord of August 28, 1992.[10] This involved drastic decentralization. The senate would be elected and effective, with equal representation by the provinces. Quebec would be guaranteed 25 percent of the seats in the House of Commons, three justices on the Supreme Court, and recognition as a "distinct society" Native self-government within the Charter of Rights and Freedoms seemed to mean recognition of tribal governments as part of the Constitution, but no one was sure. English and French language rights would be protected across Canada. Provinces would have full powers over a number of economic and social areas and each province would have a veto over constitutional changes. It was Meech with much more.

The Charlottetown Accord, after months of televised debates and "town halls" ad nauseum, went to the people in a national referendum on October 26, 1992. Before the event Pierre Trudeau once again weighed anchor and sailed forth to fire another salvo in *Maclean's* and *l'Actualité* blasting Charlottetown and calling for Ottawa to stop paying blackmail to the insatiable separatists. PQ leader Jacques Parizeau thought the accord gave too little to Quebec, especially in matters of language rights, native self-government, and the equal Senate, which Quebec rejected. The new Reform Party, mainly western, led by Preston Manning, thought it gave Quebec too much. Despite the support of all three national parties, most of the media heavyweights, and the leaders of various interest groups, Charlottetown went to a crashing defeat, rejected by 54 percent of the voters and six of the provinces, including Quebec. The attempt at sweeping constitutional reform had come to grief and with it Mulroney's political fortunes.[11]

The defeat of the Charlottetown Accord was a massive rejection of the political establishment of the country. *Maclean's* commentator Peter Newman characterized it as part of a "Canadian Revolution," the title of his 1995 book, subtitled *From Deference to Defiance*. The people said no to the elites and refused to be stampeded by dire threats of doom for the federation. It was a rejection especially of Mulroney. Newman claims that Mulroney's biggest problem was that he had no vision for the country at all.

Mulroney, cautious at first, had finally thrown his weight behind the Charlottetown formula, characterizing its opponents as "enemies of Canada." The document itself was a complicated product, in the end, brokered by national and provincial leaders. The opposition was at a great advantage. A document of sixty clauses was easy to attack. You had only to demolish one or two to produce a No vote, whereas the defenders had to defend the whole document. The Yes people were the mistrusted elites, now led by Brian Mulroney who had lost credibility, and in key areas the "compromises" made nobody happy.[12]

The result revealed the breakdown of Mulroney's coalition of Quebec and the West, already apparent in the Meech debacle. The Bloc Québécois and the Reform Party were able to exploit the antigovernment cynicism. Robert Campbell and Leslie Pal concluded that "the future of the Canadian federation was very much in doubt."[13]

Mulroney faced an election in 1993 without having cured Canada's annual deficit or its huge debt or delivering a constitutional package. His dismal showing in the polls completed the message on the wall. He resigned in June, leaving his defense minister, Kim Campbell, as the first woman prime minister, to face Jean Chrétien's Liberals in October. Starting with a high approval rating, she campaigned a ineptly, dodging specifics and failing to give assurances on employment. A week before the election a Tory advertisement focused on Chrétien's facial defect that causes him to talk out of one side of his mouth. This backfired heavily on her despite her immediate disavowal of it. Chrétien handily survived being branded as "yesterday's man" and did better. He focused on jobs and the economy and emphasized stability, sensing the weariness of Canadians with constitutional proposals.

Further, Campbell perhaps underestimated the rise of new sectional parties of Quebec and the West. In the West the shrill voice of Preston Manning rallied massive resentments of that region against the perceived arrogance and indifference of central Canada. He carried much of the old "Bible Bill" Social Credit constituency or at least their children and grandchildren. These regional parties drew off more support from the Tories than from the Liberals. Chrétien won handily. The shocker was the near obliteration of the Conservatives and the New Democrats, with two and eight seats respectively. The survival of the Conservatives as a party itself was in doubt although in early 1997 it was showing signs of revival under Jean Charest. The choice of Kim Campbell was probably a mistake. She was too inexperienced and stumbled during the campaign but probably not even the best campaign would have helped, so deep was Mulroney's unpopularity with the voters.

On those lines enlightening insights are to be found in a book by Michel Gratton, the Ottawa journalist who signed on with the Mulroney campaign in 1983 and later became the prime minister's press secretary. The book's revealing title is *"So What Are the Boys Saying?"*[14] Gratton sees Mulroney as an honest and capable man who had very bad luck and perhaps spent too much time on his image in the media. He wanted too badly to be liked. He courted the media and when they went after him he felt betrayed and blamed them for his problems. Brian and Mila, his wife, radiated charm, the kind of charm John Turner lacked. Canadians were looking for another Camelot. But his image started to slip even during the first campaign. John Turner had made a number of patronage appointments, apparently because of prior commitments to Trudeau. They included Bryce Mackesey, not exactly a star player. Mulroney, chatting with reporters, said "There's no whore like an old whore. If I'd been in Bryce's place I'd have been the first with my nose in the trough, just like all the rest of them."[15] He apparently thought he was among friends and it wouldn't get out. It did and Mulroney came off as damning patronage in public but accepting it in private. Mulroney "felt betrayed," but it was his own fault. Gratton writes, "How could he have thought the reporters were his friends, his confidants?"[16] This hurt him, but the day was saved by John Turner, who patted the rear of Liberal president Iona Campagnolo in public. "Suddenly old whores were old hat. Bum-patting was now the media rage. Here was the Prime Minister behaving like a buffoon in public."[17] Mulroney and the Tories went on to a stunning victory on September

4, winning 211 out of the 282 seats in the Canadian Parliament.

But things started to go wrong. The response of the Prime Minister's Office (PMO) on the question of a nanny at the prime minister's residence was heavyhanded and looked like a coverup. Few would have cared about the issue but the response raised eyebrows. There followed a series of scandals involving cabinet members, some waffling on issues like old-age pensions. Then, after a government retreat on pensions, an American icebreaker, the *Polar Sea*, steamed through the Northwest Passage, which Canada claimed as territorial water. It was embarrassing to a prime minister who prided himself on his friendship with President Reagan. The government began to get heat from the press. Then came the tuna scandal: a million tons of rancid tuna were sent to Canadian markets on the word of Fisheries Minister John Fraser, against the advice of his own inspectors. Mulroney tried to keep Fraser on until Fraser contradicted him in a session with reporters. The prime minister had done the right thing and was not to blame, but the press savaged him. "His personal credibility was gurgling down the drain."[18] Communications Minister Marcel Massé was investigated for allegedly exceeding campaign-spending limits. He was acquitted but the damage was done. Environment Minister Suzanne Blais-Grenier was cited in the press for expensive trips. International Trade Minister James Kelleher, responding to a question, said he didn't think Nova Scotia had a textile industry, which must have come as a surprise to former Conservative leader Robert Stanfield of Stanfield's Underwear of Nova Scotia. These were relatively minor, but the press seized on them and the reputation of the prime minister was slowly undermined. There were triumphs, such as the "Shamrock Summit" with President Reagan at Quebec City in March 1985 and the Nassau Commonwealth Summit Conference in October, but even these seemed to be overshadowed by the bad news. The Tories had lost their lead in the polls by January 1986. When Mulroney and Reagan met in Washington in March, the press was almost totally distracted by the wife of the Canadian ambassador to the United States slapping her social secretary in front of a crowd, including reporters. "This could only happen to us," Gratton mourned, "we'd become like the tar baby: everything stuck to us."[19]

Gratton was concerned that Mulroney didn't seem to have any grand plan or strategy. If he did he kept it quiet. He wanted to be liked and his administration was increasingly one of damage control. "For all his personal skills, Mulroney never seemed to realize that pretty pictures of himself and his wife in the Canadian boondocks were not a substitute for a coherent political philosophy."[20] Problem followed problem. Conservative support in the West suffered when the government awarded the CF-18 aircraft contract to Canadair in Quebec instead of Bristol

Aerospace in Manitoba. Then there was the Oerlikon affair, involving a land deal by the administrator of a blind trust set up for cabinet member André Bissonette.

By the end of the second term, the Conservatives would face a revived Liberal challenge now led by the charismatic and popular Jean Chrétien. The result was the PC disaster.

One commentator explains the volatility of the Canadian voter in sports terms:

> In the land of hockey, as in most parliamentary democracies, voter attention during election times is frequently diverted from the scoreboard. The spotlight is on the new lineup of players and on promises of new plays to come. The emphasis is on change rather than reflection, on style rather than issues, on process rather than substance. It is usually after the noise of the campaign has subsided that citizens turn back to look at the scoreboard, only to find that they are still not winning.[21]

This bears out Gratton's and Newman's sense that the Mulroney had no commanding vision for Canada but was playing to what he thought the voters wanted to see, responding day to day. He was undoubtedly hurt by the defection of Lucien Bouchard and the loss of Quebec support even before the Charlottetown disaster and of course the economic shrinkage in the country partly due to a changing global economy over which heads of governments have little control.


REFERENDUM II

Honoring a campaign promise, Quebec Premier Jacques Parizeau scheduled another referendum on Quebec sovereignty for October 30, 1995. That referendum proved to be a wake-up call to Canada. As the date neared, Chrétien advised people not to get excited, fearing an overreaction in Anglo Canada would strengthen the hand of the separatists. Under Parizeau the polls early on indicated a defeat for the PQ. But in the closing weeks of the campaign Lucien Bouchard led the Yes forces and proved so charismatic that the odds changed. The No forces won by a very narrow margin: 50.4-49.6, less than a one percent victory. This catapulted national unity back onto center stage in Canada. It shared that stage with ongoing concerns about jobs and the national deficit.

The narrowness of the referendum victory was a serious blow to the federal Liberals. Chrétien received severe criticism for having been complacent and ignored the danger almost too long. Had Jacques Parizeau remained in charge of the Yes campaign that might have been the right course. But when the charismatic Lucien Bouchard came back to Quebec to lead it, separatist sentiment climbed so fast it could no longer be ignored and almost won the day. Peter Newman, commenting in *Maclean's* on November 13, 1995, pointed to the Swiss confederation of twenty-three quasi-independent cantons and a limited federal role as a possible model for Canada. "There comes a point," he said, "when national institutions can't be fixed any more. They have to be replaced." Preston Manning and company denounced Chrétien for not preparing a contingency plan for Quebec separation. A spate of books by academics called on Anglo Canada to accept Quebec's departure as inevitable and to plan for the aftermath and its own survival.[22]

Canadians had expressed in one way or another great fatigue with constitutional questions but they would not go away. On November 26, 1995 Chrétien called on provincial premiers and Parliament to recognize Quebec as a distinct society and to give it a veto over constitutional changes along with Atlantic Canada, Ontario, and "The West." British Columbia, stung at being lumped in with the prairie provinces, reacted angrily and Chrétien quickly added British Columbia to the veto list in its own right. Feelings were not soothed, however, as the original proposal seemed to British Columbians typical of eastern ignorance and indifference to the fastest-growing province.

Bouchard, leaving national politics to replace Jacques Parizeau as leader of the Parti Québecois and premier of Quebec, predictably denounced the Chrétien olive branch as too little, too late. *Maclean's* editor, Robert Lewis, rose to its defense, however. Clearly, he wrote on December 11, without such recognition Quebec will secede. Ontario will then have 45 percent of the remaining seats in Parliament. British Columbia and Alberta will be angry about that and move toward affiliation with the United States. "Breakup is not out of the question."

At the start of 1996 a joint *Macleans*/CBC poll found Canadians lacking faith in their political leaders' ability to stop the deterioration. A third of Canadians and a half of Quebeckers believed that Canada as then constituted would not exist by the year 2000. Despite Chrétien's best efforts, he lacked support in the issue. Polls indicated that French Quebeckers increasingly saw nothing to lose by separating while Anglo Canadians saw no reason to make any further concessions. In the light of these findings, pollster Allan Greg recommended acceptance of some form of sovereignty-association with Quebec and the redesign of a decentralized Canada.[23] But if Chrétien should move to do this possibly sensible thing, he would be vilified as the man who broke up Canada.

More than Quebec has been on Canadian minds. Chrétien has failed to deliver on one campaign promise: elimination of the 7 percent Goods and Services Tax (GST), which, for many, comes on top of hefty provincial taxes and drives Canadians over the border to American malls in great numbers. In February 1996 Chrétien shuffled his cabinet, bringing in Pierre Pettigrew as minister for intergovernmental affairs. The cabinet drew up a package of nonconstitutional changes involving decentraliza-tion of powers and a hard line toward Quebec separatists. There would be no dual citizenship in the event of Quebec's separation. Also Que-bec's borders would be open to question since northern Quebec was added to the province only in 1912 and western Quebec is heavily English in makeup. Cabinet minister Marcel Massé said, "If Canada is divisible, so is Quebec."

In by-elections on March 25, Liberals did well but the Bloc, now led by Michel Gauthier, held onto official opposition by a hair. A clear dan-ger was that now the Liberals, the only national partly left, might quickly lose favor because of unpopular but unavoidable measures to confront the deficit. Finance Minister Paul Martin confessed in Parlia-ment that the promise to drop the GST had been a mistake. Sheila Copps, deputy prime minister, had promised her constituents she would resign if the GST was not scrapped. At first she hesitated but then, in May 1996, was forced to keep her promise. The by-election was critical for Liberal prestige. A drastic loss of Liberal support at this time would leave the field to the Bloc Separatists and the Reform Party, opposed to any concessions to Quebec, and might well presage the separation of Quebec. Copps won handily and returned to her job in June.

Manning's Reform Party was beset with divisions between homo-phobic rightists and Manning who needed to keep his party closer to the mainstream. Bloodletting saw the resignation of party whip Bob Ringma and the suspension of Dave Chatters of Alberta from the caucus.[24]

In 1996 the big question remained Quebec separatism. If it occurred it would be messy and possibly violent. Even if it were smooth and peaceful, Anglo Canada would be left with a federation dominated by Ontario, with half the population, and with Atlantic Canada cut off. Then the question marks would then be British Columbia and Alberta, rich and resentful of Ottawa. The federation could survive only in a drastically decentralized form. Despite their seeming instransigence, it is hard to believe the Liberal government would refuse flatly to negotiate with a Quebec that had voted for sovereignty. Canadians are more prag-matic than that. Some sort of negotiation would be needed to guarantee minority rights in both countries.

In early 1997 the Conservatives had made some headway against the Liberals according to the Angus Reid poll of the Southam newspa-pers.[25] The Liberal support appeared to have dropped to 47% from a high of 63% in February 1995.Chrétien was expected to call elections in 1997. Charest's PCs were up to 18% from 5% in February 1995. Inter-net news of January 10, 1996 showed polls estimating the Conservatives might take at least 30 seats in the coming election and even return to the official opposition if the Bloc and Reform continue to slip. Reform had slipped from a high of 19% to 11% in November 1996. The New Democrats seem to be moving up on the left to 11% from a low of 7% in 1993. Chrétien had moved to the right in fiscal policy since the last election. Chrétien's posture toward Quebec stiffened. Public statements in November 1996 indicated he would not accept a simple narrow majority for separation in the next Quebec referendum as binding. He did not indicate how large a majority would be considered sufficient. He also has insisted that a future referendum question be a clear choice in "leaving Canada," rather than the "partnership with Canada" offer put forward by the PQ. Support of separatism in Quebec seemed to be waning in early 1997 but this could change with a single incident or a charismatic leader. All the signs were in place and Chrétien surprised no one when he announced, on April 27, an election for June 2, 1997. It was only three and a half years into the mandate but the polls at the time made the Liberals the overwhelming favorite. They might, however, lose ground on the left to a resurgent NDP and on the right to a resurgent Progressive-Conservative Party. The race was for which party would become the official opposition. Tories and Reform promised to cut taxes. The NDP promised to restore services. The Bloc Québecois promised an end to Canada as we know it, and stood lowest in the polls at the call for the election.

The June 2, 1997 election confirmed the Liberals' majority but by a slender margin. Chrétien's party took 155 of the 301 seats, not a comfortable one but still a majority. Solid Ontario gave the Liberals 99 of their seats, two thirds of their caucus. Preston Manning's Reform Party moved into the official opposition with 60 seats but it remained strictly a western party with no seats east of Manitoba. Despite a lackluster performance by its leader, Gilles Duceppe, the Bloc came third, with 44 seats strictly in Quebec, down from its previous 54. Fourth, with 21 seats, came the New Democratic Party under Alexa McDonough, most of the seats, drawn from the Liberals in Atlantic Canada, where unemployment remained the central issue. The NDP recovered official party status as did Jean Charest's Tories also with a surprisingly good showing in Atlantic Canada but few gains elsewhere. The House of Commons, now Italianate, with five official parties, confirms the regional nature of Canadian politics with the two leading opposition parties uncompromisingly regional, the governing Liberals mostly Ontario-based, and the Conservatives on the Atlantic fringe. The future of the once-formidable Progressive-Conservative Party is in doubt. Charest brought it back to official status but failed to cut into Reform strength in Ontario or the West. Nevertheless all the partly leaders declared themselves satisfied. Television gave us the spectacle of five smiling winners and their cheering supporters. Fine, but who speaks for Canada? Ottawa analyst Bruce Campbell says leadership will be an issue in the coming years. Chrétien was widely criticized for nearly losing the Quebec referendum in 1995 and for calling an early election in which the Liberals were set back and confined to central Canada. He is not popular in Quebec. Quebec polls in early 1998 indicated that Jean Charest would win in an election against Lucien Bouchard but that the current Liberal leader, Daniel Johnson, would not. Pressure developed quickly for Charest to leave the leadership of the federal Conservatives and ride into the lists as leader of the Quebec Liberals thereby to save Canada. Polls also indicated that, while Bouchard retains a solid following, most Quebeckers do not want another referendum. After first refusing the overtures, Charest began to hedge and, on March 26, announced his decision to lead the Liberals in Quebec. He probably had little choice. A refusal to accept the provincial challenge would have weakened his popularity in the rest of Canada and left him further from the Prime Minister's chair than his shift did. This, at last, gives Quebec voters a clear choice. If Bouchard wins in the coming election, due by the fall of 1999, it will be a clear mandate for another referendum and for secession. It cannot be laid to colorless or inept Liberal campaigning by an unpopular leader. Charest seemed to see no ideological problem in this shift, explaining that the Quebec Liberal Party is independent of the federal one.

The idea of nation-state has been a hard one to sell in Canada since its foundation in 1867. Local and ethnic loyalties, firmly entrenched then, have not withered away, railway, highway, telephone, television, and e-mail notwithstanding. The English–French divide has remained sharp, especially since the French minority is largely concentrated in Quebec and is older in its history than Anglo Canada. But even within Anglo Canada there are distinct regional communities with distinct characters and interests, most with roots that predate Confederation.

Newfoundland has a strong sense of its otherness. Tied economically and culturally to the British Isles, the island has only been in Canada since 1949. The three maritime provinces, traditionally oriented to New England and old England, were reluctant partners in Confederation and retain a suspicion of the central Canadians. Ontario, the most populous province, is also the most vociferously Canadian. The three prairie provinces simmer in perpetual discontent at perceived indifference or malevolence from Canadian government too much under the influence of Quebec and Ontario. Preston Manning is their voice. British Columbia, the fastest-growing province, has its distinct character and interests, especially trade around the Pacific Rim. It resents Ottawa and central Canada for a number of perceived slights.

From the start national leaders strove to inculcate a sense of Canadian nationality, pulling away from Britain toward independence, complete with the 1982 Constitution Act. But it has been uphill sledding against the regional loyalties and jealousies. Nova Scotia was the first province to try to secede, immediately after the formation of Canada. Quebec's first provincial nationalist party, Le Parti Nationale was formed in 1886 in the wake of the execution of a francophone rebel in Saskatchewan. And the mainstream provincial Liberals and Conservatives have been separate organizations with tenuous ties to the national parties. Charismatic leadership like that of John A. Macdonald, Wilfred Laurier, and Pierre Eliot Trudeau has been able to articulate a national vision but not to give it permanence. Regional loyalties have always rebounded and seem sharper than ever and the only leader with remotely charismatic potential recently was Jean Charest, who abandoned the limping Tories to lead the Quebec Liberals.

Canadians have never been as strongly identified with political parties as Americans. The sharp swings in the Mulroney decade underline this. There is today no Canadian party with a truly national constituency. Chrétien's Liberals have little currency in Quebec, little west of Ontario, and hardly any left in Atlantic Canada. The three largest parties are regional in constituency. Jean Charest hoped his rebounding Tories would be able to fill this gap. They have a long climb ahead of them out of the pit dug by Mulroney and Campbell. Charest's charisma combined with growing disillusionment with the Liberals won some seats in Atlantic Canada on June 2 but failed to gain in the West against Reform. Charest promised to cut income taxes by 10 percent, cut unemployment insurance premiums, and create a million jobs by 2005, a task critics in Reform and Liberal camps dismiss as impossible.[26] The recent *Maclean's* poll indicates a growing lack of faith in the "ability of parties to grapple with the big problems." If Peter Newman is right, the erosion of faith in all institutions, including the churches, is so massive and decisive as to constitute a revolution in Canadian attitudes.

Party leaders have certainly *tried* to initiate changes—witness Trudeau and the Constitution Act, which alienated Quebec leaders once again. Witness the attempts of Mulroney and friends to redress the Quebec grievance, which alienated Anglo Canada. Meech Lake and Charlottetown were resounding failures, which may explain the reluctance of the Chrétien government to initiate change or to tinker with the Constitution. Economic realities have intruded upon the agenda and fiscal austerity had been an inescapable response to mounting deficits. This is true now in Quebec where labor leaders have threatened to abandon separatism if it means cutbacks in social programs.

Parties are not able in Canada to mediate effectively between the electorate and the national government due to their regional constituencies and the same kind of weakening of party role one sees in the United States. This is partly due to the parliamentary system itself. A party with a solid majority is difficult to oppose given the traditional party discipline of such systems. And that solid majority may come from one or two regions as indeed it has on June 2, 1997, leaving the others out of power. Opposition parties are hard put to be mediators. Television has led to more direct and personal appeals to the people. Prime ministers have been accused of "presidential politics" for doing this but they all have in recent years, sometimes to their regret as in Chrétien's recent embarrassment when he publicly denied having promised to do away with the seven percent goods-and-services tax only to be confronted with himself on TV making the promise.

Canada's unique geography and history make for unique political problems that make Canada-watching, from this northern New York vantage point, the most interesting game in town.

## NOTES

1. Review by Andrew Phillips in *Maclean's*, April 29, 1996.
2. Toronto: HarperCollins, 1996.
3. *Maclean's*, April 29, 1996.
4. Wayne C. Thompson, *Canada 1995* (Harpers Ferry, W.V.: Stryker-Post, 1995), p. 180.
5. Peter C. Newman, *The Canadian Revolution: From Deference to Defiance* (Toronto: Penguin, 1995), p. 300.
6. Thompson, *Canada 1995*, p. 61.
7. Robert M. Campbell and Leslie A. Pal, *The Real Worlds of Canadian Politics* (Peterborough, Ont.: Broadview Press, 1994), p. 17.
8. *Maclean's*, October 30, 1995.
9. Louis Balthazar, "Within the Black Box: Reflections from a French Quebec Vantage Point," *The American Review of Canadian Studies*, Winter 1995, pp. 519–41.
10. Campbell and Pal, *Real Worlds*, p. 18.
11. Thompson, *Canada 1995*, p. 63.
12. Campbell and Pal, *Real Worlds*, pp. 177–81.
13. Ibid.
14. Michel Gratton, *"So What Are the Boys Saying?"* (Toronto: McGraw-Hill Ryerson, 1987), p. 28.
15. Ibid., pp. 123, 124, 127.
16. Segal, *No Surrender*.
17. Gratton, *The Boys*, p. 28.
18. Ibid., pp. 123, 124, 127.
19. Gratton, *The Boys*, pp. 163, 166.
20. Ibid., pp. 190, 191.

21. Andrew B. Gollmer and Daniel Salee (eds.), *Canada under Mulroney* (Montreal: Vehicule Press, 1988), pp. 10, 11.

22. Jeffrey M. Ayres, "A Reluctant Nation Finds Its Voice," *The American Review of Canadian Studies*, Spring 1996, pp. 115–26.

23. *Maclean's*, December 25, 1995–January 1, 1996.

24. *Maclean's*, May 13, 1996.

25. Reuters, December 11, 1996.

26. *Maclean's*, March 17, 1997.

# CHAPTER 7

# *Australia:*
# *An Old Order Manages Change*

## Rodney Smith

The last three Australian national elections have brought cries of "party crisis." The 1990 election saw the combined major party primary vote dip to 83 percent, its lowest level since 1943. For some, the end of Australia's two-party system was nigh.[1] In 1993, the Liberal-National Coalition parties lost an election they were widely tipped to win against an unpopular Labor government struggling with high unemployment levels. Many saw the Liberal and National parties as over, or at least in need of radical rethinking and reform.[2] Three years later, without any such reform, the Coalition parties swept to office, winning 47 percent of the primary vote and 94 of the 148 lower house seats. The size of the Coalition win and Labor's decimation in its blue-collar heartlands brought claims that Labor would be consigned to the political wilderness.[3]

Were these elections signs of a real crisis for the Australian parties, or just a *maladie imaginaire*? This chapter argues the latter case. Certainly some of the key supports of the old party political order in Australia have shifted since that order was established in 1909 and consolidated in the 1940s. These changes accelerated during Labor's thirteen years of government from 1983. Nonetheless, in 1998 the major parties of the 1940s—Labor and the Liberal-National Coalition—remain the key institutions competing over government, policy choices, and electoral support in Australia. They do not look exactly as they did in the 1940s, but to expect them to do so in Australia's changed social, economic, and geopolitical context would be naive. Australia's major parties have avoided real crisis—as opposed to temporary dips in their individual or combined party votes—partly because of the strength of the old order, partly because they have recognized and managed the changes affecting them reasonably effectively, and partly because they remain protected by institutional arrangements within the political system.

## THE OLD ORDER

The spur to formation of Australia's party order was the establishment of the Labor Party (ALP) in 1890. Labor's electoral support grew rapidly to 31 percent in 1903, giving it national minority government in 1904. The non-Labor parties remained relatively disorganized and divided over Labor's challenge until 1909, when they fused into Australia's original Liberal Party. Labor's primary vote in 1910 was now 50 percent.[4] This fusion produced the bipolar lower house electoral competition—Labor versus non-Labor—that has essentially continued into the late 1990s, although the name of the main non-Labor party has changed several times (see table 7.1). The potential electoral complication caused by the formation between 1920 and 1922 of the Country Party as a nationwide rural anti-Labor Party was reduced by coalition agreements between the rural and urban anti-Labor parties. These agreements left the dominant electoral contest that between Labor and the Coalition parties.[5]

TABLE 7.1
Average Australian House of Representatives Vote
by Decade, Labor, Coalition, and Minor Parties

| Decade | Labor | Coalition | Minor |
|--------|-------|-----------|-------|
| 1910–19 | 47 | 50 | 3 |
| 1920–29 | 45 | 49 | 6 |
| 1930–39 | 32 | 50 | 18 |
| 1940–49 | 47 | 41 | 12 |
| 1950–59 | 46 | 48 | 6 |
| 1960–69 | 45 | 45 | 10 |
| 1970–79 | 45 | 47 | 8 |
| 1980–89 | 47 | 45 | 8 |
| 1990– | 41 | 45 | 14 |

Sources: Calculated from C. Macintyre, *Political Australia* (Melbourne: Oxford University Press, 1991), pp. 1–13; M. Mackerras, "Statistical Analysis of the Results," in *The Politics of Retribution: The 1996 Federal Election*, ed. C. Bean, M. Simms, S. Bennett, and J. Warhurst (Sydney: Allen and Unwin, 1997), p. 210.

The strength of this party order lay partly in electoral arrangements and partly in the prominence of class over other socioeconomic divisions as the basis for political mobilization. The electoral apparatus supporting the party order included single-member electorates that locked out geographically dispersed minority opinions from House of Representatives elections. The "winner-take-all" systems used for Senate elections also worked to eliminate the chances of minority party representation. Preferential voting from 1918 aided the emergence of the Coalition by allowing the non-Labor parties to exchange preferences. Virtually universal suffrage from 1902 helped to ensure the full mobilization of party support. Compulsory voting from 1924 reduced the effort needed by parties to get out the vote.[6]

Aside from these formal arrangements, Australia's socioeconomic structure lent itself to bipolar electoral and interest group mobilization along broad class lines. As a consciously "new" society, Australia retained few vestiges of the precapitalist order. The key political conflicts of late-nineteenth-century Australia revolved around economic issues. Employers and workers were mobilized in these conflicts by business organizations and trade unions. These organizations became key backers of the fledgling parties, with many significant unions formally affiliating with the ALP and businesses mobilizing funds and support for the non-Labor parties.[7] Against such conflicts, purely regional, ethnic, and religious issues had little purchase on the parties. In any case, the Catholic-Protestant and English-Irish divides largely reinforced class divisions.[8]

In this period, the parties consolidated the ideological and policy consensus and conflict that marked party relations until at least the 1960s. Marsh identifies six themes of party consensus:

> the "White Australia" policy, which preserved the ethnic character of Australia and insulated the workforce from "unfair" competition; justiciable industrial relations and needs based wages; tariff based manufacturing development; per capita equalisation of revenues between States; and finally, the adoption of welfare and national development roles for the federal government.[9]

The parties often pursued different emphases within these themes, and on other policy and ideological issues—particularly government socialization of industries and the role of trade unions—their differences were quite sharp. Nonetheless, these themes established an Australian "liberal-egalitarian project" to which both parties were broadly committed.[10] Thus although the parties had different class bases, the potentially divisive effects of these bases for national integration were muted by considerable consensus on the nation-building goals sketched above.

From this outline, it would be tempting to see the party order as complete by at least 1922, if not 1909. Two points mitigate against such a conclusion. The first concerns party organization. The urban non-Labor party only found a stable organizational form in 1944 with the formation of the Liberal Party under Robert Menzies's leadership. Moreover, in the 1930s the ALP had to weather a split in which the defectors set up in competition for working-class votes rather than joining the non-Labor ranks. Thus the stability of the party order was only confirmed in the 1940s (see table 7.1). Second, one key element of the party consensus was only achieved in the 1940s with the establishment of a national welfare state. The 1940s also saw arguably the greatest party ideological conflicts over socialization of industry with Coalition opposition to the Chifley Labor government's attempts to nationalize medicine and banking. By the mid-1940s, then, a strong bipolar party order with solid organizational, parliamentary, voting base, interest group, policy, ideological, and electoral system dimensions was established.

## 1944–98: THE OLD ORDER MANAGES CHANGE

The longevity of Menzies's prime ministership—1949 to 1966—and the even longer incumbency of Coalition federal governments—1949 to 1983, with the exception of the three years between 1972 and 1975—suggest that the party order remained frozen for much of the postwar period. Despite gloom among some at Labor's repeated national election failures, the party easily held its status as the second major party.[11] Similarly, in the thirteen years of Labor government from 1983, the Coalition remained the only viable opposition (see table 7.1).

Such apparent stability should not obscure the fact that the parties managed considerable change. One significant change was the 1948 switch to proportional representation for Senate elections. This gave minor parties a realistic chance of gaining the statewide vote needed to elect a senator. The first beneficiary of this change was the Democratic Labor Party (DLP), a conservative labor party whose founders left or were expelled from the ALP in the mid-1950s. These DLP activists used their new party to continue campaigns against what they saw as the Labor leadership's lack of resolve against domestic and international communism, including communism within the ALP itself. At elections between 1955 and 1970 the DLP won up to three Senate seats and held the balance of power in the Senate from 1965 to 1974. The DLP generally supported the Coalition, reducing any disruption to the bipolar party system.[12]

The same could not be said for the second major beneficiary of the Senate election rules, the Australian Democrats. Formed in 1977, the Democrats have won Senate seats in every subsequent Senate election and held the balance of power alone or with other minority senators from 1981. On many issues they have acted as a centrist watchdog over both major parties; however on "new politics" issues such as the environment, human rights, and gender equality, they have stood apart from both major parties. They have used their legislative balance of power more creatively than the DLP, presenting a greater challenge for the old party order. The major parties have, however, done much to accommodate upper-house balance-of-power politics, including the Democrats and other minor parties in legislative negotiations and parliamentary committees to build majority support for government legislation.[13]

At the national level, then, Australian parliamentary party politics now has a split quality, with the lower house retaining majoritarian politics and the upper house exhibiting a rather different coalition-building pattern. During the past decade, such coalition-building politics has entered the state lower houses. Every state except Victoria has seen lower-house minority government, with either Labor or the Coalition relying on the support of independents to stay in power. In no state has the electoral dominance of the major parties been seriously threatened, but enough voters have supported minor candidates to produce minority governments.[14] The limit of this development was probably reached in Tasmania between 1989 and 1992, when Labor governed with the support of five Green independent parliamentarians on the basis of a policy accord.[15] In New South Wales, independents negotiated an institutional "Charter of Reform" in return for supporting a minority Coalition government between 1991 and 1995.[16] Although the major parties complained that minority government obstructed their mandate to govern, they generally adapted to the new circumstances and negotiated their legislative programs through parliament.

In turn, opinion poll evidence and voting figures suggest that a sizeable group of Australian voters welcomes the role played by minor parties in weakening the power of major party governments. Polls taken at various times since 1975 have shown majority support for minor parties in the Senate combining with the opposition to block government bills. The most recent such polls concerned the Democrats' intention in 1996 to block the Coalition government's part-privatization of Telstra, the government telecommunications arm. Between 50 and 64 percent of those polled supported the Democrats' right to block the bill.[17]

Voter support for minor parties appears to be linked to judgments about those parties' likely electoral success. In Senate elections, for example, where the vote quota needed for success is 14.3 percent, the minor party vote has peaked at 20 percent. The main beneficiary is the Democrats, who win around half the minor party vote and the bulk of the minor party seats in any election. In New South Wales, on the other hand, the upper house quota is only 4.6 percent. At the 1995 NSW election, 26 percent of voters gave minor parties their primary vote. The Democrats only won one eighth of this vote and were one of five minor parties to have a candidate elected. A section of the electorate thus appears to engage in tactical voting based on the effects of voting rules. This tactical voting has modified rather than overturned the old Australian party order.[18]

The emergence of parties like the DLP and Democrats points to changes within the Australian electorate. The DLP drew its support largely from devout Catholics who were upwardly socially mobile or were Eastern European immigrants.[19] Democrat voters are more diverse; however, they are slightly concentrated among the young, professionals, and the tertiary educated.[20] Between them, these minor party profiles point to some of the key shifts in the postwar Australian electorate. These include large shifts in the workforce from the primary to the secondary and tertiary sectors; increased social and geographical mobility; raised educational levels, greater gender equality in education, employment, and social opportunity; larger and more diverse non-Anglo-Celtic communities; declining levels of church attendance; and a decline in the rural population.[21] By the 1980s, the composition of the Australian electorate was increasingly fluid and diverse.

The major parties have managed these changes with a combination of reluctance and dexterity, competing for each new group of voters while attempting to retain the loyalties of their old support bases. From the late 1960s, Labor moved its image away from that of a blue-collar union party in an attempt to capture votes from white-collar and professional workers. This strategy appeared to increase Labor's non-manual vote but saw some manual voters desert the party. By the late 1980s, Labor gained almost the same proportions of votes from public sector workers—largely white-collar and professional—as it did from its traditional manual-worker base.[22] By 1993, the Coalition was explicitly competing for Labor's traditional class base, arguing that Labor had deserted "the battlers" during the Hawke-Keating era. At the 1996 election, this rhetoric appeared to pay off, with Labor seats in lower socioeconomic areas falling to the Coalition.[23]

In a connected trend, Labor captured larger proportions of the tertiary-educated vote from the 1970s. Labor also narrowed the electoral gender gap, reducing the Coalition's lead among women voters and winning almost the same proportion of men's and women's votes throughout the 1980s and early 1990s.[24] The pursuit of gender equality policies by Whitlam's Labor government (1972–75) was largely continued by Fraser's Coalition government (1975–83), allowing both parties to compete for the votes of female voters. In a similar way, the introduction of multicultural policies by the Whitlam government and Labor's more consistent commitment over the following two decades to multiculturalism and nondiscriminatory immigration policy appeared to gain it increasing electoral support from non-Anglo-Celtic communities. This shift to Labor was so marked that in the 1996 election campaign, Liberal leader Howard distanced himself from his 1980s skepticism regarding immigration and multiculturalism.[25] The decline in regular churchgoing has significantly reduced the reach of one of the conservatizing forces on the vote, to Labor's overall advantage. On the other hand, the traditionally solid Catholic vote for Labor eroded as more Catholics experienced upword social mobility.[26]

The party that has struggled most to accommodate recent socioecomonic changes has been the National Party. It remains locked into a rural constituency that is declining in size as urban populations and cities and towns encroach on previously country areas. The National Party vote has not declined as much as might have been expected, partly because the rural population reduction has been disproportionately among rural workers who supported Labor, and partly because the National Party has embarked on strategies to broaden its appeal beyond farming communities.[27]

The power of different groups to mobilize sections of the electorate behind the major parties has also shifted in recent decades. The reach of business groups has arguably increased with a growing number of small businesses, although the electoral impact of these groups was dampened by disagreements between industry sectors over the merits of competing major party policies.[28] The reduced electoral reach of churches was noted above. The direct workplace mobilizing power of trade unions has also declined. Total union membership among workers fell 12 percent between 1982 and 1993, with declines in all industry sectors.[29] Unions are still key players in mobilizing support for Labor policies. In the Hawke-Keating period (1983–96), the Labor government and the Australian Council of Trade Unions (ACTU) negotiated a series of accords, one of whose main achievements was to bind workers to reductions in real wages. The ACTU's efforts to convince workers to accept wage restraint were important in maintaining support for the Labor government.[30] At a more specific level, unions continued to support Labor's election campaigns.[31]

Since the 1970s, unions and other traditional vote mobilizers have been competing with a range of new "issue movements," whose electoral reach has proved impressive. Environmental groups such as the Australian Conservation Foundation (ACF), for example, have used their potential to mobilize a large support base to make policy demands on both major parties. In 1990, Labor strategists accepted that the large green vote mobilized by the ACF and other groups was going to be directed first to Australian Democrat and Green candidates. The ALP ran an advertising campaign asking green voters to give their second preferences to Labor, a strategy endorsed by environmental groups. Ultimately, the strategy appeared to work for Labor, making the difference between its winning and losing an extremely close election with a high minor party vote.[32] In 1996, key environmental groups approved Coalition policies, a factor that probably added weight to the landslide against Labor.[33]

While environmental groups appear to have been the largest new source of electoral mobilization, diverse groups mobilizing women, gays and lesbians, Aboriginal and Torres Strait Islanders, other ethnic minorities, civil libertarians, pensioners, students, and particular local communities have all emerged or become more influential since the 1970s.[34]

The parties' attempts to manage a more dynamic electorate and a wider array of mobilizing pressure groups have meant changes to and expansion of party policies, some of which have already been mentioned. If they have not become "catch-all" parties, the Labor and Liberal parties have certainly become "catch-more" parties. Attempts by the parties to attract international trade and investment in a more open world market provided another source of party policy change, particularly during the Hawke-Keating era.

These electoral, pressure group, and market forces combined to undo much of the "liberal egalitarian project" around which the Australian party order was developed.[35] The White Australia policy was dismantled in the 1960s by the Coalition government, replaced with nondiscriminatory immigration policy and, under Labor in the early 1970s, a multicultural program that challenged the cultural protection of Anglo-Celtic Australians. In the 1980s and 1990s, first the Liberal Party, then Labor, began to question the protection of a centralized wage-fixing system. In 1990, the Hawke Labor government introduced enterprise bargaining as one strand of its accord agreements with the ACTU. Howard's Coalition government (1996–) legislated to reduce union involvement in decentralized wage bargains. As part of attempts to reduce taxation and the size of government, the Hawke and Keating governments tightened eligibility for social transfers such as unemployment benefits, old age pensions, family allowances, and student subsidies. At the same time as the major parties abandoned the vision of individual prosperity via full employment, they undermined expectations that the state would support its citizens as of right.

Government support for business was similarly reevaluated. Until

Hawke's prime ministership, Labor and the Coalition did little to question seriously levels of industry protection. Hawke, Keating, and Howard all reduced protection, leaving businesses and workers more open to foreign competition. The Hawke and Keating governments overturned other Labor economic orthodoxies. Rather than pursuing the traditional Labor ideal of government ownership of industry, they and their state counterparts engaged in privatization of government utilities. Government controls over areas such as banking and finance, traditionally thought by both major parties to be essential to government management, were relaxed in favor of self-regulation. The Howard government again continued these policy approaches.

By the mid-1990s, the liberal egalitarian project of Australian party politics was largely replaced by a new project in which Australian government had a reduced role and Australian society and economy were opened up to global flows of economic and cultural capital. An important feature of this new political settlement was that although many of its key ideas emerged in or around the Liberal Party, it was Labor governments under Hawke and Keating that began to implement these ideas. In the 1980s, the party order shifted from a bipolar contest over the old liberal egalitarian project to a bipolar contest over this new liberal market project. Neither party upheld the old project against the new. Rather, the debate was about which party was best equipped to sweep away the old project and set up Australia for a future of increased economic deregulation and competition.[36]

These changes disenchanted sections of the parties' memberships. Both the Liberal and Labor parties have experienced strong membership declines in the past two decades.[37] Even here, the parties have counteracted the most debilitating effects of membership decline through a combination of taxpayer funding of the parties' electoral campaigns and the use of polling and targeted mail-outs to reach voters.[38]

Despite the considerable changes outlined above, the old party order persists in Australia. The parties of the old order have managed change, incorporating new supporters, crafting new rhetorics, and pursuing new policies. The question that remains is how the parties were able to undertake such extensive changes without losing the support of voters for whom "Labor" and "Liberal" meant different things in the 1980s and 1990s than they had in the 1960s or 1970s.

## PARTY IDENTIFICATION IN AUSTRALIA

Orthodox accounts of the Australian party order would see party identification as the only answer needed here. McAllister puts the position baldly: "In Australia, party identification is the basis for the stability of the party system."[39] For the orthodox, the links between party identification, voting behavior, and the party system stability are clear and direct. As Graetz and McAllister put it:

> Just as individuals identify with particular social, religious or ethnic groups during their lives, so . . . feelings of party loyalty endure throughout the individual's lifetime and provide the continuity and structure on which the stability of the party system rests. This concept of party loyalty is known as party identification. . . .
>
> Since political parties, like other social groups, do not change the fundamental premises on which they stand, partisanship represents a longtime influence on political behaviour.[40]

Supporters of this approach cite survey research conducted between 1967 and 1993, the main findings of which can be summarized simply. In this period, around 90 percent of Australian adults apparently identified with a party, and almost all with a major party. Respondents usually claimed a lifelong identification. Around 90 percent of identifiers voted for their party in any election, and 60 to 70 percent claimed to have done so al their voting lives. A vote for a minor party, or indeed for the major party other than the one with which a voter identified, should be understood as short-term protest votes. Partisanship provided a "homing tendency" for errant voters.[41]

Moreover, partisanship passed successfully from parents to their children, resulting in a stable two-party system unassailable by third forces.[42] As Aitkin summarized the argument from his pioneering 1967 and 1969 Australian surveys:

> At the time of his [sic] first vote, then, the typical Australian is equipped with a store of political information and a recently formed preference for one party, a preference which is remarkably likely to be also that of his parents. But his inheritance from his parents does not stop here. His identification with one party is likely to remain with him for the rest of his life.[43]

The Australian orthodoxy thus provided a cradle to grave account of partisan attachment that locked the bipolar party order tight. Political events, governments, issues, leaders would come and go, individuals' personal circumstances would change, the socioeconomic structure would alter, but the extent and distribution of party identification would remain stable and hold the party order to the pattern set in the early decades of the century.[44]

The one slight fly in the ointment concerned an apparent decline in the *intensity* of partisanship in Australia during the 1980s (see table 7.2). This decline was generally seen as unimportant and even short-

TABLE 7.2
Strength of Party Identification in Australia: 1967–1996
(ANPA, NSSS, and AES figures)

|              | 1967 | 1979 | 1984–85 | 1987 | 1990 | 1993 | 1996 |
|--------------|------|------|---------|------|------|------|------|
| Very Strong  | 30   | 31   | 26      | 19   | 17   | 17   | 16   |
| Fairly Strong| 40   | 43   | 40      | 45   | 44   | 43   | 37   |
| Not Very     | 21   | 17   | 23      | 31   | 33   | 28   | 30   |
| None         | 8    | 8    | 10      | 5    | 6    | 12   | 17   |

Sources: Recalculated from D. Aitkin, *Stability and Change in Australian Politics*, 2nd ed. (Canberra: Australian National University Press, 1982), p. 287; C. Bean, "Politics and the Public: Mass Attitudes towards the Australian Political System," in *Australian Attitudes*, ed. J. Kelley and C. Bean (Sydney: Allen and Unwin, 1988), p. 46; C. Bean and I. McAllister, "Long-Term Electoral Trends and the 1996 Election," in *The Politics of Retribution: The 1996 Federal Election*, ed. C. Bean, M. Simms, S. Bennett, and J. Warhurst (Sydney: Allen and Unwin, 1997), p. 175.

term, with McAllister predicting that it "will not continue."[45] Moreover, the evidence on which the orthodox view rested indicated that neither the overall *extent* of party identification, nor its long-term effects on voting behavior, nor its intergenerational transmission had weakened. If anything, they were stronger than ever.[46] Declining partisan intensity thus did not cause a reevaluation of the orthodox argument. With increasing evidence of partisan decline in the United States and the United Kingdom, Australia was seen as an exception among the Anglo democracies in maintaining a strong party system via high levels of party identification.[47]

## THE AUSTRALIAN ORTHODOXY CHALLENGED

Despite its pervasiveness, the orthodox account contained empirical and conceptual weaknesses. A useful starting point here concerns the evidence for Australian party identification as the foundation of Australian party stability. As Leithner points out, there is no evidence on Australian partisanship prior to the Australian National Political Attitudes (ANPA) sample collected by Aitkin in 1967. To extrapolate stable partisanship into previous decades—as Aitkin as others have done—is to make an assumption.[48] This assumption is rather risky, given Goot's finding of greater overall net volatility in voting between 1910 and 1940 than in the period since 1967 and Leithner's discovery of considerable fluctuations in voting support for parties between 1910 and 1969 on a polling booth by polling booth basis.[49] Partisanship *may* have been stable during the formation and consolidation of the Australian party order, but it may equally have possessed a volatility paralleling these fluctuations in voting behavior.

In understanding party stability since 1967, the orthodox account has used the national face-to-face ANPA samples of 1967 and 1979 as a baseline against which to compare the series of national Australian Electoral Study (AES) mailback surveys conducted for each federal election since 1987. The 1984–85 National Social Science Survey (NSSS) data, drawn from a mixed face-to-face and mailback survey, is sometimes included as part of this series.[50] Until 1996, the NSSS and AES data showed little if any decline in the overall extent of partisanship in Australia (see table 7.2). Nonetheless, the AES data indicate a progressive weakening of partisan bonds in Australia since 1979. In that period, the proportion of "very strong" partisans halved, and the proportion with either "not very strong" or no party identification grew from around one-quarter in 1979 to one-third in 1984–85 and 1987 and almost one-half in 1996 (table 7.2). If the absolute extent of party identification is the focus, then something new (and perhaps only temporary) appears to be happening in the Australian electorate in the mid-1990s. If, on the other hand, attention is given to the whole pattern of partisan bonds, then the 1996 AES results are part of a pattern of progressively weakening partisanship beginning in the 1980s.

The latter argument gains strength when data sources other than the AES studies are taken into account. These suggest that a decline in absolute levels of partisanship was under way in the early to mid-1980s. They include a large number of telephone interviews of random voter samples in specific electorates conducted throughout the 1980s by Chaples. Summarizing these studies, he writes:

> Many of these surveys have shown that, particularly at a time somewhat removed from a general election, substantially greater numbers of voters than had previously been indicated in Australian surveys now have no major party identification. . . . [I]n the past five years, the percentage of voters who now indicate no major party ID has risen to average about 33 percent, seldom falls below 25 percent in any electorate and on occasion has gone over 40 percent.[51]

One of Chaples's largest surveys, of 2,976 voters from seven urban and rural marginal electorates conducted during the 1990 federal election, found nonpartisans comprised 27 percent of the electorate. Chaples's figures are similar to the 28 percent of nonpartisans in my 1993 telephone survey of a random sample of 552 Sydney voters. These results lie between the 36 percent of nonpartisans in the 1986 national Class

Structure of Australia Project survey and the 18 percent of nonidentifiers in the 1988 national Issues in Multicultural Australia (IMA) survey (table 7.3)[52]

Some of the differences between the AES and other studies are due to question-wording and data-collection effects. Charnock estimates that these effects artificially reduced the level of nonidentification in the 1987 and 1990 AES surveys by about 10 percent.[53] Adding that 10 percent would bring the AES series into closer line with the other studies, particularly the 1988 IMA survey. The IMA survey used face-to-face interviews, employing interpreters for respondents with poor English.[54] It is particularly interesting (and curiously neglected in the literature), since it is the only study employing the same question and survey method as Aitkin. Its indication of an erosion of partisanship by the late 1980s is thus telling. Overall, while the non-AES studies give varied readings of the precise extent of the decline of partisanship in Australia, all point to a process of voter dealignment more extensive and beginning earlier than the AES studies.

Other Australian evidence suggests that partisanship may be less firm than the orthodoxy argues. Direct evidence of individual partisan volatility is hard to find due to the general absence of Australian voter panel research. The two reported instances of such panel research indicate that some Australians' party identifications do change in the short term. Between 1967 and 1969, 13 percent of Australian voters in the ANPA panel study had changed their party identification. Between 1984 and 1987, 9 percent of the NSSS panel study had changed party horses.[55]

TABLE 7.3

Strength of Party Identification in Australia: 1988–93 (alternative surveys)

|  | *1988* | *1990* | *1993* |
|---|---|---|---|
| Very Strong | 16 | 22 | 15 |
| Fairly Strong | 41 | 36 | 37 |
| Not Very | 25 | 14 | 19 |
| None | 18 | 27 | 28 |

Sources: Recalculated from E. Chaples, "A Decade of Voter Dealignment: Party Identification and Electoral Volatility in Australia in the 1980s" paper presented to the Annual Meeting of the Southern Political Science Association, Atlanta, November 10, 1990; I. McAllister and T. Makkai, "The Formation and Development of Party Loyalties: Patterns among Australian Immigrants," *Australian and New Zealand Journal of Sociology* 27.2 (August 1991): 202; R. Smith, *1993 Sydney Corruption Survey: Codebook and Frequencies* (Sydney: School of Political Science, University of New South Wales).

The suggestion that around 10 percent of voters switch partisan allegiances in the average time between federal elections indicates more individual partisan volatility than the lifetime partisanship argument would allow.

What of the argument that party identification is fixed by family childhood socialization? Australian research on immigration, religion, occupational mobility, and unemployment indicates that adult socialization experiences such as these can disrupt or alter individuals' formation of party identification.[56] In 1993, only 43 percent of voters matched their partisanship with the recalled partisanship of both their parents, considerably less than the figure required to ensure stability in the party order.[57] The only research on the formation of Australian children's party identifications, conducted by Connell in 1969, showed that many Australians developed a partisanship by their teenage years. Despite the interpretation sometimes drawn from this finding, nothing in Connell's study suggested that partisanship could not change later in life. Connell argued that the *structure* of Australians' political orientations were set by the end of childhood but not that the *content* of those orientations would be fixed.[58]

Connected with these empirical doubts are conceptual issues that the orthodox account has never properly resolved. "Party identification" was always a conceptually foreshortened answer to the question of Australian party stability. It begged the question: "*Why* is partisanship stronger in Australia than elsewhere?" This issue was sometimes acknowledged in the literature, but its serious consideration was continually put off.[59]

McAllister and others habitually list up to six briefly explained reasons for the apparently higher levels of partisanship in Australia than in other countries. These are compulsory voting, preferential voting, frequent elections, increased political interest, stronger class voting, and a weaker economic crisis than in the United Kingdom or the United States.[60] Oddly, this list omits any direct reference to parties, their policies, their ideologies, or the political contest between them. I shall return to this omission below. First, the explanations in the list need to be considered.

Compulsory, preferential and regular voting are poor explanations for Australia's pattern of partisanship. Compulsory voting forces the attention of more citizens on the electoral contest than does voluntary voting, but this is quite a different thing from building identification. Moreover, the argument that having to vote for a party leads to identification reverses the causal relationship between vote and partisanship on which party identification models rely and suggests that partisanship might be a post-hoc justification of a voting choice. Preferential voting certainly forces voters to choose between candidates, including those of the major parties. Again, it is unclear why this should lead to identification, rather than to an assumption on voters' parts that the electoral contest is ultimately about which of the two Australian parties with the historical and media-supported status of alternative governments should govern at a given time. The argument that Australia has more frequent elections than Anglo democracies with lower partisanship suffers from the same difficulties and is also empirically dubious. Australian federal elections occur every three years and most state elections every three or four years. This is less frequent than in the United States. Finally, since these long-established features of the Australian electoral system have remained unchanged in the 1980s and 1990s, they cannot explain why partisanship should have declined in this period.

Arguments from political culture are potentially more convincing, particularly as class and political interest have both shown movement in Australia in recent decades. The difficulty is that the movements both run in the wrong direction. If interest in politics supports partisanship, then Australian partisanship should have increased with political interest since the 1960s.[61] If the class-party relationship supports partisanship, then the Australian evidence on the weakening relationship between class and party suggests that partisanship should have been declining in recent decades.[62]

The economic crisis argument is suggestive, although it is not clear that Australia's plunge into high unemployment and inflation in the mid-1970s was less dramatic than those in the United States or the United Kingdom. The inflation and unemployment jumps of the 1970s had an enormous impact on party politics and policy-making in Australia.[63] In any case, subjective perceptions of an economic crisis, rather than its objective measurement, are what count in electoral terms. Voters are more likely to make parochial economic judgments than detailed international comparisons. The evidence from the 1970s onwards suggests that some Australian voters have used their economic experiences to evaluate the parties in power and to guide their party loyalties.[64]

## WHY THE PATTERN OF
## PARTISANSHIP CHANGE IN AUSTRALIA?

If the decline in party identification cannot easily be traced to these six factors, how is it to be explained? My argument centers on the parties themselves. As Graetz and McAllister noted (see above), the partisanship model assumes that "political parties . . . do not change the fundamental premises on which they stand." As we have seen, however, the major

Australian political parties have changed their "fundamental premises," so we would expect to see shifts in partisanship of the sort found above. The question that follows is why Australian partisanship declined during the 1980s, while the drop in U.S. and British party identification took place in the 1960s and 1970s.

The answer put forward here is the presence of a policy crisis over which both major parties govern. The United States experienced such crises with the Vietnam War and economic recession in the 1960s and 1970s; the United Kingdom with the economic instability and industrial unrest of the 1970s. Partisanship fell at these times. Australia experienced similar crises; however, until the 1980s the two parties did not share government over them. The Coalition's dominance of federal government from 1949 to 1983 meant Labor did not have the chance to show what it would do to deal with policy crises. The euphoria in 1972 surrounding Labor's first chance at federal power for twenty-three years, the controversial manner of Whitlam's 1975 dismissal, but most importantly the brevity of Labor's time in office, thus delayed the decline of party identification in Australia. Until the Hawke and Keating Labor governments, the inability of both parties to deal effectively with major economic crises was not sufficiently clear in the electorate to produce a weakening of partisan bonds. By contrast, the Democrats and Republicans had shared policy responsibility during the 1960s and 1970s, as had the Conservative and Labour parties in the United Kingdom. When Hawke and Keating began undoing Labor orthodoxy in the 1980s and were unable to produce substantially better economic outcomes than the Coalition, partisanship decline set in.

## CONCLUSION: NO THREAT TO THE OLD ORDER?

The foregoing analysis has argued that the Australian party order has resisted crisis largely because of the ability of the major parties to manage change within Australia's society, economy, and political system. To manage these changes, the parties have had to respond to new electoral and interest group demands and to alter their policy platforms and rhetorics. These processes have in turn produced disillusionment among many party members and tensions between the parties and their traditional interest-group allies. The texture and content of much Australian party politics are thus substantially different from those of fifty or even thirty years ago. Nonetheless, the structure of the old order has remained solid. Although the Australian Democrats have established themselves as an apparently permanent minor party in the system, their impact on the party order has been restricted to a brokering role in the

Senate. The old parties of Labor and the Coalition remain the only ones capable of forming a government.

The parties' political management has been associated with a decline in partisan bonds since the 1980s. Their governing over a transformed public policy landscape has undermined the levels and strength of support they enjoyed in the 1960s. While most Australians still profess a party identification, it is now more likely to be weak than strong. The major parties' new liberal market settlement is, as yet, incapable of mobilizing national support to the same extent as the liberal egalitarian party settlement of early this century. In this sense, the parties are now less capable than they were of integrating citizens in a positive way into the Australian political system.

The old order will almost certainly survive despite these weakened loyalties. The electoral system severely penalizes new parties. The news media present elections as a contest for government between the two parties, painting the Democrats and other minor parties as curiosities. The vast bulk of voters appear to accept this logic, at least for House of Representatives elections. None of these factors appears likely to change in the near future, leaving the party order to persist on a mixture of old loyalties, new contingent votes and an inability to imagine serious alternatives.

## NOTES

1. On 1990, see E. Papadakis, "Does the New Politics Have a Future?" in *Australia Compared*, ed. F. Castles (Sydney: Allen and Unwin, 1991). More generally, see I. Marsh, *Beyond the Two Party System* (Cambridge: Cambridge University Press, 1995).

2. For a good critique of the doomsayers, see P. Coleman, "Illiberal Thoughts on Our Present Discontents," *Australian Quarterly* 66.4 (Summer 1994): 91–98.

3. See contributions to C. Bean, M. Simms, S. Bennett, and J. Warhurst (eds.), *The Politics of Retribution: The 1996 Federal Election* (Sydney: Allen and Unwin, 1997).

4. Figures from C. Macintyre, *Political Australia* (Melbourne: Oxford University Press, 1991), pp. 1–2.

5. D. Jaensch, *Power Politics*, 2nd ed. (Sydney: Allen and Unwin, 1989), chap. 4.

6. L. F. Crisp, *The Parliamentary Government of the Commonwealth of Australia* (London: Longmans, 1949), pp. 65–73.

7. P. Loveday, A Martin, and R. Parker (eds.), *The Emergence of the Australian Party System* (Sydney: Hale and Iremonger, 1977).

8. D. Aitkin, *Stability and Change in Australian Politics*, 2nd ed. (Canberra: Australian National University Press, 1982).

9. Marsh, *Beyond the Two Party System*, pp. 17–18. See also P. Kelly, *The End of Certainty* (Sydney: Allen and Unwin, 1992), pp. 1–16.

10. Marsh, *Beyond the Two Party System*, p. 19.

11. D. Rawson, *Labor in Vain?* (Croydon, U.K.: Longmans, 1966).

12. P. Reynolds, *The Democratic Labor Party* (Milton, Jacaranda, 1974).

13. J. Warhurst (ed.), *Keeping the Bastards Honest* (Sydney: Allen and Unwin, 1997).

14. J. Moon, "Minority Government in the Australian States: From Ersatz Majoritarianism to Minoritarianism?" *Australian Journal of Political Science* 30 (special issue) (1995): 142–63.

15. See M. Haward and P. Larmour (eds.), *The Tasmanian Parliamentary Accord and Public Policy 1989–92* (Canberra: Federalism Research Center, Australian National University, 1993).

16. R. Smith, "Parliament," in *Reform and Reversal*, ed. M. Laffin and M. Painter (Melbourne: Macmillan, 1995).

17. M. Goot, *Pulling the Plug: Competition Policy, Privatisation and the Electoral Politics of Telstra* (Sydney: Department of Politics, Macquarie University, unpublished paper).

18. On Senate voting, see S. Bowler and D. Denemark, "Split Ticket Voting in Australia: Dealignment and Inconsistent Votes Reconsidered," *Australian Journal of Political Science* 28.1 (March 1993): 19–37.

19. Reynolds, *Democratic Labor Party*, pp. 48–71.

20. C. Bean and E. Papadakis, "Minor Parties and Independents: Electoral Bases and Future Prospects," *Australian Journal of Political Science* 30 (special issue) (1995): 111–26.

21. For an overview, see B. Graetz and I. McAllister, *Dimensions of Australian Society*, 2nd ed. (Melbourne: Macmillan, 1994).

22. I. McAllister and A. Ascui, "Voting Patterns," in *Australia Votes*, ed. I. McAllister and J. Warhurst (Melbourne: Longman Cheshire, 1988), p. 230.

23. A. Robb, "The Liberal Party Campaign," in Bean et al., *Politics of Retribution*, pp. 40–41.

24. For concise evidence of these trends, see Graetz and McAllister, *Dimensions*, pp. 368–77.

25. C. Bean and I. McAllister, "Long-Term Electoral Trends and the 1996 Election," in Bean et al., *Politics of Retribution*, pp. 179–80.

26. D. Kemp, *Society and Electoral Behaviour in Australia* (St Lucia: University of Queensland Press, 1978), chap. 6; Aitkin, *Stability and Change*, chaps. 10, 22.

27. Kemp, *Society and Electoral Behaviour*, chap. 8; B. Costar, "The Future of the National Party of Australia," in *The Paradox of Parties*, ed. M. Simms (Sydney: Allen and Unwin, 1996).

28. J. Ravenhill, "Business and Politics," in *Politics in Australia*, ed. R. Smith, 3rd ed. (Sydney: Allen and Unwin, 1997), pp. 303–5.

29. H. Manning, "The Labor Party and the Unions: Organisation and Ideology during the Labor Decade," in Simms, *Paradox of Parties*, p. 33.

30. Kelly, *End of Certainty*, especially chap. 3.

31. N. Minchin, "South Australia," in Simms, *Paradox of Parties*, pp. 62–63.

32. Kelly, *End of Certainty*, chaps. 27–31.

33. J. Warhurst, "Promises and Personalities: The House of Representatives Election in 1996," in Bean et al., *The Politics of Retribution*, p. 13.

34. Marsh, *Beyond the Two Party System*, chap. 2.

35. The policy changes in this paragraph and the next are dealt with in detail in B. Head and A. Patience (eds.), *From Fraser to Hawke* (Melbourne: Longman Cheshire, 1989); Kelly, *The End of Certainty*; and Marsh, *Beyond the Two Party System*.

36. See G. Maddox, *The Hawke Government and Labor Tradition* (Ringwood, Australia: Penguin, 1989) and Kelly, *The End of Certainty*.

37. See, for example, A. Scott, *Fading Loyalties* (Leichhardt, Pluto, 1991); Marsh, *Beyond the Two Party System*, pp. 109–13; Minchin, "South Australia," p. 62.

38. E. Chaples, "Public Funding of Elections in Australia," in *Comparative Political Finance in the 1980s*, ed. H. Alexander (Cambridge: Cambridge University Press, 1989); L. Bathgate, L. Crosby, and I. Henderson, "New Campaigning Strategies," in Simms, *Paradox of Parties*.

39. I. McAllister, *Political Behaviour* (Melbourne: Longman Cheshire, 1992), p. 38.

40. B. Graetz and I. McAllister, *The Dimensions of Australian Society* (Melbourne: Macmillan, 1988), p. 267.

41. See, for example, Aitkin, *Stability*, p. 47; C. Bean and J. Kelley, "Partisan Stability and Short-Term Change in the 1987 Federal Election: Evidence from the NSSS Panel Study," *Politics* 23.2 (November 1988): 83–85; McAllister and Ascui, "Voting Patterns," pp. 243–44; I. McAllister and C. Bean, "Explaining Labor's Victory," in *The Greening of Australian Politics*, ed. C. Bean, I. McAllister, and J. Warhurst (Melbourne: Longman Cheshire, 1990), p. 178; Graetz and McAllister, *Dimensions*, pp. 361–62; Bean, "Partisanship and Electoral Behaviour in Comparative Perspective," in Simms, *Paradox of Parties*.

42. Graetz and McAllister, *Dimensions*, p. 365.

43. Aitkin, *Stability*, p. 93.

44. Ibid., passim.

45. McAllister, *Political Behaviour*, p. 42.

46. McAllister and Ascui, "Voting Patterns," pp. 243–44; Graetz and McAllister, *Dimensions*, pp. 364–67.

47. McAllister, *Political Behaviour*, pp. 38–42.

48. C. Leithner, "Stability and Change at Commonwealth Elections, 1910–69: A Test of the Conventional Wisdom," *Australian Journal of Political Science* 29.3 (November 1994): 460–83.

49. M. Goot, "Class Voting, Issue Voting and Electoral Volatility," in *Developments in Australian Politics*, ed. J. Brett, J. Gillespie, and M. Goot (Melbourne: Macmillan, 1994), pp. 175–79.

50. See, for example, Bean, "Partisanship and Electoral Behaviour."

51. E. Chaples, "A Decade of Voter Dealignment: Party Identification and Electoral Volatility in Australia in the 1980s," paper presented to the Annual Meeting of the Southern Political Science Association, Atlanta, November 10, 1990, pp. 9–10.

52. Percentage calculated from J. Western, M. Western, M. Emmison, and Janeen Baxter, "Class Analysis and Politics," in *Class Analysis and Contemporary Australia*, ed. J. Baxter, M. Emmison, J. Western, and M. Western (Melbourne: Macmillan, 1991), p. 331. This study asked a somewhat different partisanship question to the others and did not ask a partisan strength question (see p. 367), so it could not be included in table 7.3.

53. D. Charnock, "Party Identification in Australia, 1967–1990: Implications of Method Effects from Different Survey Procedures," *Australian Journal of Political Science* 27.3 (November 1992): 510–16; and "Question-Wording Effects on the Measurement of Nonpartisanship: Evidence from Australia," *Electoral Studies* 15.2 (1996): 267.

54. Social Science Data Archives, *Issues in Multicultural Australia Survey 1988* (Canberra: Social Science Data Archives, 1989).

55. These figures exclude shifts between the Coalition parties. Aitkin, *Stability*, pp. 40–41; Bean and Kelley, "Partisan Stability," p. 85.

56. See, for example, Aitkin, *Stability*, pp. 143–54; I. McAllister and T. Makkai, "The Formation and Development of Party Loyalties: Patterns among Australian Immigrants," *Australian and New Zealand Journal of Sociology* 27.2 (August 1991): 195–217; R. Smith, "Dislocating Citizens: The Young Unemployed," in *Equity and Citizenship under Keating*, ed. M. Hogan and K. Dempsey (Sydney: Public Affairs Research Centre, University of Sydney, 1995).

57. Figure calculated from Graetz and McAllister, *Dimensions*, pp. 366–67.

58. R. Connell, *The Child's Construction of Politics* (Melbourne: Melbourne University Press, 1971).

59. A recent example is Bean, "Partisanship and Electoral Behaviour."

60. Usually only three or four appear in any one list. See, for example, McAllister and Makkai, "Formation and Development," p. 201; McAllister, *Political Behaviour*, p. 39; Graetz and McAllister, *Dimensions*, pp. 364–65; Charnock, "Question-Wording Effects," pp. 265–67.

61. See McAllister, *Political Behaviour*, p. 34.

62. See Kemp, *Society and Electoral Behaviour*; Aitkin, *Stability*.

63. K. Davis, "Managing the Economy," in Head and Patience, *From Fraser to Hawke*.

64. D. Gow, "Economic Voting and Postmaterialist Values," in *The Greening of Australian Politics*, ed. C. Bean, I. McAllister, and J. Warhurst (Melbourne: Longman, 1990).

## BIBLIOGRAPHY

Aitkin, D. *Stability and Change in Australian Politics*. 2nd ed. Canberra: Australian National University Press, 1982.

Bathgate, L. Crosby and I. Henderson. "New Campaigning Strategies." In *The Paradox of Parties*, ed. M. Simms. Sydney: Allen and Unwin, 1996.

Bean, C. "Politics and the Public: Mass Attitudes towards the Australian Political System." In *Australian Attitudes*, ed. J. Kelley and C. Bean. Sydney: Allen and Unwin, 1988.

———. "Partisanship and Electoral Behaviour in Comparative Perspective." In *The Paradox of Parties*, ed. M. Simms. Sydney: Allen and Unwin, 1996.

Bean, C. and J. Kelley. "Partisan Stability and Short-Term Change in the 1987 Federal Election: Evidence from the NSSS Panel Study." *Politics* 23.2 (November 1988): 80–94.

Bean, C. and I. McAllister, "Long-Term Electoral Trends and the 1996 Election." In *The Politics of Retribution: The 1996 Federal Election*, ed. C. Bean, M. Simms, S. Bennett, and J. Warhurst. Sydney: Allen and Unwin, 1997.

Bean, C. and E. Papadakis. "Minor Parties and Independents: Electoral Bases and Future Prospects." *Australian Journal of Political Science* 30 (special issue) (1995): 111–26.

Bean, C., M. Simms, S. Bennett, and J. Warhurst (eds.). *The Politics of Retribution: The 1996 Federal Election*. Sydney: Allen and Unwin, 1997.

Bowler, S. and D. Denemark. "Split Ticket Voting in Australia: Dealignment and Inconsistent Votes Reconsidered." *Australian Journal of Political Science* 28.1 (March 1993): 19–37.

Chaples, E. "A Decade of Voter Dealignment: Party Identification and Electoral Volatility in Australia in the 1980s. Paper presented to the Annual Meeting of the Southern Political Science Association, Atlanta, November 10, 1990.

Charnock, D. "Party Identification in Australia, 1967–1990: Implications of Method Effects from Different Survey Procedures." *Australian Journal of Political Science* 27.3 (November 1992): 510–16.

———. "Question-Wording Effects on the Measurement of Nonpartisanship: Evidence from Australia." *Electoral Studies* 15.2 (1996): 263–68.

Coleman, P. "Illiberal Thoughts on Our Present Discontents." *Australian Quarterly* 66.4 (Summer 1994): 91–98.

Connell, R. *The Child's Construction of Politics*. Melbourne: Melbourne University Press, 1971.

Costar, B. "The Future of the National Party of Australia." In *The Paradox of Parties*, ed. M. Simms. Sydney: Allen and Unwin, 1996.

Crisp, L. F. *The Parliamentary Government of the Commonwealth of Australia*. London: Longmans, 1949.

Davis, K. "Managing the Economy." In *From Fraser to Hawke*, ed. B. Head and A. Patience. Melbourne: Longman Cheshire, 1989.

Goot, M. "Class Voting, Issue Voting and Electoral Volatility." In *Developments in Australian Politics*, ed. J. Brett, J. Gillespie, and M. Goot. Melbourne: Macmillan, 1994.

———. *Pulling the Plug: Competition Policy, Privatisation and the Electoral Politics of Telstra*. Sydney: Department of Politics, Macquarie University, unpublished paper.

Gow, D. "Economic Voting and Postmaterialist Values." In *The Greening of Australian Politics*, ed. C. Bean, I. McAllister, and J. Warhurst. Melbourne: Longman, 1990.

Graetz, B. and I. McAllister. *Dimensions of Australian Society*. Melbourne: Macmillan, 1988.

———. *Dimensions of Australian Society*, 2nd ed. Melbourne: Macmillan, 1994.

Haward, M. and P. Larmour (eds.). *The Tasmanian Parliamentary Accord and Public Policy 1989–92*. Canberra: Federalism Research Centre, Australian National University, 1993.

Head, B. and A. Patience (eds.). *From Fraser to Hawke*. Melbourne, Longman Cheshire, 1989.

Jaensch, D. *Power Politics: Australia's Party System*, 2nd ed. Sydney: Allen and Unwin, 1989.

Kelly, P. *The End of Certainty*. Sydney: Allen and Unwin, 1992.

Kemp, D. *Society and Electoral Behaviour in Australia*. St Lucia: University of Queensland Press, 1978.

Leithner, C. "Stability and Change at Commonwealth Elections, 1910–69: A Test of the Conventional Wisdom." *Australian Journal of Political Science* 29.3 (November 1994): 460–83.

McAllister, I. *Political Behaviour*. Melbourne: Longman Cheshire, 1992.

McAllister, I. and A. Ascui. "Voting Patterns." In *Australia Votes*, ed. I. McAllister and J. Warhurst. Melbourne: Longman Cheshire, 1988.

McAllister, I. and C. Bean. "Explaining Labor's Victory." In *The Greening of Australian Politics*, ed. C. Bean, I. McAllister, and J. Warhurst. Melbourne: Longman Cheshire, 1990.

McAllister, I. and T. Makkai. "The Formation and Development of Party Loyalties: Patterns among Australian Immigrants." *Australian and New Zealand Journal of Sociology* 27.2 (August 1991): 195–217.

Macintyre, C. *Political Australia*. Melbourne: Oxford University Press, 1991.

Maddox, G. *The Hawke Government and Labor Tradition*. Ringwood, Penguin, 1989.

Manning, H. "The Labor Party and the Unions: Organisation and Ideology During the Labor Decade." In *The Paradox of Parties*, ed. M. Simms. Sydney: Allen and Unwin, 1996.

Marsh, I. *Beyond the Two Party System*. Cambridge: Cambridge University Press, 1995.

Minchin, N. "South Australia." In *The Paradox of Parties*, ed. M. Simms. Sydney: Allen and Unwin, 1996.

Moon, J. "Minority Government in the Australian States: From Ersatz Majoritarianism to Minoritarianism?" *Australian Journal of Political Science* 30 (special issue) (1995): 142–63.

Papadakis, E. "Does the New Politics Have a Future?" In *Australia Compared*, ed. F. Castles. Sydney: Allen and Unwin, 1991.

Ravenhill, J. "Business and Politics." In *Politics in Australia*, ed. R. Smith. 3rd edition. Sydney: Allen and Unwin, 1997.

Rawson, D. *Labor in Vain?* Croydon, U.K.: Longmans, 1966.

Reynolds, P. *The Democratic Labor Party*. Milton, Jacaranda, 1974.

Robb, A. "The Liberal Party Campaign." In *The Politics of Retribution: The 1996 Federal Election*, ed. C. Bean, M. Simms, S. Bennett, and J. Warhurst. Sydney: Allen and Unwin, 1997.

Scott, A. *Fading Loyalties*. Leichhardt, Pluto, 1991.

Smith, R. "Dislocating Citizens: The Young Unemployed." In *Equity and Citizenship under Keating*, ed. M. Hogan and K. Dempsey. Sydney: Public Affairs Research Centre, University of Sydney, 1995.

————. "Parliament." In *Reform and Reversal*, ed. M. Laffin and M. Painter. Melbourne: Macmillan, 1995.

Social Science Data Archives. *Issues in Multicultural Australia Survey 1988*. Canberra: Social Science Data Archives, 1989.

Warhurst, J. "Promises and Personalities: The House of Representatives Election in 1996." In *The Politics of Retribution: The 1996 Federal Election*, ed. C. Bean, M. Simms, S. Bennett, and J. Warhurst. Sydney: Allen and Unwin, 1997.

————, (ed.). *Keeping the Bastards Honest*. Sydney: Allen and Unwin, 1997.

Western, J., M. Western, M. Emmison, and Janeen Baxter. "Class Analysis and Politics." In *Class Analysis and Contemporary Australia*, ed. J. Baxter, M. Emmison, J. Western, and M. Western. Melbourne: Macmillan, 1991.

# CHAPTER 8

# *Mexico:*
# *The End of One-Party Pluralism?*

## Michael W. Foley

Mexico's Institutional Revolutionary Party (the PRI) boasts the longest tenure in power of any party in the world. It has survived revolutionary upheavals in its own structure, military revolts, and three dramatic economic collapses, two of them in the last fifteen years.[1] Mexico is the only country in Latin America not to have experienced a successful military coup in the years since the Mexican Revolution (1910–19). And the regime's control over organized labor allowed it to carry through economic austerity measures that were unthinkable in the volatile political environment of most Latin American countries. Yet in the midterm elections of July 1997 the party lost its grip on both the Chamber of Deputies and the Senate, and control over the Federal District (Mexico City) went to the center-left Democratic Revolutionary Party's longtime presidential candidate Cuauhtémoc Cárdenas. In the wake of the election, prospects for yet another presidential victory, in the year 2000, appeared seriously in question.

Any account of the PRI's failing grasp on power must also account for its longevity. This chapter, accordingly, will offer an interpretation of the PRI's long rule geared to explain the reasons for its woes as the century in which it was born comes to a close. The first two sections describe the role of the party within the Mexican regime and the multiple signs of the demise of this system. In the third section, I attempt to explain the party's decline and, in the conclusion, assess where Mexico is headed.

### THE PRI AND THE MEXICAN REGIME

Analysts have differed sharply over how to characterize the Mexican regime and how to explain its staying power. In 1963, when *The Civic*

*Culture* was first published, Gabriel Almond and Sydney Verba described their choice of Mexico, alongside Britain, the United States, West Germany, and Italy, as a subject for the study of "the political culture of democracy," "in order to have at least one 'non-Atlantic community' democracy."[2] At the time, it was common to refer to the Mexican system as a democracy. The student revolt of 1968, however, with its violent dénouement in the massacre of Tlatelolco, highlighted the authoritarian side of the regime and thrust a whole generation into oppositional politics, with consequences still being felt today.[3] Academic observers were slow to catch up, but by the late seventies most referred to Mexico as an "authoritarian" regime.[4]

Just how the system worked and the nature of the relations between party and state have been matters of dispute. In a 1977 essay, the distinguished Mexican historian Lorenzo Meyer outlined the major features of the dominant view among Mexicanists, which sees the party as primarily an instrument of the state, and of the president in particular:

> In theory, the system through which today's leadership is selected is democratic, but the reality is very different. Since the creation of the Partido Nacional Revolucionario (PNR) in 1929, the Mexican party system has had a purpose that is not democratic. The official party—the PNR and its successors, the Partido de la Revolución Mexicana (PRM) and the Partido Revolucionario Institucional (PRI)—was not created to win elections but to maintain a permanent campaign of propaganda in favor of the revolutionary leadership and to enforce the discipline among the "revolutionary family" that support it.[5]

Electoral campaigns were a formality, and the system was highly centralized. The Executive dominated both the legislative process and judicial outcomes. Federalism was weak, with even powerful state political bosses easily eliminated at the president's whim. "Generally speaking, the state governors are the center of the local political system, but all their important decisions are made in consultation with the President and some of his ministers. The entire political life of a governor is controlled by the center, from his nomination by the Party to the selection of his successor."[6] Though the charismatic character of the presidency had been transferred to the office itself ("institutionalized," in Samuel Huntington's terms), the president enjoyed extensive paternalistic powers, including the choice of a successor. The frequent arbitrariness of Mexican politics, in this view, along with its pervasive corruption, follows from such centralization.

Against this view witness that of Mexican writer Carlos Monsiváis, reflecting not only changes in Mexican politics over the intervening ten years but a new, more sober view of presidential power. Monsiváis asks, "What is presidentialism in contemporary Mexico?" and he answers:

It is the concentration of "omni-modal" powers and the impossibility of fully using them; it is the autocratic ability to name the next president and it is the fantasy of detailed control over a bureaucracy that is every day more autonomous; it is the singular personal power to throw the nation into debt and it is impotence in the face of the deepening problems of the country.[7]

The remarkable extraconstitutional powers of the presidency have not vanished. Indeed, almost as if to refute Monsiváis's depiction, Carlos Salinas de Gortari (1988–94) unseated more state governors than any previous president (17), reshuffled his cabinet at will, deposed two of the most powerful union leaders in the country, and jailed the first head of the Mexican stock exchange. His public policy initiatives were bold and carried through largely without opposition. He privatized some two thousand state enterprises, including the banks, and pushed through constitutional amendments that foreclosed future land reform and normalized church-state relations after seventy-five years of mutual hostility. He also imposed on his party a hand-picked successor, and upon the latter's assassination in March 1994, chose a second.

Despite this display of presidential prerogative, the constraints on presidentialism were as evident during the Salinas *sexenio* (six-year term) as its traditional scope and arbitrariness. Though Salinas opened his term at war with the traditional labor sector of the PRI, jailing one prominent leader, forcing another to step down, and favoring independent labor federations over the powerful Confederation of Mexican Workers (CTM), by midterm he had patched up relations with the CTM's ancient boss, Fidel Velázquez, and allowed CTM goons to break independent organizing efforts at major plants in Mexico City and on the border. His efforts to restructure the party around individual membership and the new citizen's committees of the National Program of Solidarity (PRONASOL), his massive public works welfare initiative, were rebuffed by the party's old guard, whose power was and is based on corporatist structures built on peasant, labor, and middle-class professional organizations. The assassination of Luis Donaldo Colosio, Salinas's chosen successor, was probably the work of the party's Baja California old guard, incensed at Colosio's role in forcing the party to accept the opposition National Action Party's (PAN) victory in gubernatorial elections in 1989.

Thus, though the party structure that was able to impose such limits even upon Salinas has lost ground in the last two decades, its role in the Mexican political system cannot be relegated to that of a mere "electoral agency" of the Mexican executive.[8] Divided into peasant, labor, and "popular" sectors in the party's expansion under President Lázaro Cárdenas (1934–40), the PRI functions even today as a "corporativist" party based primarily on the sectorial organizations.[9] These organizations are not just organs of control; they also provide important rewards to the party faithful and significant, though not determinative, channels of communication from bottom to top.[10]

The rewards for the leadership of the constituent organizations have always been clear: for faithful leaders, the party delivered political positions, from municipal presidencies to seats in the Senate and the Chamber of Deputies to governorships and cabinet posts. For party members with some degree of education, the party reserved government jobs which multiplied in the general expansion of the state from the late 1960s onwards. For union members, there were job security and a growing list of social welfare benefits, whose continuous extension often depended upon tough bargaining between union bosses and party leaders. For peasants, land, access to credit and agricultural inputs, and, for some, health and housing benefits, were all rewards for party loyalty. Such benefits were often the result of a certain voice, which found expression in sectoral meetings, sanctioned and unsanctioned demonstrations, and the elaborately staged electoral tours of the party's presidential candidates. As John Bailey comments, "Overall, the sectors operate in the difficult terrain of supporting government programmes and serving as a conduit to secure goods and services for their members, while at the same time criticising the relevant agencies and advocating greater attention to their clients' needs."[11] That they continue to generate loyalty even today is evident in the more than 1.2 million party militants the PRI fielded on election day in August 1994.[12]

The centralization of power in the hands of the president means that such exchanges are largely clientelist in nature, because control depends upon the identification and reward of a loyal leadership at all levels of the system. Thus, the warlords of the early postrevolutionary period were bought off and transformed into political bosses at the state or regional level, with considerable autonomy to buy the loyalty of smaller local machines below them.[13] The relative inclusiveness of the system meant that opposition groups would be brought in where possible, with concessions to their constituencies and rewards for the leadership, including the possibility of influencing policy in a favored direction. Corporatism and clientelism are thus intertwined. Both imply redistribution. But, as José Luis Reyna comments, "the distinctive characteristic of this redistribution is its selective implementation. Moreover, benefits, redistribution policies, and the like come from above, frequently before demands are formulated."[14] The declining fortunes of peasants (from the 1940s on) and workers (particularly after 1976) attest to this selectiveness; the increasing role of the state, post-1970, in providing credit, inputs, and marketing outlets for peasants and housing, health care, and pension benefits for labor underlines the top-down quality of the system.[15]

Nevertheless, the party is scarcely independent of the governmental apparatus; and its ability to function as an effective electoral mechanism was cast in doubt once genuine competition became possible. A growing sense of crisis among Mexico's top leadership, combined with increased pressure from reformers inside and outside the party, led to a series of electoral reforms starting in 1979, when 100 seats in the Chamber of Deputies were set aside for opposition party candidates elected according to principles of proportional representation. For a brief moment in 1981–83, the government allowed opposition parties, principally the conservative PAN, to win a number of important municipal elections. By 1986, it was clear that the PRI could be seriously challenged, and a further electoral reform added an additional 100 proportional representation seats and, in return, the so-called "governability clause," which insured that the party with a plurality would still command a majority of seats in Congress.[16]

Then, in 1988, came the cataclysm, when a coalition of left-wing and nationalist parties led by Cuauhtémoc Cárdenas, son of the revered former President Lázaro Cárdenas and leader of the Democratic Current recently expelled from the PRI, came close to winning the presidential election and deprived the PRI of the two-thirds legislative majority needed to pass constitutional amendments.[17] Though the PRI was able to dominate politics for the next *sexenio* under the dynamic leadership of Carlos Salinas de Gortari and win the 1994 elections handily, the crisis of the party was manifest in the events of the last year of Salinas's presidency, and party fortunes have fallen steadily under his successor, Ernesto Zedillo Ponce de León. The next two sections assess the current state of the party and trace the reasons for its current vulnerability.

## THE END OF ONE-PARTY PLURALISM?

Writing at the beginning of the 1960s, Almond and Verba saw Mexico and Italy as "examples of less well-developed societies with transitional political systems,"[18] and they went on to describe what they saw as Mexico's distinctive characteristics:

> In contrast to Italy, where a large portion of the population tends to view the political system as an alien, exploitative force, many Mexicans tend to view their revolution as an instrument of ultimate democratization and economic and social modernization. At the same time, the Mexican democratic infrastructure is relatively new. Freedom of political organization is more formal than real, and corruption is widespread

throughout the whole political system. These conditions may explain the interesting ambivalence in Mexican political culture: many Mexicans lack political experience and skill, yet their hope and confidence are high; combined with these widespread participant aspirational tendencies, however, are cynicism about and alienation from the political infrastructure and bureaucracy.[19]

Some 30 percent of Almond and Verba's respondents expressed pride in their governmental system, relatively high by comparison with Italy (3 percent) or Germany (7 percent) but low next to Britain's 46 percent and the United States' 85 percent.[20] On the other hand, more than half the respondents did not expect equal treatment by the bureaucracy and police (as opposed to 13 and 10 percent respectively among Italians and 7 and 6 percent among citizens of Great Britain).[21] In fact, Almond and Verba found little relationship between pride in the system and evaluation of governmental performance, an anomaly they attribute to the symbolism of the Mexican Revolution and its identification with the regime.[22]

Thirty-five years later, Mexico may still be described as "in transition," this time with greater evidence of a genuine swing in the balance of political power. At the same time, the "ambivalence" that Almond and Verba found in their data persists. In polls conducted in early 1995, 80 percent of respondents described the economic situation as "bad" or "very bad"; 73 percent thought the country was "in deep and serious trouble"; and only 31 percent were "confident" or "very confident" in the government's ability to handle the nation's economic problems. In a similar poll in early 1996, 68 percent of those surveyed said the situation was "worse" or "much worse" than the previous year, and they put hopes for a turnaround not in government, but in the private sector.

On the other hand, Mexicans showed little less support for the system than they had shown thirty-five years earlier. Some 25 percent said that they were satisfied with how democracy was working in Mexico (versus the 30 percent who expressed pride in the system in 1963). Only 40 percent thought a change of party would be better for the country. Forty-eight percent gave President Zedillo a "favorable" rating in one poll, and 75 percent rated his performance as "fair" or better in another. The PRI, on the other hand, garnered a "favorable" rating from only 33 percent of the population surveyed.[23]

Such statistics give little sense of the vast distance that separates 1963 from 1997. In 1963, the PAN, the only genuinely independent political party in the field, gained just one municipal election; they held only 5 seats in Congress. In 1988, the party gained 38 seats in the expanded legislature, and in 1989 it was awarded its first gubernatorial victory. By November 1995, notes Cornelius, "the PAN had made such gains in state and local elections that it governed some 35 million Mexicans—over one-third of the country's population."[24] By 1988, 42.3 percent of electoral districts were genuinely competitive; by 1994 the number had reached 81.4 percent.[25] In the eight significant local elections in 1996, opposition parties won 52.3 percent of the popular vote, as opposed to the PRI's 47.6 percent. And in early 1997, opposition parties won a majority in the state Congress of Morelos, a traditional PRI stronghold, and 13 of 23 mayor's races, including Cuernavaca, Cuautla, and Tepotzlán.[26] With the July 1997 elections, the PRI's proportion had fallen to just 39.1 percent of the vote, losing its majority in the Chamber of Deputies and the two-thirds majority in the Senate needed for constitutional reforms. Together, in the wake of these elections, the two major opposition parties governed seven states and 559 municipalities, which together produce some 47.8 percent of GDP.[27]

What has changed is not "system affect" (which deviates little from that recorded by Almond and Verba) or the degree of political cynicism (which has remained remarkably stable), but "political opportunity"— the availability of alternatives to the party in power.[28] In order to flesh out this argument, we look more closely in the next section at the unfolding crisis of the PRI over the last twenty years.

## FROM HEGEMONIC PARTY TO POLITICAL DINOSAUR

The sources of the PRI's current vulnerability have been variously identified, from a "crisis of legitimacy" of the system as a whole, to a "crisis of presidentialism," to the failure of the party itself as an electoral machine. As for legitimacy, Mexicans are little more cynical about the political system today than they were in the heyday of the PRI's power. The current crisis undoubtedly owes much to both the failings of presidentialism and structural weaknesses in the party. As in much of the Western world, it also stems in part from the revolt of business against the "historic compromise" between labor, capital, and the state of the post–World War II era and thus to the decreasing ability of traditional parties to reward their constituents.[29] Nevertheless, these factors must be understood in terms of the evolution of Mexican politics since the student revolt of 1968 and the new opportunities for oppositional politics developed during this period.

As elsewhere in the Western world, the student movement in Mexico gave fresh impetus to critical analysis of prevailing institutions, particularly from a Marxist point of view, centered in a long-running debate on the true significance of the Mexican Revolution, the centerpiece of official claims to legitimacy.[30] At the same time, the violent repression of the student movement provoked a retreat from normal politics on a massive scale. Young people otherwise destined by their education for membership in the party and a government job turned instead to nascent parties of the left, brief episodes of guerrilla warfare against the state, and community organizing. Still others helped build opposition sentiment among powerful, PRI-controlled unions. Even among those who sooner or later ended up in government service, old school ties, memories of the movement of '68, and personal conviction led them to champion new relations between state and *campesino* or urban poor, sometimes offering support to the independent organizing efforts of their peers outside the bureaucracy.[31]

Former student activists and their followers helped build powerful urban and rural movements in the years following 1968, and they built democratic movements within some of the most important unions in the country, including the National Teachers Union and the Union of Federal and State Employees.[32] These movements, which represented the most potent challenge to PRI hegemony since former president Lázaro Cárdenas loaned his support to the National Liberation Movement of 1962–63,[33] grew to maturity in a complex and changing environment of political opportunities and incentives that began with the presidency of Luis Echeverría Alvarez (1970–76). Echeverría, who had been intimately involved in the repression of the student movement, moved quickly to rebuild the PRI's legitimacy and revive the faltering Mexican economy. He expanded the government's economic role through purchase of new companies, heavy investment in priority sectors, new subsidies and price support programs, and new institutions designed to restart the stagnant peasant economy, Mexico's primary source of foodstuffs. Politically, his short-lived "democratic opening" encouraged democratic movements within the official unions. He backed increasingly radical demands for land reform among peasant groups and ended his term by expropriating almost 100,000 hectares of prime agricultural land in the Yaqui and Mayo valleys of Sonora state. Blocked in his effort to shift the tax burden to the business sector, he turned to deficit spending and foreign borrowing, policies that set the stage for the declining power of the government to meet popular demands over the next three administrations.

Echeverría's policies provided new openings for labor and peasant mobilization, but they also provoked a powerful reaction, reflected in growing defections to the PAN on the part of the business class. His successor, José López Portillo (1976–82), attempted to calm business fears by reversing the latest land reforms and dealing harshly with land invasions and the independent peasant organizations behind them. He quickly reached an agreement with the IMF to reduce government spending and control wages in an effort to stop inflation. At the same time, he held out an olive branch to opposition parties with the 1977 electoral reform that enlarged the legislature in the opposition's favor.

López Portillo's austerity measures were short-lived, as the discovery of significant new oil reserves led to an expansion of government borrowing and spending on the promise of future oil revenues. The new programs included significant investments in the oil industry, ports, and other infrastructure, but also new social welfare initiatives designed to compensate for wage restraints and raise living standards of the poorest third of the population. Some of these programs, like those of Echeverría, involved important components of local participation, often promoted by government personnel hired from among the generation of '68. Efforts to build more productive "Unions of Ejidos" (the *ejido* is the basic unit of the land reform, involving anywhere from 25 to 500 families) often contributed to independent organizing among peasants. The "Community Food Councils" of the Mexican Food System (SAM) initiative often fed into nascent urban and rural popular organizations, providing material incentives and salaries for activists and organizers.[34]

Under both administrations, moreover, expansion of the state into marketing, credit, housing, and urban and rural provisioning undermined the older clientelistic arrangements on which the PRI's local control was built. Government bureaucrats sometimes replaced local political bosses (*caciques*) as patrons in new patron-client relationships, but often clientelism itself came into question. In either case, the old bases of political power were challenged by the growing power of technocrats and independent-minded organizers and leaders. The resulting conflicts account for growing repression at the local level in the late 1970s and 1980s and for the emergence, in the early 1980s, of a grassroots human rights movement.[35]

In November 1982, falling oil revenues coupled with rising international interest rates provoked the announcement that Mexico could not meet its next international debt payment (the effective beginning of the global "debt crisis"), sparking both political reversals for the PRI and new incentives for independent organizing by the opposition of left and right. The political opening under López Portillo had made possible the first significant opposition victories in municipal elections in 1981. New victories followed, particularly for the PAN, in 1982 and 1983. Business outrage at López Portillo's nationalization of the banks, a last-ditch effort to control the hemorrhaging of foreign exchange, fueled the growth of the PAN. Financial and moral support from business was complemented by the charismatic organizing efforts of Manuel Clouthier, who would become the PAN's presidential candidate in 1988 (and die in a still unexplained auto accident shortly thereafter). As president of the National Confederation of Fruit and Vegetable Producers, the major exporters' association, Clouthier had toured the country, incorporating peasant producers and small farmers into an organization hitherto dominated by big agriculture. In the process, he generated a substantial personal following, crucial for the PAN's growth in the 1980s.

Dissent within the PRI centered less on its slipping grasp on popular sympathies than a renewed battle between the "technocrats" who dominated the government of Miguel de la Madrid and *"políticos"* associated with the "revolutionary nationalist line." The Democratic Current led by former head of the PRI, Porfirio Muñoz Ledo, and Cuauhtémoc Cárdenas drew on traditional notions of economic nationalism and social justice against reformers bent on modernizing the economy and reducing the state apparatus in favor of more market-oriented policies. When their calls for democratic selection of candidates were shouted down in the PRI's 1987 national convention and their bête noire, Carlos Salinas de Gortari, was unveiled as the party's presidential candidate, much of the center-left followed Cárdenas and Muñoz Ledo as they established the National Democratic Front (FDN) to contest the 1988 elections.[36]

The FDN drew off significant support from the PRI, despite the continued official loyalty of the sectorial organizations. It also drew on the support of three smaller parties, traditionally allied to the PRI, which saw their role significantly diminished by the recent electoral reform and which likewise identified themselves with a version of the revolutionary nationalist vision.[37] A more significant addition to the coalition that eventually propelled Cárdenas to the brink of victory was the Mexican Socialist Party (PSM), the product of a decade of fusions of the Mexican Communist Party with lesser parties of the left. When the smoke of the election cleared, the older pro-state parties returned to the fold, but the FDN and the PSM officially merged in the Party of the Democratic Revolution (PRD), though not without bitter internal struggles.

The new party, however, did not easily incorporate the "social left" of the popular movements. At the time of the 1988 election, intense debate over participation in the electoral process engulfed most of the popular sector organizations, which had traditionally been contemptuous of the electoral process. For many, Cárdenas's candidacy promised to unseat the PRI and bring a return to the revolutionary promise of Mexican politics. Others, particularly those tied to the organizations created in the 1970s, remembered the ill treatment they had suffered precisely at the hands of Muñoz Ledo and other former members of the PRI in the FDN's ranks. Some of these aligned themselves with Salinas. Others argued for abstention. Others eventually created the Labor Party

(PT), which would play a small role as a "spoiler" on the left flank of the PRD in 1994.[38] The continued dominance of the PRD by Muñoz Ledo and other ex-PRI *políticos* imposed a distance between the organizations of the social left and the new party that persists today.

Even before the election, Salinas had recruited key figures from the social left to work with him in the Secretariate for Budget and Planning and in the campaign. These included Carlos Rojas, the first director of PRONASOL. Another was Gustavo Gordillo, former adviser to one of the most successful of the new peasant organizations, the Coalition of Collective Ejidos of the Yaqui and Mayo Valleys, who became head of the Subsecretariate for Social Policy of the Secretariate of Agriculture and who organized a series of agreements between Salinas and peasant leaders for government assistance for economic and social projects. Hugo Andrés Araujo, a founder of the independent National Union of Autonomous Peasant Organizations, was made head of the PRI's peasant organization, the National Confederation of Campesinos. Salinas's ability to coopt these leaders was founded on both personal ties and ideological conviction. Salinas himself was associated with the Política Popular group as a student, and his brother Raúl had used his government positions to promote some of the ideas of the movement.[39] Moreover, Salinas had become convinced in the course of his thesis research among peasant communities in central Mexico that a new relationship between the state and the peasantry had to be forged, based not on clientelism but on the encouragement of independent organization.[40]

The new relationship between state and poor people's organizations was thus to be based not on political affiliation but on mutual respect and real possibilities for development. Salinas's election-year promises were quickly transformed into programs, as Gordillo, Rojas, and others began to formalize procedures for access to government poverty funds. The emerging mechanism became the National Program of Solidarity (PRONASOL), through which the administration eventually channeled more than $2 billion annually to Mexico's poor.[41] Although PRONASOL officials generally eschewed the usual quid-pro-quo of the clientelistic system, both the president's personalistic use of the program and patterns of regional variation soon made clear an electoral agenda—rebuilding party support on (generally) new lines. As Salinas remarked, shortly into his term, "We must seek new bases of support for the party. We must build alliances with new groups, some of which are unorganized now; others are organized for various purpose, but don't want to participate in political parties. We must convince them to participate."[42] A central mechanism was "Committees of Solidarity" that were required for a group or community to gain access to PRONASOL funds. The committees were designed to skirt old clientelistic mechanisms and

insure genuine community participation. Their success in doing so varied, but eventually the administration attempted to build a political
movement on the committees to yield an electoral payoff for the PRI. In
intention, at least, if PRONASOL was to win votes it was not through
the old clientelistic practices of the PRI but through "the pork barrel
common to all electoral democracies."[43]

The Salinas team's search for new bases of support was made the
more urgent by the defection of traditional constituencies threatened
both by the political direction advocated by the president and by economic and administrative reforms that undermined the state's ability to
provide party faithful with economic resources, social benefits, and jobs.
The PRONASOL strategy, moreover, tended to undermine local political bosses, who struggled, sometimes violently, against the newer organizations that PRONASOL officials were courting or creating. The president of the PRI at the beginning of Salinas's term was his close friend
Luis Donaldo Colosio, who went on to head the Secreatariat for Social
Development (SEDESOL) when PRONASOL acquired cabinet-level status, and eventually become Salinas's choice for the presidency. Under
Colosio, the PRI gave up its first gubernatorial election to the PAN, an
event that enraged the party's old guard. Together, Salinas and Colosio
set about the reform of the party, opening it up to individual membership, creating a territorial structure to incorporate individuals and the
new "Popular Urban Movement" to incorporate the Committees of Solidarity, and restructuring the relationship between party and traditional
sectors.[44]

By and large, these efforts failed. The old Popular Sector organizations (in reality, mainly middle-class and professional groups) refused to
give way to the new territorial structure, the Popular Urban Movement
failed to come together, and a projected Worker-Peasant Alliance never
amounted to much. Salinas himself found it necessary to recoup ties
with the old guard as his administration went on. Having been publicly
shunned by CTM leader Fidel Velázquez at the time of his nomination,
by 1992 he had embraced the old labor leader. At the same time, the
CTM's rank and file proved increasingly restive, and the traditional
May Day parade became a scene of embarrassing confrontations
between labor dissidents and the president, until the CTM announced
their cancelation in 1994 and each year thereafter.[45] PRONASOL was
forced to accommodate the goals of old-guard governors in response to
growing hostility between the governors and local PRONASOL officials, exacerbating the suspicions of more independent-minded participants throughout the country.[46]

The economic program of the Salinas administration took its own
toll, as it called for severe belt-tightening on the part of labor, the with-

drawal or contraction of government subsidies and services to consumers, peasant and commercial farmers, and industry, cutting government employment, and legal reforms that rapidly opened the Mexican economy to international competition and investment, well in advance of the North American Free Trade Agreement (NAFTA). The result was a disaster for much of the country's agriculture and for small and medium industry, which registered hundreds of business failures every year of the Salinas *sexenio*. Consumer prices grew only modestly, thanks to an overvalued exchange rate, but job-growth did not match new investment in the economy, and wages remained below their 1976 levels. Agricultural prices dropped and imported commodities (mainly U.S.) overwhelmed domestic production in many crops. The resulting debt crisis affected peasant and commercial producers alike, eventually prompting the emergence of a nationwide debtors movement.

Under such conditions, the efforts of PRONASOL to support innovative projects among the rural poor only underlined the desperation of peasant farmers. The crowning blow came in early 1992, with constitutional reforms designed to put a definitive end to land reform. Gustavo Gordillo was forced to muster peasant support for the "reform" of Article 27 of the Constitution, which effectively foreclosed any future land reform. He left government at the end of the Salinas administration thoroughly alienated from his old comrades on the left. The Zapatista rebellion, which broke out on the day NAFTA went into effect, had as a central demand the restoration of the old Article 27.[47]

Although the Salinas strategy yielded an electoral recovery in 1991, the slide toward other parties seemed destined to continue, particularly in the countryside, the PRI's last bastion of support. Indeed, PRI support in the poorer and more rural southern states, which stood at close to 90 percent in 1982, and 70 percent in 1988, converged with other regions by 1994 to a low of around 52 percent.[48] As Wayne Cornelius notes, "in 1994 the average percentage vote for PRI candidates in rural districts fell by 11 percentage points, continuing a trend that began with the 1982 national elections. Moreover, in all states where the PAN won gubernatorial elections in 1995, the party took a large share of the rural vote, for the first time in its history."[49] Coupled with the secular decline in support in Mexico's urban centers, the new electoral profile of the country bodes ill for continued PRI dominance.

## THE END OF THE BEGINNING?

With the election of Ernesto Zedillo Ponce de León in August 1994, the Mexican political system entered a new era. The violence of the last year of the Salinas administration, which included the Zapatista uprising and the assassination of presidential candidate Luis Donaldo Colosio in March, contributed to the success of Zedillo's campaign, with its appeal to public fears of change, but it also helped undermine public perception of the "Salinas miracle." The assassination of PRI Secretary General Francisco Ruíz Massieu, just after the election, followed by the collapse of the peso in November 1994, a few weeks into Zedillo's administration, and the economic downturn that accompanied it put a definitive end to the public romance with *salinismo*. At the same time, the economic debacle created a public image of Zedillo's incompetence. Zedillo publicly blamed Salinas for the crisis. The arrest of Carlos Salinas's brother Raúl as the "intellectual author" of the Ruíz Massieu assassination in early 1995 and the revelation that Raúl had deposits valued between $120 and $300 million in foreign banks, let loose an unprecedented flood of resentment against the former president, whose questioning and prosecution was even proposed by PRI legislators.

At the same time, Zedillo's political weakness provoked speculation that he might be overthrown in a military coup. The president was forced to delay public presentation of the austerity plan developed to deal with the new economic crisis because of recalcitrance on the part of CTM and private sector leaders. The plan was further threatened when fifty PRI legislators balked at the increase in the value-added tax, and Zedillo had to actively lobby Congress, a virtually unheard-of ordeal for a Mexican president. When Zedillo agreed with PAN and PRD leaders to intervene in what they contended were fraudulent gubernatorial elections in Chiapas and Tabasco, PRI supporters in Tabasco, led by the governor, staged an open rebellion, forcing cancelation of the agreement. Even documented proof that the governor had illegally spent over $50 million on the campaign was rejected by the government, once the local PRI had flexed its muscles. Though Zedillo has continued the program of economic liberalization that he shares with his predecessor, efforts to carry out the privatization of the petroleum industry were blocked by party opposition.[50]

Zedillo has withdrawn himself from interference in candidate selection within the PRI, and local party organizations have held open conventions to select candidates for the first time since an abortive experiment in democratization in the early 1980s. More significantly, Zedillo appears to have made good on his pledge to avoid interference in the electoral process, pushing through legislation that puts the administration of elections in nonpartisan hands for the first time. One clear result has been the wave of opposition victories noted at the beginning of this chapter.

At the same time, the president has surrounded himself with elements of the PRI's old guard. He responded to the wave of crime that followed the economic collapse of 1995 by replacing much of the police apparatus of Mexico City with military personnel. The emergence of a new guerrilla challenge in several of Mexico's poorest states prompted the militarization of significant areas of the countryside and the harassment of legal peasant organizations and their supporters.[51] Despite the general openness of the elections of July 1997, irregularities abounded in southern states, and harassment of civilian opposition groups continues to be a feature of daily life.[52] And Mexico's military has been strengthened further under the Zedillo administration with significant imports of new weaponry from the United States, ostensibly for drug interdiction purposes, but capable of deployment in counterinsurgency operations, as well.[53]

Any estimate of Mexico's political future, accordingly, must be guarded. At the same time, we can draw on the analysis so far to judge the bases for continued collapse of the old order and the achievement of democratization in Mexico today. First constructed as a vehicle for managing inter-elite conflicts in postrevolutionary Mexico, then broadened to channel and control the demands of broad sectors of the public, the PRI is ill-suited for electoral competition. Nevertheless, the real sources of the PRI's current crisis lie in the emergence of visible and viable alternatives to continued rule by the party. Thus the collapse of the old order is not simply a matter of the "modernization" of Mexican society. Nor has it resulted in any straightforward way from the achievement of an economic level conducive to democratization, as many theorists of democratization still argue. Indeed, the most decisive period politically has been one of economic crisis, characterized by a shrinking middle class and growing polarization. Nor does the global revolt of capital against the "populist" state explain the particulars of the decline of the PRI, however well it accounts for some of the pressures facing the party.

The sources of the PRI's decline lie in the character of the Mexican regime itself and in the independent mobilization of the population that the state has alternately promoted and repressed. First, business's traditional independence from the party became salient politically through two, at times contradictory, processes. The revolt of business at the inflationary and populist policies of the Echeverría regime produced the first signs of a break, which became decisive with the nationalization of the banks in 1982. The new face of the PAN, which moved from being the party of Catholic dissent from the secular and anticlerical project of the PRI to the party of business demanding political reform and economic freedom in the name of economic liberalism, was created in these years. At the same time, in many areas of northern Mexico the PAN appeared the only viable alternative to the PRI, often incorporating popular classes that in other areas would bow to the abstentionist sentiments of the social left. These two streams came together in the candidacy of Manuel Clouthier in 1988, only to drift apart as the PAN played a more conciliatory role in Congress under Salinas.

But, second, the PAN's growing competitiveness would have been meaningless without significant regime concessions at the ballot box. These grew out of an attempt to stem the tide of opposition, initially granting a place in Congress for the opposition, without ceding genuine power. The first such concessions responded more to pressures from below and to a logic of co-optation than to democratizing sentiments within the PRI. Later, especially under Salinas, the widespread perception that the PRI could no longer deliver the votes strengthened the hand of democratizing reformers within the party, who attempted to rebuild its base of support through such instruments as PRONASOL. Both efforts responded to growing mobilization outside the ranks of the PRI, on the left as well as the right.

The most significant threat to the PRI, in fact, came from the left, because it competed for the very constituency on which the PRI had built its coalition. Until the July 1997 elections, when virtually all of the PRI's losses registered as gains for the PRD, this threat was mitigated by its fragmentation. When in 1988 Cuauhtémoc Cárdenas forged a coalition that seemed poised to win power, the presidency and the PRI turned all their forces against the Cardenistas, working out a modus vivendi with the PAN that lasted through the Salinas administration and into the first years of the Zedillo administration. The growth of an electoral alliance of the center-left had been uncertain from the start and remained so even after Cárdenas's earth-shaking performance in 1988. The left-wing parties, while benefiting from the expansion of opportunities that the electoral reform of 1977 represented, remained weak, with only small constituencies in labor or the peasant sector. Cárdenas's expulsion from the PRI provided an opportunity to forge a new alliance, but Cárdenas was determined to chart his own course, and it was little more than a month before the July 1988 election that the Mexican Socialist Party decided to throw its weight behind Cárdenas. It took two more years before the two groups merged to form the PRD. And the split between the PRD and large elements of the social left is still not entirely resolved.

Despite these fits and starts, and the still shaky relationship between the PRD and its "natural" constituency on the left, the PRD, like the PAN, has achieved the status of a genuine alternative in Mexican politics. In July 1997, it surged to 25.7 percent of the vote, against the PAN's (almost stagnant) 26.6 percent and the PRI's 39.1 percent. Once again, the regime's concessions on control over the electoral process have been crucial, as first Salinas, then Zedillo, worked out a series of pacts with an increasingly powerful opposition—and, implicitly, an increasingly demanding public—for freer and fairer elections. This could not have been accomplished without presidential control over the party, particularly the party-in-Congress. Zedillo has evidently found ways to reward the party's top leadership while buying time for reform to make the process irreversible. Mexico may indeed have reached that point with the July 1997 elections, and, if so, this will represent an unprecedented transformation.

Though foreign observers tend to take it for granted that the transition is now well under way, Mexicans remain divided on the issue, with some pointing out that the PRI can still put together a comfortable majority in both chambers through alliances with the "Green" Party, the PT, and, most important, the PAN, which has not abandoned its earlier strategy of accommodation.[54] The PRI, moreover, is not only the party-in-Congress, and not only the party as corporatist umbrella for a welter of still important organizations in civil society. It is also the party-in-government, at both national and local levels, and as such it retains potent sources of power with which to resist further reform. It also has powerful motives to do so in the corruption that is characteristic of a clientelistic system, but that expanded exponentially in the late '80s and early '90s thanks to the enormous windfalls of privatization and the growing importance of Mexico in the drug trade.

No one knows whether Mexico can be governed in the teeth of opposition by the PRI. Indeed, increased violence is likely as the bases of the old system continue to come apart; in this, the military plays a decidedly ambiguous role, particularly in areas under siege such as Chiapas, Guerrero, and Oaxaca, by and large upholding the *ancien régime* against more vulnerable upstarts. Voters chose not to attempt the experiment in 1994; they came much closer to replacing the PRI in 1997. If that experiment proves successful, and if economic conditions improve, they may be tempted to try to live without the PRI in the year 2000. But they may also return to the old wisdom, which held that governing Mexico requires the maintenance of an equilibrium, something that only the PRI has the experience to achieve.

## NOTES

1. For a brief account of the turbulent conditions surrounding the genesis of the party, see Michael C. Meyer and William L. Sherman, *The Course of Mexican History*, 3rd ed. (New York: Oxford University Press, 1987), pp. 582–608.

2. Gabriel A. Almond and Sidney Verba, *The Civic Culture: Political Attitudes and Democracy in Five Nations* (Newbury Park, Calif.: Sage, 1989), p. 38.

3. Judith Adler Hellman, *Mexico in Crisis*, 2nd ed. (New York: Holmes and Meier, 1983).

4. José Luis Reyna Richard S. Weinert (eds.), *Authoritarianism in Mexico* (Philadelphia: Institute for the Study of Human Issues, 1977); Soledad Loaeza, "México, 1968: Los Orígenes de la Transición," in *La Transición Interrumpida: México 1968–1988*, ed. Ilán Semo (Mexico City: Universidad Iberoamericana/Nueva Imagen, 1993). Nevertheless, Roger Hansen, writing in 1971, had already noted the distance between scholarly characterizations and the reality. See Roger D. Hansen, *The Politics of Mexican Development* (Baltimore: Johns Hopkins University Press, 1971), 120.

5. Lorenzo Meyer, "Historical Roots of the Authoritarian State in Mexico," in *Authoritarianism in Mexico*, ed. José Luis Reyna and Richard S. Weinert (Philadelphia: Institute for the Study of Human Issues, 1977) p. 10. For a more extreme version,see Luis Javier Garrido, "The Crisis of Presidentialismo," in *Mexico's Alternative Political Futures*, ed. Wayne A. Cornelius, Judith Gentleman, and Peter H. Smith. Monograph Series (La Jolla, Calif.: Center for U.S.-Mexican Studies, University of California, San Diego, 1989), pp. 417–34.

6. Meyer, "Historical Roots," p. 12.

7. Carlos Monsiváis, "'En Virtud de las Facultades Que Me Han Sido Otorgadas.' Notas Sobre el Presidencialismo a Partir de 1968," in *La Transición Interrumpida: México 1968–1988*, ed. Ilán Semo (Mexico City: Universidad Iberoamericana/Nueva Imagen, 1993), p. 113.

8. The phrase is that of Manuel Moreno Sánchez, *La Crisis Política de México* (Mexico City: Editorial Extemporáneos, 1970), pp. 51–63, quoted in Meyer, "Historical Roots," p. 10. It reflects the general view of all those who share the "presidentialist" characterization of the Mexican system sketched by Lorenzo Meyer above.

9. In a party reorganization in 1992, Salinas opened the doors to individual membership, officially enabling members of Mexico's business class to enter the party. Nevertheless, this reform scarcely altered the fundamental structures of the party.

10. Vivane Brachet-Marquez, *The Dynamics of Domination: State, Class, and Social Reform in Mexico, 1910-1990* (Pittsburgh: University of Pittsburgh Press, 1994), p. 39; Clarisa Hardy, *El Estado y los Campesinos: La Confederación Nacional Campesina (CNC)* (Mexico City: Nueva Imagen, 1984).

11. John J. Bailey, *Governing Mexico: The Statecraft of Crisis Management* (London: Macmillan, 1988), p. 105.

12. Wayne A. Cornelius, *Mexico: The Breakdown of a One-Party-Dominant Regime*. Monograph Series (La Jolla, Calif.: Center for U.S.-Mexican Studies, University of California, San Diego, 1996), p. 59.

13. Pablo González Casanova, *Democracy in Mexico* (London: Oxford University Press, 1970), pp. 32–36; Cornelius, *Mexican Politics in Transition*, pp. 39–44.

14. José Luis Reyna, "Redefining the Authoritarian Regime," in *Authoritarianism in Mexico*, ed. José Luis Reyna and Richard S. Weiner (Philadelphia: Institute for the Study of Human Issues, 1977), p. 162.

15. This description confirms the views of most comparativists comment-

ing on the Mexican system. The centrality of presidential power and prestige to the Mexican political system has often been remarked, but most comparativists have attributed the regime's longevity to the success of the party in mobilizing and channeling political action. Samuel P. Huntington, *Political Order in Changing Societies* (New Haven, Conn.: Yale University Press, 1968), for instance, singled out the PRI as one of the most successful parties (second, perhaps, only to the Communist Party of the USSR) in "institutionalizing" participation in a rapidly modernizing society. Huntington attributed the "institutionalization of the revolution" through the party to Plutarco Elias Calles, the party's founder and longtime boss. But it was Lázaro Cárdenas, president from 1934 to 1940, who created the modern PRI, successfully incorporating into the party structure and the political system labor, the peasantry, and a middle class whose livelihood over the next forty years would increasingly depend on a growing state. See Nora Hamilton, *The Limits of State Autonomy: Post-Revolutionary Mexico* (Princeton, N.J.: Princeton University Press, 1982). In Ruth Berins Collier and David Collier's extended comparative study of the political trajectories of eight major Latin American countries, Mexico stands out for its success at integrating the diverse elements of national society under the umbrella of the dominant party and managing conflict thereby through almost seventy years of unbroken civilian rule. See Ruth Berins Collier and David Collier, *Shaping the Political Arena: Critical Junctures, the Labor Movement, and Regime Dynamics in Latin America* (Princeton, N.J.: Princeton University Press, 1991).

16. For the changing strategies of electoral engineering carried out by the PRI from 1963 onwards, see Juan Molinar Horcasitas, "Changing the Balance of Power in a Hegemonic Party System: The Case of Mexico," in *Institutional Design in New Democracies: Eastern Europe and Latin America*, ed. Arend Lijphart and Carlos H. Waisman (Boulder, Colo.: Westview Press, 1996), pp. 137–60.

17. On the basis of the limited polling data available and analysis of the electoral results that were released, Cornelius, *Mexican Politics in Transition*, p. 5, concludes that, despite clear evidence of fraud in the mysterious "computer crash" that halted counting of ballots in the 1988 election, "Salinas probably did win." Nevertheless, a comparison of newspaper accounts the day after the election, which reflected a massive voter turnout, with the official vote count alleging the highest rate of abstention since 1946 (51 percent), suggests that millions of votes were literally thrown away during the week it took to issue even a preliminary vote count.

18. Almond and Verba, *Civic Culture*, p. 37.

19. Ibid., p. 39.

20. Ibid. p. 64.

21. Ibid., p. 70.

22. Ibid.,p. 203.

23. "Polling Abroad—The Tumult in Mexico," *The Public Perspective*, April/May 1995, pp. 41–42. The 1996 poll was carried out by Gallup de México, as reported in "No confían los mexicanos en las medidas del gobierno contra la crisis," *La Jornada*, March 7, 1996.

24. Cornelius, *Mexican Politics in Transition*, p. 8.

25. See table 3 in Cornelius, *Mexican Politics in Transition*, p. 65. Figures for 1995 were calculated by Cornelius using Bailey's criteria for competitiveness, where the PRI vote was less than 70 percent and the difference between the PRI and its competitor was less than 40 percentage points.

26. Diego Cevallos, "Mexico: Nuevo Avance de la Oposición en Elecciones," *InterPress Service*, March 17, 1997 (Montevideo, Uruguay: InterPress Service, 1997).

27. Roberto González Amador and Juan Antonio Zúñiga M., "Gobernarán PAN y PRD zonas económicas claves," *La Jornada*, July 21, 1997.

28. "Political opportunity" is a crucial variable in the emergence and success of social movements. See Sidney Tarrow, *Power in Movement: Social Movements, Collective Action and Politics* (Cambridge: Cambridge University Press, 1994). As Adam Przeworski has argued in a seminal article, what matters in transitions from authoritarian rule is less a crisis of "legitimacy" (however defined) than the emergence of alternatives that give people both hope for change and options. See Adam Przeworski, "Some Problems in the Study of the Transition to Democracy," in *Transitions from, Authoritarian Rule: Comparative Perspectives*, ed. Guillermo O'Donnell, Philippe C. Schmitter, and Laurence Whitehead (Baltimore: Johns Hopkins University Press, 1986) pp. 50–53.

29. John Walton and David Seddon, *Free Markets and Food Riots: The Politics of Global Adjustment* (Cambridge, Mass.: Blackwell, 1994); Peter Gourevitch, *Politics in Hard Times: Comparative Responses to International Economic Crises* (Ithaca, N.Y.: Cornell University Press, 1986).

30. Adolfo Gilly's characterization of the Revolution as "the interrupted revolution" stood at the center of the debate. See Adolfo Gilly, *The Mexican Revolution*, 2nd ed., trans. Patrick Camiller (London: Verso, 1983); Adolfo Gilly, *La Revolución Interrumpida* (Mexico City: El Caballito, 1971). See also Adolfo Gilly et al., in *Interpretaciones de la Revolución Mexicana* (Mexico City: Nueva Imagen, 1980); Arnaldo Córdova, *La Revolución y el Estado en México* (Mexico City: Ediciones ERA, 1989).

31. The role of the movement of '68 in recent Mexican politics has still not received comprehensive treatment. Early accounts include Elena Poniatowska, *La Noche de Tlatelolco* (Mexico City: Ediciones ERA, 1971); Evelyn P. Stevens, *Protest and Response in Mexico* (Cambridge, Mass.: MIT Press, 1974); Sergio Zermeño, *México: Una Democracia Utópica. El Movimiento Estudiantil de 1968* (Mexico City: Siglo XXI 1978). Information on the trajectory of various outgrowths of the movement are scattered in a number of sources. The best overview in English is that of Julio Moguel, "The Mexican Left and the Social Program of Salinismo," in *Transforming State-Society Relations in Mexico: The National Solidarity Strategy*, ed. Wayne A. Cornelius, Ann L. Craig, and Jonathan Fox (La Jolla, Calif.: Center for U.S.-Mexican Studies, University of California, San Diego, 1994), pp. 167–78. See also Vivienne Bennett, "Orígenes del Movimiento Urbano Popular Mexicano: Pensamiento Político y Organizaciones Políticas Clandestinas, 1960–1980," *Revista Mexicana de Sociología* 55.3 (July–September 1993): 89–102; Neil Harvey, "La Unión de Uniones de Chiapas y los Retos Políticos del Desarrollo de Base," in *Autonomía y Nuevos Sujetos Sociales en el Desarrollo Rural*, ed. Julio Moguel, Carlota Botey, and Luis Hernández (Mexico

City: Siglo XXI/Centro de Estudios Históricos del Agrarismo en México, 1992), 219–32; Neil Harvey, "Rebellion in Chiapas: Rural Reforms, Campesino Radicalism, and the End of Salinismo," in *Transformation of Rural Mexico*, no. 5 (La Jolla, Calif.: Center for U.S.-Mexican Studies, University of California at San Diego, 1994), pp. 30–35; Paul Haber, "Political Change in Durango: The Role of National Solidarity," in *Transforming State-Society Relations in Mexico: The National Solidarity Strategy*, ed. Wayne A. Cornelius, Ann L. Craig, and Jonathan Fox (La Jolla, Calif.: Center for U.S.-Mexican Studies, University of California, San Diego, 1994) pp. 255–308.

32. Jeffrey W. Rubin, "Popular Mobilization and the Myth of State Corporatism," in *Popular Movements and Political Change in Mexico*, ed. Joe Foweraker and Ann L. Craig (Boulder, Colo.: Lynne Rienner, 1990), pp. 247–70; Graciela Flores Lúa, Luisa Paré, and Sergio Sarmiento Silva, *Las Voces del Campo. Movimiento Campesino y Política Agraria, 1976–1984* (Mexico City: Siglo XXI, 1988); Michael W. Foley, "Agenda for Mobilization: The Agrarian Question and Popular Mobilization in Contemporary Mexico," *Latin American Research Review* 26.2 (1991): 39–74; Luis Hernández, "Autonomía y Desarrollo. La Lucha en el Campo en la Hora de la Concertación," in *Los Nuevos Sujetos del Desarrollo Rural*, ed. Armando Bartra et al. Cuadernos Desarrollo de Base (Mexico City: ADN Editores, 1991), pp. 101–34; Gustavo Gordillo, *Campesinos al Asalto del Cielo* (Mexico City: Siglo XXI, 1988); Joe Foweraker, *Popular Mobilization in Mexico: The Teachers' Movement, 1977–87* (Cambridge: Cambridge University Press, 1993); Maria Lorena Cook, *Organizing Dissent: Unions, the State, and t:he Democratic Teachers Movement in Mexico* (University Park, Pa.: Pennsylvania State University Press, 1996).

33. See Lorenzo Meyer, "La Encrucijada," in *Historia General de México*, vol. 2 (Mexico City: Editorial HARLA/El Colegio de México, 1988), pp. 1333–34; and Julio Moguel (ed.), *Política Estatal y Conflictos Agrarios (1950–1970)*. Historia de la Cuestión Agraria Mexicana, vol. 8 (Mexico City: Siglo XXI/Centro de Estudios Históricos del Agrarismo en México, 1989). With the withdrawal of Cárdenas's support and the co-optation of several of the constituent organizations, the movement dissolved in a short time.

34. Jonathan Fox, *The Politics of Food in Mexico: State Power and Social Mobilization* (Ithaca, N.Y.: Cornell University Press, 1992).

35. Blanca Rubio, *Resistencia Campesina y Explotación Rural en México* (Mexico City: Ediciones ERA, 1987), pp. 144–54.

36. Wayne A. Cornelius, Judith Gentleman, and Peter H. Smith, "Overview: The Dynamics of Political Change in Mexico," in *Mexico's Alternative Political Futures*, ed. Wayne A. Cornelius, Judith Gentleman, and Peter H. Smith. Monograph Series (La Jolla, Calif.: Center for U.S.-Mexican Studies, University of California, San Diego, 1989), pp. 16–18.

37. Juan Molinar Horcasitas, "The Future of the Electoral System," in *Mexico's Alternative Political Futures*, ed. Wayne A. Cornelius, Judith Gentleman, and Peter H. Smith. Monograph Series (La Jolla, Calif.: Center for U.S.-Mexican Studies, University of California, San Diego, 1989), p. 284.

38. Luis Hernández, "El Partido del Trabajo: Realidades y Perspectivas," *El Cotidiano* 7.40 (March–April 1991): 21–28.

39. Moguel, "The Mexican Left and the Social Program of Salinismo," p. 173.

40. Carlos Salinas de Gortari, "Political Participation, Public Investment, and Support for the System: A Comparative Study of Rural Communities in Mexico," Research Report Series (La Jolla,Calif.: Center for U.S.-Mexican Studies, University of California, San Diego, 1982).

41. Wayne A. Cornelius, Ann L. Craig, and Jonathan Fox, "Mexico's National Solidarity Program: An Overview," in *Transforming State-Society Relations in Mexico: The National Solidarity Strategy*, U.S.-Mexico Contemporary Perspectives Series (La Jolla, Calif.: Center for U.S.-Mexican Studies, University of California, San Diego, 1994), pp. 3–28.

42. Quoted in Cornelius, Gentleman, and Smith, "Dynamics of Political Change," p. 28.

43. Cornelius, Craig, and Fox, "Mexico's National Solidarity," p. 17; Juan Molinar Horcasitas and Jeffrey A. Weldon, "Electoral Determinants and Consequences of National Solidarity," in *Transforming State-Society Relations in Mexico: The National Solidarity Strategy*, U.S.-Mexico Contemporary Perspectives Series (La Jolla, Calif.: Center for U.S.-Mexican Studies, University of California, San Diego, 1994), pp. 124–41; Jonathan Fox, "The Difficult Transition from Clientelism to Citizenship: Lessons from Mexico," *World Politics* 46 (January 1994): 151–84; Denise Dresser, "Bringing the Poor Back In: National Solidarity as a Strategy of Regime Legitimation," in *Transforming State-Society Relations in Mexico: The National Solidarity Strategy*, ed. Wayne A. Cornelius, Ann L. Craig, and Jonathan Fox (La Jolla, Calif.: Center for U.S.-Mexican Studies, University of California, San Diego, 1994), pp. 143–66.

44. Partido Revolutionario Institucional (PRI), *Documentos Básicos* (Mexico City: PRI, 1993).

45. "Mexico: Sindicatos Suspenden Marcha del 1 de Mayo por Tercera Vez," *InterPress Service*, March 10, 1997.

46. Jonathan Fox, "Targeting the Poorest: The Role of the National Indigenous Institute in Mexico's Solidarity Program," in *Transforming State-Society Relations in Mexico: The National Solidarity Strategy*, U.S.-Mexico Contemporary Perspectives Series (La Jolla, Calif.: Center for U.S.-Mexican Studies, University of California, San Diego, 1994), p. 213.

47. George A. Collier, *Basta! Land and the Zapatista Rebellion in Chiapas* (Oakland, Calif.: Institute for Food and Development Policy, 1994); Michael W. Foley, "Forcing the Political Agenda: The Zapatista Rebellion and the Limits of Ethnic Bargaining in Mexico," *International Negotiation* 2 (1997): 123–46.

48. Stephen D. Morris, *Political Reformism in Mexico: An Overview of Contemporary Mexican Politics* (Boulder, Colo.: Lynne Rienner, 1995), pp. 160–61.

49. Cornelius, *Mexican Politics in Transition*, p. 64.

50. Eduardo Garcia, "Mexico to Sell Stakes in Petroleum Plants" (Bloomberg Business Wire, October 14, 1996); Nick Anderson, "Mexico Cancels Plant Auctions" (Associated Press, October 13, 1996).

51. Joel Simon, "Militarization of Mexico. Part I: Mexican Army Escalates Patrols in Reputed Rebel Stronghold" (Pacific News Service, August 28, 1996);

David Luhnow, "Rights Abuses Growing, Charges Watchdog" (The News [Mexico City], October 6, 1996).

52. In a sampling of polling places, the Federal Electoral Institute (IFE) found that in 11.7 percent conditions were "not optimal" for the exercise of a free and secret ballot. This was particularly true in the southern states, including Chiapas, where electoral irregularities and disputes were concentrated. Mireya Cuéllar, "En sur y sureste, la menor calidad electoral: IFE," *La Jornada*, July 19, 1997.

Meanwhile, some 600 *campesinos* in Chiapas alone have been killed by paramilitary bands ("white guards") between 1995 and 1997, according to a report submitted to the United Nations Human Rights Commission; but the problem reaches across the country, with the poorest states exhibiting the highest levels of violence. Marco Antonio Aguirre, "Zonas indígenas, las que sufren más acciones de represión: FIDH," *La Crónica de Hoy*, August 17, 1997.

53. Jeffrey St. Clair, "U.S.-Mexico. The 'Drug War' against the Zapatistas" (*InterPress Service*, January 14, 1997).

54. Luis Javier Garrido, "La Hidra," *La Jornada*, July 11, 1997.

## BIBLIOGRAPHY

Aguirre, Marco Antonio. "Zonas indígenas, las que sufren más acciones de represión: FIDH." *La Crónica-de Hoy*, August 17, 1997.

Almond, Gabriel A. and Sidney Verba. *The Civic Culture: Political Attitudes and Democracy in Five Nations.* Newbury Park, Calif.: Sage, 1989.

Anderson, Nick. "Mexico Cancels Plant Auctions." Associated Press, October 13, 1996.

Bailey, John J. *Governing Mexico: The Statecraft of Crisis Management.* London: Macmillan, 1988.

Bennett, Vivienne. "Orígenes del Movimiento Urbano Popular Mexicano: Pensamiento Político y Organizaciones Políticas Clandestinas, 1960–1980. "*Revista Mexicana de Sociología 55.*3 (July–September 1993): 89–102.

Brachet-Marquez, Vivane. *The Dynamics of Domination: State, Class, and Social Reform in Mexico, 1910–1990.* Pittsburgh: University of Pittsburgh Press, 1994.

Cevallos, Diego. "Mexico: Nuevo Avance de la Oposición en Elecciones." *InterPress Service*, March 17, 1997. Montevideo, Uruguay: InterPress Service.

Collier, George A. *Basta! Land and the Zapatista Rebellion in Chiapas.* Oakland, Calif.: Institute for Food and Development Policy, 1994.

Collier, Ruth Berins and David Collier. *Shaping the Political Arena: Critical Junctures, the Labor Movement, and Regime Dynamics in Latin America.* Princeton, N.J.: Princeton University Press, 1991.

Cook, Maria Lorena. *Organizing Dissent: Unions, the State, and the Democratic Teachers Movement in Mexico.* University Park, Pa. Pennsylvania State University Press, 1996.

Córdova, Arnaldo. *La Revolución y el Estado en México.* Mexico City: Ediciones ERA, 1989.

Cornelius, Wayne A. *Mexican Politics in Transition: The Breakdown of a One-Party-Dominant Regime*. Monograph Series. La Jolla, Calif.: Center for U.S.-Mexican Studies, University of California, San Diego, 1996.

Cornelius, Wayne A., Ann L. Craig, and Jonathan Fox. "Mexico's National Solidarity Program: An Overview." In *Transforming State-Society Relations in Mexico: The National Solidarity Strategy*. U.S.-Mexico Contemporary Perspectives Series, 3–28. La Jolla, Calif. Center for U.S.-Mexican Studies, University of California, San Diego, 1994.

Cornelius, Wayne A., Judith Gentleman, and Peter H. Smith. "Overview: The Dynamics of Political Change in Mexico." In *Mexico's Alternative Political Futures*, ed. Wayne A. Cornelius, Judith Gentleman, and Peter H. Smith. Monograph Series, 1–54. La Jolla, Calif.: Center for U.S.-Mexican Studies, University of California, San Diego, 1989.

Cuéllar, Mireya. "En sur y sureste, la menor calidad electoral: IFE." *La Jornuda*, July 19, 1997.

Dresser, Denise. "Bringing the Poor Back In: National Solidarity as a Strategy of Regime Legitimation." In *Transforming State-Society Relations in Mexico: The National Solidarity Strategy*, ed. Wayne A. Cornelius, Ann L. Craig, and Jonathan Fox, 143–66. La Jolla, Calif.: Center for U.S.-Mexican Studies, University of California, San Diego, 1994.

Flores Lúa, Graciela, Luisa Paré, and Sergio Sarmiento Silva. *Las Voces del Campo: Movimiento Campesino y Política Agraria, 1976–1984*. Mexico City: Siglo XXI, 1988

Foley, Michael W. "Agenda for Mobilization: The Agrarian Question and Popular Mobilization in Contemporary Mexico." *Latin American Research Review* 26.2 (1991): 39–74.

———. "Forcing the Political Agenda: The Zapatista Rebellion and the Limits of Ethnic Bargaining in Mexico." *International Negotiation* 2 (1997): 123–46.

Foweraker, Joe. *Popular Mobilization in Mexico: The Teachers' Movement, 1977–87*. Cambridge: Cambridge University Press, 1993.

Fox, Jonathan. "The Difficult Transition from Clientelism to Citizenship: Lessons from Mexico." *World Politics* 46 (January 1994): 151–84.

———. *The Politics of Food in Mexico: State Power and Social Mobilization*. Ithaca, N.Y.: Cornell University Press, 1992.

———. "Targeting the Poorest: The Role of the National Indigenous Institute in Mexico's Solidarity Program." In *Transforming State-Society Relations in Mexico: The National Solidarity Strategy*. U.S.-Mexico Contemporary Perspectives Series, 179–216. La Jolla, Calif.: Center for U.S.-Mexican Studies, University of California, San Diego, 1994.

García, Eduardo. "Mexico to Sell Stakes in Petroleum Plants." Bloomberg Business Wire, October14, 1996.

Garrido, Luis Javier. "The Crisis of Presidentialismo." In *Mexico's Alternative Political Futures*, ed. Wayne A. Cornelius, Judith Gentleman, and Peter H. Smith. Monograph Series, 417–34. La Jolla, Calif.: Center for U.S.-Mexican Studies, University of California, San Diego, 1989.

———. "La Hidra." *La Jornada*, July 11, 1997.

Gilly, Adolfo. *The Mexican Revolution*. 2nd ed. Translated by Patrick Camiller. London: Verso, 1983.

———. *La Revolución Interrumpida*. Mexico City: El Caballito, 1971.

Gilly, Adolfo, et al. *Interpretaciones de la Revolución Mexicana*. Mexico City: Nueva Imagen, 1980.

González Amador, Roberto and Juan Antonio Zúñiga M. "Gobernarán PAN y PRD zonas económicas claves." *La Jornada*, July 21, 1997.

González Casanova, Pablo. *Democracy in Mexico*. London: Oxford University Press, 1970.

Gordillo, Gustavo. *Campesinos al Asalto del Cielo*. Mexico City: Siglo XXI, 1988.

Gourevitch, Peter. *Politics in Hard Times: Comparative Responses to International Economic Crises*. Ithaca, N.Y.: Cornell University Press, 1986.

Haber, Paul. "Political Change in Durango: The Role of National Solidarity." In *Transforming State-Society Relations in Mexico: The National Solidarity Strategy*, ed. Wayne A. Cornelius, Ann L. Craig, and Jonathan Fox, 255–308. La Jolla, Calif.: Center for U.S.-Mexican Studies, University of California, San Diego, 1994.

Hamilton, Nora. *The Limits of State Autonomy: Post-Revolutionary Mexico*. Princeton, N.J.: Princeton University Press, 1982.

Hansen, Roger D. *The Politics of Mexican Development*. Baltimore: Johns Hopkins University Press, 1971.

Hardy, Clarisa. *El Estado y los Campesinos: La Confederación Nacional Campesina (CNC)*. Mexico City: Nueva Imagen, 1984.

Harvey, Neil. "Rebellion in Chiapas: Rural Reforms, Campesino Radicalism, and the End of Salinismo." In *Transformation of Rural Mexico*. No. 5, 1–43. La Jolla, Calif.: Center for U.S.-Mexican Studies, University of California at San Diego, 1994.

———. "La Unión de Uniones de Chiapas y los Retos Políticos del Desarrollo de Base." In *Autonomía y Nuevos Sujetos Sociales en el Desarrollo Rural*, ed. Julio Moguel, Carlota Botey, and Luis Hernández, 219–32. Mexico City: Siglo XXI/Centro de Estudios Históricos del Agrarismo en México, 1992.

Hellman, Judith Adler. *Mexico in Crisis*. 2nd ed. New York: Holmes and Meier, 1983.

Hernández, Luis. "Autonomía y Desarrollo. La Lucha en el Campo en la Hora de la Concertación." In *Los Nuevos Sujetos del Desarrollo Rural*, ed. Armando Bartra et al. Cuadernos Desarrollo de Base, 101–34. Mexico City: ADN Editores, 1991.

———. "El Partido del Trabajo: Realidades y Perspectivas." *El Cotidiano* 7.40 (March–April 1991): 21–28.

Huntington, Samuel P. *Political Order in Changing Societies*. New Haven, Conn.: Yale University Press, 1968.

Loaeza, Soledad. "México, 1968: Los Orígenes de la Transición." In *La Transición Interrumpida: México 1968–1988*, ed. Ilán Semo, 15–48. Mexico City: Universidad Iberoamericana/Nueva Imagen, 1993.

Luhnow, David. "Rights Abuses Growing, Charges Watchdog." *The News* (Mexico City), October 6, 1996.

"Mexico: Sindicatos Suspenden Marcha del 1 de Mayo por Tercera Vez." *Inter-Press Service*, March 10, 1997.

Meyer, Lorenzo. "La Encrucijada." In *Historia General de México*, vol. 2, 1273–356. Mexico City: Editorial HARLA/El Colegio de México, 1988.

———. "Historical Roots of the Authoritarian State in Mexico." In *Authoritarianism in Mexico*, ed. José Luis Reyna and Richard S. Weinert, 3–22. Philadelphia: Institute for the Study of Human Issues, 1977.

Meyer, Michael C. and William L. Sherman. *The Course of Mexican History*. 3rd ed. New York: Oxford University Press, 1987.

Moguel, Julio. "The Mexican Left and the Social Program of Salinismo." In *Transforming State-Society Relations in Mexico: The National Solidarity Strategy*, ed. Wayne A. Cornelius, Ann L. Craig, and Jonathan Fox, 167–78. La Jolla, Calif.: Center for U.S.-Mexican Studies, University of California, San Diego, 1994.

——— (ed.) *Política Estatal y Conflictos Agrarios (1950–1970)*. Historia de la Cuestión Agraria Mexicana, vol. 8. Mexico City: Siglo XXI/Centro de Estudios Históricos del Agrarismo en México, 1989.

Molinar Horcasitas, Juan. "The Future of the Electoral System." In *Mexico's Alternative Political Futures*, ed. Wayne A. Cornelius, Judith Gentleman, and Peter H. Smith. Monograph Series, 265–90. La Jolla, Calif.: Center for U.S.-Mexican Studies, University of California, San Diego, 1989.

———. "Changing the Balance of Power in a Hegemonic Party System: The Case of Mexico." In *Institutional Design in New Democracies: Eastern Europe and Latin America*, ed. Arend Lijphart and Carlos H. Waisman, 137–60. Boulder, Colo.: Westview Press,1996.

Molinar Horcasitas, Juan and Jeffrey A. Weldon. "Electoral Determinants and Consequences of National Solidarity." In *Transforming State-Society Relations in Mexico: The National Solidarity Strategy*. U.S.-Mexico Contemporary Perspectives Series, 124–41. La Jolla, Calif.: Center for U.S.-Mexican Studies, University of California, San Diego, 1994.

Monsiváis, Carlos. "'En Virtud de las Facultades Que Me Han Sido Otorgadas.' Notas Sobre el Presidencialismo a Partir de 1968." In *La Transición Interrumpida: México 1968–1988*, ed. Ilán Semo, 113–26. Mexico City: Universidad Iberoamericana/Nueva Imagen, 1993.

Moreno Sánchez, Manuel. *La Crisis Política de México*. Mexico City: Editorial Extemporáneos, 1970.

Morris, Stephen D. *Political Reformism in Mexico: An Overview of Contemporary Mexican Politics*. Boulder, Colo.: Lynne Rienner, 1995.

"No confían los mexicanos en las medidas del gobierno contra la crisis." *La Jornado*, March 7, 1996.

Partido Revolutionario Institucional (PRI). *Documentos Básicos*. Mexico City: PRI, 1993.

"Polling Abroad—The Tumult in Mexico." *The Public Perspective*, April/May 1995, 41–43.

Poniatowska, Elena. *La Noche de Tlatelolco*. Mexico City: Ediciones ERA, 1971.

Przeworski, Adam. "Some Problems in the Study of the Transition to Democracy." In *Transitions from Authoritarian Rule: Comparative Perspectives*, ed.

Guillermo O'Donnell, Philippe C. Schmitter, and Laurence Whitehead, 47–63. Baltimore: Johns Hopkins University Press, 1986.

Reyna, José Luis. "Redefining the Authoritarian Regime." In *Authoritarianism in Mexico*, ed. José Luis Reyna and Richard S. Weinert, 155–72. Philadelphia: Institute for the Study of Human Issues, 1977.

Reyna, José Luis and Richard S. Weinert (eds.). *Authoritarianism in Mexico*. Philadelphia: Institute for the Study of Human Issues, 1977.

Rubin, Jeffrey W. "Popular Mobilization and the Myth of State Corporatism." In *Popular Movements and Political Change in Mexico*, ed. Joe Foweraker and Ann L. Craig, 247-70. Boulder, Colo.: Lynne Rienner, 1990.

Rubio, Blanca. *Resistencia Campesina y Explotación Rural en México*. Mexico City: Ediciones ERA, 1987.

Salinas de Gortari, Carlos. "Political Participation, Public Investment, and Support for the System: A Comparative Study of Rural Communities in Mexico." Research Report Series. La Jolla, Calif.: Center for U.S.-Mexican Studies, University of California, San Diego, 1982.

Simon, Joel. "Militarization of Mexico. Part I: Mexican Army Escalates Patrols in Reputed Rebel Stronghold." Pacific News Service, August 28, 1996.

St. Clair, Jeffrey. "U.S.-Mexico. The 'Drug War' against the Zapatistas." Inter-Press Service, January 14, 1997.

Stevens, Evelyn P. *Protest and Response in Mexico*. Cambridge, Mass.: MIT Press, 1974.

Tarrow, Sidney. *Power in Movement: Social Movements, Collective Action and Politics*. Cambridge: Cambridge University Press, 1994.

Walton, John and David Seddon. *Free Markets and Food Riots: The Politics of Global Adjustment*. Cambridge, Mass.: Blackwell, 1994.

Zermeño, Sergio. *México: Una Democracia Utópica. El Movimiento Estudiantil de 1968*. Mexico City, 1978.

# CHAPTER 9

# Political Parties and the Emergence of Israel's Second Republic

## Asher Arian

Three parallel stories shaped the state of political parties in Israel at the end of this century. The first story involves the two major parties, Labor and the right-wing Likud. Their story is one of changing patterns of power-sharing over time, and skirmishing over security issues that have focused the country's attention since independence in 1948. The second story involves the constitutional reform that instituted the direct election of the prime minister. Since 1996, the Knesset (parliament) and the prime minister are elected in simultaneous and separate elections. The third story, related to the other two, is the persistence of parties that appeal to sectarian sentiments, based on unresolved issues of legitimacy and identity. The Israeli party system at the end of the century, and the variety of organizational forms it manifests, was fashioned by the intertwining of these three strands.

These stories relate to the three major periods of Israel's political history: (1) the period of independence and state consolidation between 1948 and 1967; (2) the period (between 1967 and 1993) of the Six Day War and the struggle to extricate the country from the fruits of that victory; and (3) the period, from 1993, that began the process of seeking accommodation with the Palestinians. The Labor Party dominated the first period, and competed with the right-wing Likud in the second. The third period, that of Israel's Second Republic, witnessed the two largest parties abandoning the smoke-filled rooms of the bosses to the open air of the public arena with the introduction of the direct election of the prime minister and the selection of the Knesset lists by the members of the major parties in primary elections. The granting of two votes to the electorate (one for prime minister and one for the parliament) instead of one, encouraged the split-ticket voting that led to a flourishing of parties' pursuing sectarian interests.

In Israel's proportional representation system of elections, many lists and parties compete. The record was set in 1981 when 31 different lists ran; in 1996, 20 lists formally competed, although two announced their withdrawal before the election began. The decrease in the number of competing parties is associated with the fact that since 1992 the minimum needed to win representation was increased from 1 percent to 1.5 percent.

Any registered party may run in the election, and 100 citizens applying to the responsible official is all that is needed to form a party. A party may not oppose the existence of Israel as a Jewish and democratic state, it may not advocate racism, and it may not be a cover for illegal activity. Once the registrar determines that the party's platform and behavior are consistent with democracy, and that it keeps appropriate records of its accounts, the party is approved.[1]

Labor's list in 1996 was made up of one party; the Likud list (formally Likud-Gesher-Tzomet) was comprised of the lists of three parties: the Likud, David Levy's Gesher, and Rafael ("Raful") Eitan's Tzomet. In the past (as recently as 1984), the Labor and Mapam parties jointly set up a single list called the Labor-Mapam Alignment, and the Likud list was made up of two autonomous parties, Herut and the Liberals. In 1988, Labor and Mapam ran separate lists, and Herut and the Liberals merged into a single party called the Likud. By 1992, Mapam had joined with two other parties, the Citizens Rights Movement and Shinui, to form a single list known as Meretz.

Labor was the dominant party, in power until 1977. After that the Likud successfully competed with Labor, and at times the close election results forced them to share power. The religious parties, and especially the National Religious Party (NRP), were almost always coalition partners in government regardless of the party in power; they were very effective in establishing aspects of Jewish religious law (Halacha) in public life, while tending to support the foreign and security policies of the party in power.

Labor's organizational efforts were central to Israel's formation, and its Zionist and socialist values epitomized the country's early development. Likud's more hard-line approach became more prominent after Labor's loss of dominance. Even as the competition persisted, Israeli society and its economy developed in a less regimented, more individualistic, more market-oriented manner. These parties were eclipsed; they ceased being mass parties and were transformed into cartel parties. As society changed, and the role of the party weakened, the politicians agreed to institute electoral reform that would change the manner in which the prime minister was elected, but would leave the election of the parliament unchanged. After the reform, the path to power still flows through the parties, but the party hierarchy has lost much of its power to control the economy, or to determine which candidate would lead the party, or who would be elected to the Knesset (parliament).

The smaller parties flourished, using older appeals and organizational forms; their voters were less mainstream, and tended to identify less completely with the heroic definition of Israel as a Zionist state whose role was to gather Jews into a modern, democratic Jewish state. Thus, the big winners of the 1996 elections were all sectarian: a non-Zionist Sephardi ultra-Orthodox party, two Arab lists, and a party appealing to new immigrants from the former Soviet Union.

## THE PARTY ACTORS

### Dominance

In the years immediately following independence, Mapai (Labor's precursor) was presented with an opportunity shared by few parties in democratic polities—that of presiding over the creation of the constitutional and political order. As a consequence, it was closely identified with the new state, and it was the party of those segments of Israeli society most involved with those heroic years. It was able to translate this identification into an organizational network that complemented and amplified the advantages conveyed by its image. Furthermore, most of this network consisted of channels maintained largely at the expense of the state, with the result that party and government tended to merge in the popular mind. The role of governmental personalities in this image-building process was most important, and until 1977 almost all were from parties associated with Labor and leftist parties. As a result, the dominant-party system was remarkably stable. The opposition could not replace the dominant coalition. The frustration of the opposition led only to superficial instability. The same parties and usually the same politicians continued to dominate the coalition. The faithful were rewarded, while the opposition was shut out from power.

In the years immediately following independence Mapai epitomized the dominant party. The largest vote-getter, the key ingredient of any government coalition, the standard-bearer of the society's goals, and the articulator of its aspirations, Mapai also had the tremendous political advantages of a united and integrated leadership, led by David Ben-Gurion; a broad-based, well-functioning, and flexible political organization; no serious political opposition; and control over the major economic and human resources flowing into the country. At independence,

Mapai (Labor's precursor) was perceived as legitimate, Herut (Likud's antecedent) as illegitimate. Mapai's eventual failures, especially internal disputes over political leadership and ineffective party organization, were as important in explaining its eventual decline as was the gradual strengthening of the Herut movement and the Likud. The weakening dominance of Mapai and Labor, and the achievement of legitimacy and an equal political status by Herut and Likud, sum up this first chapter of Israel's political history.

*Competition*

Labor's uninterrupted reign ended in 1977, after which the Likud and Labor competed for power. Likud ascended to power after years in the wilderness, and after serving an apprenticeship during the National Unity government of 1967–70, the period before and after the Six Day War. By 1973, the gap was closing between Labor and Likud, and in 1977 Likud became the largest party, largely because a wounded Labor hemorrhaged with the establishment of the Democratic Movement for Change (DMC).[2] The DMC appeared only once, but in its single appearance it won fifteen seats, mostly at Labor's expense. Likud's surge and Labor's loss led to the beginning of the period of competition.

The Likud emerged as the largest party in 1977, grew more in 1981, and then began a downward trend (see table 9.1). The growth of the two-parties' share of the vote coincided with the emergence of amalgamated parties, or lists set up by a combination of parties,[3] especially after 1965 with the emergence of the Mapai-Ahdut Haavoda Alignment and the Herut-Liberal Gahal (see figure 9.1). In 1965, in reaction to the split in Mapai caused by the setting up of Rafi by Ben-Gurion, Moshe Dayan, Shimon Peres, and others, old-time Mapai leaders, formed an electoral coalition with Ahdut Haavoda in order to avoid political defeat.[4] By 1968 Rafi, Mapai, and Ahdut Haavoda had formed the Labor Party, and in 1969 Labor joined Mapam in a broader Alignment. Meanwhile, the right Herut and center Liberals were founding an electoral bloc for the 1965 elections, expanded in 1973 under pressure from Ariel Sharon, with the acquiescence of Menachem Begin, to form the Likud.

In 1981 the race between the Likud and the Alignment was very close; between them they won almost 1.5 million of the almost 2 million votes cast, but only 10,405 votes separated them. Within the Jewish population the Likud was a bigger winner, since Arabs accounted for more than 40,000 of the Alignment total. Labor peaked in 1969; its reemergence in 1992 was only relative to the poor showing of Likud that year.

The difficulties in setting up a stable coalition led the leaders of the

TABLE 9.1

Share of 120-Member Knesset by the Two Largest Parties, 1949–1996

|  | Biggest Winner | Second Biggest Winner | Total Seats | Competitiveness Ratio[a] |
|---|---|---|---|---|
| 1949 | Mapai: 46 | Mapam: 19 | 65 | .41 |
| 1951 | Mapai: 45 | Liberal: 20 | 65 | .44 |
| 1955 | Mapai: 40 | Herut: 15 | 55 | .38 |
| 1959 | Mapai: 47 | Herut: 17 | 64 | .36 |
| 1961 | Mapai: 42 | Herut: 17 | 59 | .40 |
|  |  | Liberal: 17 |  |  |
| 1965 | Alignment:[b] 45 | Gahal:[c] 26 | 71 | .58 |
| 1969 | Alignment:[d] 56 | Gahal:[c] 26 | 82 | .46 |
| 1973 | Alignment:[d] 51 | Likud:[e] 39 | 90 | .76 |
| 1977 | Likud:[e] 43 | Alignment:[d] 32 | 75 | .74 |
| 1981 | Likud:[e] 48 | Alignment:[d] 47 | 95 | .98 |
| 1984 | Alignment:[d] 44 | Likud:[e] 41 | 85 | .93 |
| 1988 | Likud: 40 | Labor: 39 | 79 | .98 |
| 1992 | Labor: 44 | Likud: 32 | 72 | .73 |
| 1996 | Labor: 34 | Likud:[f] 32 | 66 | .94 |
| PM 1996 | Netanyahu 50.5% | Peres 49.5% | 100% | .98 |

Notes:

[a] Competitiveness ratio = second biggest winner/biggest winner.
[b] Mapai and Ahdut Haavoda.
[c] Herut and Liberals.
[d] Labor and Mapam.
[e] Herut, Liberals, and others.
[f] Likud-Gesher-Tzomet

two major parties to set up the National Unity government of 1984, which featured the rotation between Prime Minister Peres and Foreign Minister Yitzhak Shamir after two years. Despite tensions and crises, the agreement held, and Peres exchanged ministries with Shamir in 1986. After the 1988 elections, another unity government was established but this time rotation was not part of the agreement because Likud support among other potential coalition partners was greater than in 1984. But the results of the inconclusive 1988 elections become an important factor in the next phase of the story.

*After 1996*

The major parties were dealt a severe blow by the 1996 elections. With Labor electing 34 members and Likud 32 members in the 120-seat Knes-

FIGURE 9.1

The Share of the Two Largest Parties in the 120-Seat Knesset, 1949–1996

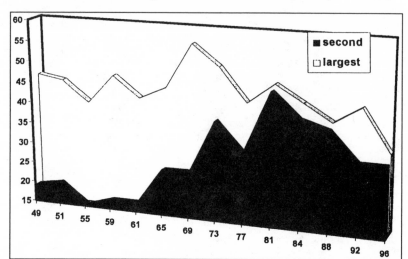

set, instead of 44 and 40 as in 1992, the party system was fragmented as never before. Never in Israeli political history had there been a winning party with such a small Knesset delegation as Labor won in 1996. Moreover, the total seats won by the two biggest parties was also unusually small. One must look to the 1949 elections and those in the early 1950s to find the two major parties commanding so few of the votes of the electorate.

The drop to 34 seats and 32 seats respectively in the 1996 election was a harsh blow to both Labor and Likud. Likud had 32 seats in 1992 also, except that in 1996 Gesher and Tzomet were partners in the joint list with Likud. Levy's Gesher had been part of the Likud until 1995, and returned to run in a joint list with the Likud before the elections. But Tzomet had independently won eight seats in the 1992 elections. Labor won 818,570 votes to the Likud- Gesher-Tzomet's 767,178 votes. In the prime minister race of 1996, the division between Netanyahu and Peres closely followed the Likud-Labor.split in 1981. With almost 3 million votes cast, Netanyahu won 1,501,023 votes, Peres 1,471,566. Among Jewish voters, Netanyahu won 55 percent. The votes of the Likud-Gesher-Tzomet list was only 51.1 percent of those that Netanyahu won; Labor won only 54.5 percent of the Peres total.

The Israeli system after 1996 became more concentrated and more fractionalized; the dual method of electing the prime minister directly and the Knesset based on a fixed-list system of proportional representation brought about this curious result. Of course, the result did not happen in a vacuum. It was precisely because public trust in political parties was so low, because reform was in the air, and because the parties had already relinquished many of their historical functions, that reform was possible. As is usually the case, the reform both reflected and accelerated processes that were already under way.

## CONSTITUTIONAL REFORM

After the inconclusive elections of 1988, it seemed that the only way to set up a governing coalition was to give in to the demands of the Orthodox religious parties (who had collectively won 15 percent of the vote) for amending the "Who is a Jew?" definition of the Law of Return and to provide substantial additional funding for their schools. It appeared that the religious parties controlled the future of Israeli politics because they could determine which of the large parties would form a governing coalition in the Knesset. Accordingly, strong appeals rose to prevent in the future the exaggerated power of the minority over the majority.

It was in this period of sharp political division over the future of the territories, and a perceived stalemate between the major parties, that the one major reform of Israeli constitutional transformation—the direct election of the prime minister—may be dated. The ills of the system became more obvious than ever because of the "dirty trick" of 1990, the name given by Yitzhak Rabin to the failed attempt by Peres to replace the Likud-led National Unity government with a Labor-led coalition.

The background of the story of the "dirty trick" was a peace initiative put forth by Israel. It gained support in Washington and Cairo, but when the Americans pressed the Israeli government to be more flexible regarding details, Prime Minister Shamir recoiled. The Knesset expressed no-confidence in its government for the first time in Israeli history and the Unity government fell by a vote of 60 to 55, with the votes of Labor, the Arabs, the left, and ultra-Orthodox Agudat Israel. The key to the "victory" of Peres and Labor was the fact that five of the six Knesset members of the ultra-Orthodox Shas party absented themselves from the vote.

A protracted series of negotiations ensued, with Peres having to placate hawks and doves within his party, and yet woo politicians from the other side of the aisle to support his bid to be prime minister. After he failed, Shamir was again asked to form a government. The high (or low) point came when Shamir promised the balking finance minister an important ministry in the new government (foreign, defense, or treasury), another for one of his colleagues, five certain places in the next Likud election list, and a $10 million security deposit to guarantee these pledges. After petitions to the judicial system, and a massive demonstration calling for constitutional reform, the finance minister backed down from his demand for a cash deposit, and agreed to make do with the signatures of all of the Likud ministers backing the agreement with him. When four of them refused to go along, negotiations were reopened with Labor. After more trading, Shamir was successful and his right-wing government served until 1992.

Reform followed. The Knesset reacted to this unseemly chain of events by passing legislation that was intended to change basic parliamentary norms. Legislation was passed making it less likely that Knesset members would resign from the party that elected them in order to achieve personal gains. The other reform to emerge from this messy political period was the direct election of the prime minister. Originally conceived of as one of a series of constitutional reforms by a group of law professors,[5] the direct election became the focus of reform and sparked a well-funded public campaign featuring petition drives and demonstrations.[6] The legislation, though passed before the 1992 elections, would be applied beginning with the 1996 elections. The "dirty trick" set the stage for this major change in Israeli political life.

The new system provided that the tenure of the prime minister and the Knesset shall be four years long, each elected by the voters. The Knesset may remove the prime minister by a special vote of eighty members, upon which new elections for the prime minister take place. The prime minister, with the agreement of the country's president, can dissolve the Knesset; such a step would also end the prime minister's tenure and would force new elections for both. The Knesset can also remove the prime minister by expressing no confidence by a majority vote (61 votes), or by failing to pass the national budget, but then new elections for both prime minister and Knesset would be held.

The behavior of the party politicians had become so outrageous that popular demand for reform was forceful. In a 1990 survey, the public's trust in institutions was tested. Of the eleven institutions asked about, political parties scored lowest with 14 percent expressing trust compared with 52 percent no trust. In contrast, the Israel Defense Force scored 94 percent trust, and 2 percent no trust, the courts, 83 percent and 5 percent, and the police 53 percent and 17 percent respectively. Even the press did better than the parties, with 20 percent trust and 43 percent no trust.[7]

## DEMOGRAPHY AND ISSUES

The peace process with Israel's neighbors, initiated in 1993, became the new reality and embraced moderates and hardliners, among both Jews and Arabs. The Likud adopted more moderate policies and a rhetoric which would have been unthinkable a few short years before. The security issue seemed to be transforming itself into the question of which party could better manage the peace, as the policies of the parties seemed to become more similar. Yet the security issue continued to discriminate among Likud and Labor voters very well, and the public saw the parties as different on this dimension.

The correlations in Table 9.2 provide important clues as to the nature of partisanship in Israel. The correlations are between the Labor/Likud vote and various demographic and issue variables for the 1969–1996 period, and the Peres/Netanyahu vote in 1996. Age has had a consistent relationship with vote, with the young somewhat more likely to vote Likud, and the old, Labor. Gender has never been related to vote choice in Israeli surveys to a statistically significant extent. Class differences mattered to a degree, although the correlations were not consistent and not very strong. Living density (the number of persons per room) and education, show that lower-class voters abandoned Labor in favor of the Likud as competition began in 1977. Income is not the best measure of class in Israel, as it is the kind of topic an Israeli is unlikely to discuss in an open manner with an interviewer-stranger.

Religion and ethnicity were much stronger correlates of the vote. The critical election year for both is 1977. Before that year, both dimensions barely distinguished Labor voters from Likud voters. In 1977, they both became important. Religion (measured by extent of religious observance) gained in importance over time, reaching an all-time high in the 1992 election and in the vote for prime minister in 1996. The relationship between ethnicity and the vote reached its highest point in the 1984 election, and has receded since.

The relationship between voting and origin is not a new one in Israeli politics. In the 1948–77 of Labor dominance, it regularly won support from most groups in the society. This was especially true of new immigrants, who were often in awe of the "miracle" that had returned them to the land of their fathers. These immigrants were dependent on the bureaucracies of the establishment for the whole gamut of economic, educational, health, social, and cultural needs. An increasingly large share of the electorate was of Sephardi origin, and Mapai maintained its dominant role as the largest plurality party and the leader of every government coalition, and attempts to appeal to the Sephardi population at election time by lists set up by Sephardim largely failed.

The twin issues of God (religion) and nationalism (the territories) are powerful predictors of the vote. On the state-religion issue, the trend of increasing correlations persists over time. The identification of Labor as an anticlerical party has strengthened, while the Likud has played to the traditional sympathies of much of its voting base, even

## TABLE 9.2
### Correlations between Likud and Labor, Demographics and Issues, 1969–1996

| Survey[c] | (N) | Demography | | | | | | | Issues | | |
|---|---|---|---|---|---|---|---|---|---|---|---|
| | | Age | Gender | Density | Education | Income | Religion | Ethnicity | No terr. for peace[d] | Capitalism/ Socialism[e] | State/ Religion[f] |
| 10/69 | (1,017) | .17 | (.05) | .07 | (.00) | (-.04) | .08 | .13 | .15 | .23 | .12 |
| 5/73 | (1,062) | .27 | (.01) | .15 | (-.02) | (-.01) | (.04) | .13 | .23 | .17 | –[g] |
| 3/77 | (620) | .29 | (-.03) | .18 | (.01) | (.06) | .18 | .32 | .28 | .22 | .17 |
| 3/81 | (798) | .13 | (.06) | .07 | .09 | (.00) | .19 | .23 | .27 | .16 | .20 |
| 7/84 | (807) | .20 | (-.03) | .25 | .22 | .08 | .37 | .53 | .57 | .32 | –[g] |
| 10/88 | (532) | .16 | (.04) | .09 | .15 | (.01) | .27 | .27 | .61 | .30 | .24 |
| 6/92 | (657) | .10 | (.07) | .13 | .24 | (-.02) | .40 | .35 | .57 | (.05) | .29 |
| 5/96 | (798) | .13 | (.04) | .18 | .21 | .12 | .36 | .30 | .65 | (.07) | .35 |
| PM96 | (1,113) | .09 | (.06) | .20 | .18 | .12 | .44 | .28 | .63 | (.08) | .41 |

(continued on next page)

TABLE 9.2 *(continued)*

Notes:

[a] Pearson correlations, significant above the .05 level, except for those in parentheses.

[b] The coding for these correlations was Likud = 1, Labor = 2; Netanyahu = 1, Peres = 2. Low scores for the other variables indicate young age, female, high density, low education, low income, high religiosity, Sephardi, unwillingness to concede territories for peace, favoring capitalism over socialism, and favoring public life in accordance with Jewish religious law, respectively.

[c] Preelection surveys used. In years for which multiple surveys were available, the one that contained the most variables used in the table was chosen.

[d] Before 1984, a question concerning the maximum amount of territory Israel should give up in order to achieve a peace settlement. In 1984 and after, constructed from two questions, the first asking preference between return of territories for peace, annexation, or status quo, and a follow-up question forcing a choice of those who chose the "status quo" option. In 1996 a 7-point answer was used.

[e] The question asked about preference for the socialist or capitalist approach. The 1973 question asked if the Histadrut labor union should both own industries and represent workers.

[f] The question asked whether the government should see to it that public life in Israel be conducted according to the Jewish religious tradition.

[g] Not asked.

though the origins and ideology of the Likud are very secular.

The trend of growing correlations for the territories issue is steady, with the critical year being 1984, the election following the war in Lebanon, and the first one in which Shamir replaced Begin as the head of the Likud. Since 1984, the correlations of the territories issue with the vote are very high and of similar magnitude. Over time, Labor has more unambiguously identified itself as the territories-for-peace party, and the platform of Labor has become less vague on this issue.

The public perception of the difference between these two parties on the territories issue did not change much; almost two-thirds of the respondents in the 1981, 1984, and 1992 surveys thought these differences were big or very big. By 1996 the figure jumped to 80 percent, although Netanyahu strained toward the middle in the election campaign. The years 1992 and 1996 were different from previous elections in that many more voters said that the territories would be an important consideration in their voting decision. In the 1996 sample, 71 percent said that the issue of the territories would very greatly influence their vote, compared with 52 percent in 1992, and less than a third in previous elections. Adding the next category of response, 90 percent in 1996 and 81 percent in 1992 said that it would influence them greatly or very greatly, compared with 63 percent in previous elections.

The correlations between the vote and the classical economic cleavage between capitalism and socialism do not follow a clear pattern over time. They were strongest in 1984 and 1988. In 1992 and 1996 there was no relationship whatsoever between voters' position on this question and their preference for Likud or Labor.

## EQUITY, LEGITIMACY, IDENTITY

Apart from the security issue, fundamental questions of equity, legitimacy, and identity remain far from settled in Israel. It was around these axes that the sectarian parties thrived. Voters could declare their policy preference on security matters by their vote for prime minister, and then, liberated by the second ballot, they could express themselves regarding other concerns. The dual ballot led to a strengthening of parties with a point of view. Shas, Israel b'Aliya, and two Arab parties all wanted more: more funds, more housing, better schools, and so forth. But there the similarities ended. Their specific appeals were quite different.

### Shas

Three religious lists won representation in 1996—Shas, the National Religious party, and United Torah Jewry. They won 20 percent of the vote and 23 Knesset seats—an unprecedented achievement. Before 1996, the highest number of seats won by religious parties had been 18 seats, which they had won in 1959, 1961, and 1969, and 1988. The 1996 display of strength was led by Shas (10 seats) and continued the pattern begun in 1988 in which non-Zionist religious parties won more seats than did the Zionist religious parties. Until 1988, the Zionist religious parties bettered the non-Zionist religious parties by a ratio of two-to-one.

Shas is *haredi* and Sephardi, and both elements are important in understanding the appeal of the party. Haredi refers to a religious party (all religious parties in Israel are Orthodox); the word *haredi* connotes awe-inspired, fearful of God's majesty, in the same way that the Christian Quakers and the Shakers use the term. The *haredi* parties do not participate in Zionist institutions, such as the World Zionist Organization. They do not consider themselves Zionists and see their role in influencing the Israeli government as similar to their role of influencing the local government in Brooklyn or Brookline. To ensure their support, Israeli governments (led by either Labor or Likud) have allowed them unusual privileges such as exempting their sons from army service while studying in yeshivas (daughters are completely exempt) and allowing them to maintain an "independent" school system partly funded by public moneys but not controlled by the Ministry of Education.

Shas has combined a nostalgia for religion in this traditional population, the provision of social services, and an appeal to ethnic pride. Many voters whose parents were born in North Africa or Asia are proud of the material concessions that Shas has been able to win from what they consider to be the Ashkenazi (European) establishment. Appealing especially to voters who are lower class, less educated, and have large families, Shas fills functions Mapai had filled in the past, but then abandoned because many social services were transferred to the state.

## Arab Parties

In the early years of statehood, Arab voters were afforded symbolic representation by having delegates in the Knesset in lists sponsored by Mapai, the dominant party. Arab leaders of a nationalist bent found outlets for their activities in lists affiliated with the Communist Party, dominated by Jews.[8] For the first time in 1988, an indigenous Arab party competed. By 1996, two Arab lists won a record nine seats.

The Arab vote has gone increasingly to Arab parties, and less to Zionist ones. The year 1996 was a record year in terms of Arab participation in the elections (about 77%), and in terms of the percent of the vote that went to Arab parties (about 70%). Arab parties have never been formerly in government coalitions and an Arab has never served as a cabinet minister. While Arab parties helped block the formation of a right-wing government after the 1992 elections, thus allowing Labor to pursue the peace accord with the PLO, they were not officially members of the government. Arabs have served as deputy ministers, but these were from Labor or left-wing Zionist parties.

## Israel b'Aliya

This list appealed to the more than one-half million new immigrants from the former Soviet Union, about 15 percent of the electorate, and won seven seats in 1996. Aliya literally means coming up, and in its ideological connotation, immigrating to Israel. The double significance of the party's name is coming to Israel, and improving the country.

## Unfinished Business

The appeals of these parties indicate the unfinished political business of Israel, including the very legitimacy of the system, and matters of identity. For many religious Jews, any state law that contradicts Jewish religious law is illegitimate. Could any secular parliament or court, no matter how constitutional the action, decide to revoke Divine law (or Halacha, Jewish religious law)? When a religious court ruled in accordance with Halacha regarding the division of property in a divorce case, what legitimate right did the Supreme Court have to overturn the ruling because it conflicted with man-made legislation regarding equality?

Regarding the future of territories taken in the 1967 Six Day War, many would oppose their return to the Arabs; some (perhaps 10 percent of the population) would also view such a decision as illegitimate. Divine promises to restore real estate cannot be ignored by elected parliamentarians, the argument would go.

Israeli Arabs also raise difficult issues of legitimacy for the system. In a system that self-consciously puzzles over the difficulties of being simultaneously Jewish and democratic, what is the appropriate reaction of the non-Jewish minority (some 18 percent of the population)? They are called upon to support a Jewish state in a period of intense Arab nationalism, and, even though most would not wish to serve, they are excluded from the army, the most important element in determining the pecking order of Israeli political and bureaucratic life.

As the country becomes less entangled with issues of the territories and of the Palestinians, it is likely that it will have to grapple with the real questions of Zionism, including the meaning of a Jewish democratic state. What is the meaning of a Jewish state—a state full of Jews, or a state filled with Jewish content? And who is to define Jewish content? For that matter, who is to define who is a Jew?

The elements of a Jewish, democratic state have been expressed in legislative declarations and are fervently believed by most Israeli Jews. When asked, "Are we in Israel an inseparable part of the Jewish people or a separate people?" 85 percent chose the first option. An overwhelming and growing majority of Jews in Israel identify themselves as both Jews and Israelis. More than two-thirds in 1965 and almost three-quarters in 1974 responded that being Jewish played an important part in their lives. When asked about the centrality of being Israeli, 90 percent of the same samples reported in both 1965 and 1974 that "Israeli-ness" plays an important part in their lives.[9]

In a 1996 survey, the overwhelming majority identified themselves as "Jewish" and "Israeli." Respondents were given four identities to rank: Jewish, Israeli, their ethnic classification (Ashkenazi or Sephardi), and religion (observant or secular). More than 40 percent of the respondents chose each of "Jewish" and "Israeli" as both first and second choice. Ethnic and religious observance identities were left far behind. There were obvious political ramifications in these cues. About 70 percent of the Likud's Benjamin Netanyahu supporters ranked "Jewish" first, and about 30 percent ranked "Israeli" first before the election of 1996. The choices of Labor's Shimon Peres supporters were the reverse, but neither camp had a monopoly on either of these two identities. For most Jews in Israel, then, there was no discrepancy between being Israeli and being Jewish.

## THE SPECTRUM OF PARTY TYPES IN ISRAEL

There is no ideal form of party organization, and forms of organization are not static. Party organization adapts to meet existing conditions. Organization reflects interests, needs, and motivations, but it also generates all of these. And in so doing, party organization itself changes. As power shifts in a society, so organization of the political party changes. When elections determine the division of power, it becomes politically advantageous to organize the electorate better than your opponents do. When the important resources are controlled by the state, it is advantageous to coalesce with opponents to assure a steady flow of money.

Various organizational forms of political parties may coexist at a given time in the same country. Parties play to different audiences, they are pressured by differing forces, and are susceptible to varying pressures. The forms used by the winners are often mimicked by other parties, but in so doing they invariably change the original forms to conform with their own special needs. The organizational structures of new winners are copied in their turn.

Parties are very malleable, and they adapt to changing conditions. The mass party in Israel was prevalent during the period of nation building; after independence the dominant Mapai, and especially Ben-Gurion, led the move to statism, a universal, inclusive view of the state and citizenship, and away from the more particularistic party-based activity that had been used so effectively by the party to catapult to power. The inevitable result of statism, however, was to shrink the party's base of patronage and influence. This especially hurt the Histadrut, the labor organization; the passage of the National Health Insurance Act in 1994 was another, and not necessarily the final, blow in a series of moves removing the Labor Party from its once prominent place in Israeli social and economic life.

The emergence of catchall parties occurred in the 1960s and 1970s as leaders of various parties began to enjoy a capacity to appeal to the electorate at large when the mass parties weakened as the media became more varied and independent, as the children of the immigrant generation came of age, and as social services were transferred from party-related organizations to the state.[10] Voters were beginning to behave more like consumers than active participants. Elections were seen to revolve around the choice of leaders rather than the choice of policies or platforms, especially in the 1980s, while the formation of those policies became the prerogative of the party leadership rather than of the party membership. Popular control and accountability were weakened as the public seemed to judge politicians prospectively rather than retrospectively, in terms of promises rather than record, in terms of what they would do in the future rather than in terms of what they had done in the past.[11] The persistence of national unity governments in the 1980s also contributed to this pattern. Parties were not over, nor were they in decline—they were changing. But against this background, it was not surprising that support was found for the moves to institute the direct election of the prime minister and to hold primaries, in which party members selected the candidates for the lists of the major parties to the Knesset.

The cadre party model presupposes that the elected notables can identify and pursue the national interest, while the model of the mass party was one of competing visions of appropriate social policy. Where the cadre party relied on the quality of supporters, the mass party relied on their quantity. The mass party became a victim of its own success as the state began to provide on a universal basis the welfare and educational services that had been the responsibility of the party. The improvement of social conditions increased social and electoral mobility. The catchall party recruited members on the basis of policy agreement rather than social identity. Parties began making universal appeals directly to voters rather than communicating principally to and through their core supporters, further weakening the ties between particular parties and particular segments of society. The party began to act as a broker between the electorate and organized interests, rather than in its traditional role of organizing and then representing interests.

The capacity of a party to perform the brokerage function depends not only on its ability to appeal to the electorate, but also on its ability to manipulate the state.[12] A party that can use the state in the interests of its clients can also use it in its own interests. In their role of law-makers it was "natural" for party leaders to turn to the state to provide and regulate financial support for political parties, and to acquire a easy access to the electronic media, controlled by the state, to pursue their goals. The introduction of party financing in 1969 and the generous amount of free television and radio time provided during election campaigns in the Israeli case, fit this model perfectly. In a sense, the state is invaded by the parties; the state rules are determined by the parties in concert, providing resources to existing parties to ensure their own survival, and aiding them to resist challenges from newly mobilized alternatives. The state becomes an institutionalized structure of support for sustaining insiders while excluding outsiders. The parties now become absorbed by the state rather than acting as brokers between the state and other groups. No longer trustees (cadre party), delegates (mass party), or even entrepreneurs (catchall party), party leaders become functionaries of semi-state agencies. In this sense a cartel emerges, in which all the existing parties share in resources and in which all survive.

Likud and Labor are good examples of cartel parties that rely on government support to persist. They still have branches and place a premium on membership, but these are holdovers from mass party forms; these are occasionally important resources in intraparty fights, but they are no longer vital for the survival of the party organization. This explains how leaders of such parties could even consider "open primaries" in which any citizen, whether a member of the party or not, could participate in choosing the party's candidates for office.

The NRP still retains the forms and functions of a mass party, although, like all parties, it too enjoys the legislation for funding parties promoted by the cartel parties. The NRP has a vibrant membership based in the synagogues affiliated with its movement; it is closely involved in religious state-supported educational institutions ranging from preschool through the university; it is identified with special training-and-Torah-learning units in the army; it prides itself on the organizational and economic commitment by the party's leaders and most of its members to the settlements in the territories; and it has a very active youth group. The NRP preserves a form of total party activity originally developed and perfected by the parties of the secular socialist left, but which has increasingly vanished in Israeli society.

The *haredi* parties are closest to cadre parties. They flourish by providing their supporters with a sense of pride and religious continuity, access to government money for the social services they often badly need, and with ideological clarity. Their ranks are fed by congregations of faithful worshippers and students of the Torah, which band together with other communities to form the myriad of sects and courtyards allegiant to diverse rabbinical authorities. Matters of policy and appointments to official positions are controlled by the Councils of Torah Sages of each party, and are not issues of participatory democracy. Membership, meetings, and primaries are out of place and unnecessary for these parties, but the party is central to the existence of the community.

Shas, the Sephardi *haredi* party, and Agudat Israel and other Ashkenazi *haredi* parties, are as close to total parties as one can find in Israel at the turn of the century, and their organizations nurture their followers in activities along much of the social, economic, and cultural spectrum. These parties are committed to the well-being of their membership, providing schools outside the national education system but largely funded from the public treasury, and both are active in procuring government funding to construct housing in communities earmarked for their membership, and in providing other goods and services. Although there are no manifestations of democratic process, the allegiance of the faithful is very impressive. Many Sephardim who had voted Likud in the past voted for Netanyahu and Shas in 1996 out of identification with or nostalgia for the world of tradition and religion that the party represented.

If the *haredi* parties want to retain their separateness, the Arab parties and Israel b'Aliya struggle to be accepted in a society that often treats them as marginal. Having tried the political path and having found it promising, if not completely satisfying, they are likely to persist. In an organizational sense, Israel b'Aliya probably will have a harder time of it, because many of its voters will likely succeed in their efforts to be integrated in Israeli society and it remains to be seen if they will retain their loyalty to this immigrant party, which is, after all, a declaration of marginality. The Arabs are much less likely to solve their dilemmas of legitimacy and identity, and hence the potential for their parties is great.

The parallel stories of different political agendas, various organizational responses, and the impact of constitutional manipulation frame the state of political parties in Israel at the end of the century. The issues they address are so fundamental and complex that it is relatively clear that future chapters of the drama will appear familiar, although they may well take wholly unexpected twists.

# NOTES

1. Dan Avnon (ed.), *The Parties Law in Israel: Between a Legal Framework and Democratic Norms*, in Hebrew (Jerusalem: Israel Democracy Institute and Kibbutz Hameuhad, 1993).

2. Amnon Rubinstein, *A Certain Political Experience*, in Hebrew (Jerusalem: Idanim, 1982); Nachman Orieli and Amnon Barzilai, *The Rise and Fall of the DMC*, in Hebrew (Tel Aviv: Reshafim, 1982); Miri Bitton, "Third Reformist Parties" (Ph.D. dissertation, City University of New York, 1995).

3. Jonathan Mendilow, "Party Cluster Formations in Multi-Party Systems," *Political Studies* 30 (1982): 485–503.

4. Nathan Yanai, *Split at the Top*, in Hebrew (Tel Aviv: Lewin-Epstein, 1969).

5. U. Reichman, B. Bracha, A. Rosen-Zvi, A. Shapira, D. Friedman, B. Susser, K. Mann, A. Maoz, and A. Klagsveld, *A Proposal for a Constitution for the State of Israel* (Tel Aviv: A Constitution for Israel, 1987).

6. Tamar Hermann, "The Rise of Instrumental Voting: The Campaign for Political Reform," in *The Elections in Israel—1992*, ed. A. Arian and M. Shamir (Albany: State University of New York Press, 1995), pp. 275–97; Gideon Doron, and Barry Kay, "Reforming Israel's Voting Schemes," in *The Elections in Israel—1992*, ed. A. Arian and M. Shamir (Albany: State University of New York Press, 1995), pp. 299–320; Guy Bechor, *A Constitution for Israel*, in Hebrew (Or Yehuda: Maariv, 1996).

7. Yochanan Peres and Ephrain Yuchtman-Yaar, *Trends in Israeli Democracy: The Public's View* (Boulder, Colo.: Lynne Reinner, 1992), p. 21.

8. Jacob Landau, *The Arabs in Israel* (London: Oxford University Press, 1990).

9. Simon Herman, *Jewish Identity in the Jewish State* (Beverly Hills: Sage, 1977); Yair Auron, *Jewish-Israeli Identity* (Tel Aviv: Sifrait Poalim, 1993); Asher Arian, *The Second Republic: Politics in Israel* (Chatham, NJ: Chatham House, 1998).

10. Otto Kirchheimer, "The Transformation of West European Party Systems," in *Political Parties and Political Development*, ed. Joseph LaPalombara and Myron Weiner (Princeton, N.J.: Princeton University Press, 1966), pp. 177–200.

11. Morris Fiorina, *Retrospective Voting in American National Elections* (New Haven, Conn.: Yale University Press, 1981).

12. Richard S. Katz, and Peter Mair "Changing Models of Party Organization and Party Democracy," *Political Parties* 1 (1995): 5–27.

# CHAPTER 10

# South Africa:
# Rise and Demise of Political Parties

## Christopher Thornhill

South Africa's political arena has been characterized by centuries of divisions between the white, black, colored, and Indian[1] inhabitants. The distinction between the different groups have been intensified and legally entrenched since 1948 when the National Party was voted into power on its policy of segregating the races, popularly known as the *apartheid* policy.

To be able to comprehend the development of the political parties that exist presently, reference has to be made to the political history of South Africa. This will be done by referring to the development of the political parties that developed amongst the white population, the colored population, the Indian population, and the black population. Nonracial political parties only came to fruition since 1990 with the unbanning of a number of organizations and the advent of the fully democratic elections of April 26–28, 1994.

The historical review will be followed by a brief discussion of the results of the 1994 elections. Thereafter attention will be devoted to the aftermath of the elections. It will be indicated that the major liberation movement, namely, the African National Congress (ANC), appears to retain its support. The National Party, which mainly consisted of white members and wielded political power for forty-eight years, suffered a significant loss of support. The Inkatha Freedom Party also appeared to experience a loss in popularity.

### HISTORICAL ANTECEDENTS

*White Political Development*

The political dispensation followed by the different colonial powers (British and Dutch) since the establishment of a refreshment post in

South Africa in 1652, provided for the separate political developments of the European and the indigenous population groups. Even the indentured Indian sugarcane workers that arrived in South Africa in 1860 could not freely participate in the country's political activities.

**Pre-unification politics.** The social and economic effects of colonial policies on the South African society as a result of the policy of fragmented political participation are not discussed. However, it should be emphasized that political development amongst the indigenous groups was seriously hampered as a result of this. Therefore, it could be argued that some political parties taking part in the legislative processes are rather inexperienced in formal political activities. Political participation in South African governmental matters was mainly limited to people of European descent. Thus the major part of the historical overview represents the politics of the white or European electorate.

Political differences toward the end of the nineteenth century and the early part of the twentieth century were on the one hand mainly characterized by British colonialism. On the other hand a strong nationalism developed. This eventually resulted in the establishment of the Union of South Africa through the South Africa Act (1909), passed by the British Parliament. Language also played a significant role in the political scene in South Africa. On one side of the political spectrum, those who favored links with Great Britain preferred the English language. Those with a strong nationalistic view favored Dutch and later Afrikaans. A political grouping, the Afrikaner Bond, was established in 1879 to promote Dutch as an official language and succeeded in obtaining this goal in 1884.[2]

**Unification of South Africa.** Political parties were largely unknown in the Dutch and later the Afrikaans-speaking community (Afrikaans is a language that developed from Dutch and related languages). It was actually only after the Anglo-Boer War that political parties developed amongst the Dutch—or Boers—under the guise of agricultural societies. The first political parties included *inter alia* the Volkskongres (Congress of the People), the Responsible Government Party (later known as the National Association), the Orangia Unie (Orange Union), the Het Volk (the Nation), the Unionist Party, and the Labour Party.[3] Developments saw an intensification of the differences amongst the main political parties based on the language issue. In fact the differences were between the establishment of a single South African nation on the one hand and the retention of two separate identities (English-speaking and Dutch- or Afrikaans-speaking). The Union of South Africa established in 1910 did not bring a reconciliation between the two main language groups. This *inter alia* led to the establishment of the National

Party on July 1, 1914. The party favored a separate South African entity free from the British Empire.

One of the first acts passed by the newly established Parliament in 1910 was aimed at creating a Department of Native Affairs to deal with the affairs of South Africa's black population.[4] This approach of distinguishing specific institutions indeed formed the basis of public sector organizational structures until the democratic elections of April 1994. It is considered necessary to take note of this fact to be able to comprehend the composition of the governmental system and the public sector that existed for nearly eighty years.

The first general election after unification was held in 1915 resulting in the South African Party winning 54 seats of the 130, with the National Party 27, the Unionist Party 39, the Labour Party 4, and 6 Independent representatives.[5] Another general election held in 1921 increased the South African Party's majority to 79 and the National Party to 45 with the Labour Party 9 and one Independent.[6] Labor unrest and opposition to government's handling of the situation resulted in an election being called in 1924 that saw the South African Party obtaining 26 seats less (i.e., 53 seats), the National Party gaining 18 (i.e., 63 seats), the Labour Party 18 seats, and one Independent member.[7] This afforded the National Party the opportunity to form a government and to introduce its first policy proposals, resulting in the entrenchment of the "color bar." The latter provided, as the term indicates, different methods and mechanisms to deal with labor issues based on color or race.

A chronological review of party political development is omitted due to political fluidity in affiliations at the early stages of political developments. However, some highlights are provided to track the development of South African politics until 1994. Thus a significant event could be identified which saw Generals J. C. Smuts and J. B. M. Hertzog entering the political arena in 1933. The election witnessed the amalgamation of two major parties winning 144 seats (South African Party 61 and National Party 75 respectively with eight other supporters) with an opposition complement of only six.[8] Toward the end of the year the merging led to the establishment of the United South African National Party, popularly known as the United Party. Dissatisfied members of the United Party later formed the purified National Party with 19 supporters.

The government elected in 1933 passed a number of acts, such as the Black Representation Act (1936) which removed black people from the common voters roll (in one province blacks could vote for members of Parliament). The Black Trust and Land Act (1936) is worth mentioning as it provided for the purchase of 6.3 million hectares of land from black indigenous people, thus laying the geographical foundation for the apartheid policy introduced in 1948.

**The Second World War era.** The Second World War in 1939 created a unique situation in South Africa. It again brought to the fore South Africans favoring the support of Great Britain against those proposing a nonalignment. This division brought a clash in cabinet between the two groups in the United Party cabinet. Six members who supported Hertzog chose neutrality at the cabinet meeting of September 4, 1939. Smuts's seven supporters chose participation in the war and support of Britain. Even in Parliament, of the 147 members present, 80 supported the Smuts groups and 67 supported Hertzog's proposed neutrality. Prime Minister Hertzog tendered his resignation. The governor-general as head of state refused to dissolve Parliament and requested Smuts to form a new cabinet.[9]

During the war election of 1943 Smuts won an easy victory. After the Second World War the first election was called in 1948. At this election the National Party obtained a slight majority of 70 seats against the United Party's 65 with the Afrikaner Party 9 and the Labour Party 6.[10] The National Party's role remained unchallenged for the next forty-eight years with a steady increase in its majority in Parliament for decades. Simultaneously the United Party steadily lost ground and since the death of Smuts failed to attract prominent leaders. It continued to lose support and ultimately saw new parties developing to take over its niche.

Since 1949 the National Party introduced various measures to give effect to its election manifesto. This included *inter alia* the Group Areas Act (1949), which provided for segregated residential areas for whites, coloreds, Indians, and blacks. The Separate Representation of Voters Act (1951) effectively prevented people of one racial origin from participating in the political activities of another group.

After 1948 various other political parties developed. For instance, in 1953 the Union Federal Party emerged with the redistribution of government powers as its main objective. The Liberal Party promoted a common voters roll for all South Africans. However, neither made an impact and the latter had to disband following the Prohibition of Political Interference Act (1968), which actually prevented the promotion of a common voters roll. Disgruntled members of the United Party established the Progressive Party in 1958. Although it played a major role in the realignment of political allegiance it only won one seat—that of Ms. Helen Suzman—in the 1961, 1966, and 1970 elections.

**Republican period.** In 1960 a referendum was called and the Republic of South Africa was established on May 31, 1961, through the Constitution of the Republic of South Africa Act, 1961 (Act 32 of 1961). Ties with Great Britain were finally severed, a state president was elected, and South Africa left the British Commonwealth. The new Constitution and the majority of 126 seats against the official opposition's 39 seats opened the road for the National Party to give full effect to its apartheid policy.[11] Its support in Parliament remained unchallenged until a serious rift developed in the party in 1969 with the invitation of a multiracial sports team to South Africa. Twelve members were expelled from the National Party and eventually formed the Herstigte Nasionale Party (Reconstituted National Party). However, in the first election following this event and for that matter in all the following elections (except 1985), they failed to win a single seat in Parliament.

The National Party's apartheid policy succeeded in attracting more and more supporters and its prominent place in white politics remained until 1979. At this stage one of its senior members (Dr. C. P. Mulder) resigned and established the National Conservative Party.[12] The latter party never succeeded in making serious inroads into the National Party's power base. It appears as though the white electorate preferred the clear policy guidelines provided by the National Party.

**The period 1980–1994.** The 1980's were characterized by a number of changes in white political alliances, resignations from parties, and an increase in the support of some parties. In 1981 it was decided to introduce a new Constitution that would make provision for colored and Indian communities to join the white electorate in electing members to sit in a Parliament consisting of three chambers—one for each group. However, the black population was still excluded from this arrangement. The elections to decide on the proposed constitution saw the National Party winning 131 seats, the Progressive Federal Party 26, and the New Republic Party (an offshoot of the disbanded United Party) 8 seats.

During 1982 another prominent member of the National Party resigned and established a new rightist party, the Conservative Party,[13] with sixteen members either having been expelled from the National Party or having resigned. With a further member resigning from the National Party, the Conservative Party with seventeen members formed a formidable rightist party promoting separate development and vehemently opposing the proposed tricameral parliament.

The Progressive Federal Party (PFP), as one of the newer entrants into the party political scene, challenged the Prohibition of Political Interference Act (1968), and decided to admit any member irrespective of his or her racial classification. When this act was abolished in 1985, the PFP had a clear road ahead, but did not succeed in attracting a significant number of members from other population groups. This may have been due to the fact that such members would still have been required to exercise their political rights in one of the chambers of Parliament created for them through the Constitution of the Republic of South Africa Act, 1983 (Act 110 of 1983). In 1986 the first real multiracial political party—the United Christian Conciliation Party (UCCP)—was established. However, as black people could still not exercise a vote in Parliament, the UCCP did not make a significant contribution to the party political scene in South Africa.

The first general elections after the 1983 Constitution that admitted coloreds and Indians to the legislature at the central level of government took place in 1986. However, it should be pointed out that this election provided for whites to elect whites for the House of Assembly only. (Coloreds voted for colored members in the House of Representatives and Indians for members in the House of Delegates). During this election the Progressive Federal Party proposed a political alliance with the New Republic Party. However, this did not come to fruition and thus no serious threat developed for the National Party's dominance in white politics. The right-wing parties (Conservative Party and Herstigte Nasionale Party) also endeavored to unite for the election campaign, but failed to reach consensus. During this period the Afrikaner Weerstandsbeweging (Afrikaner Resistance Movement) under a charismatic leader, Eugene Terreblanche, was formed, but never became a political party and is therefore not discussed. It is worth mentioning as it united the far right or ultraconservative whites under the banner of "Afrikaner."

The elections of 1986 saw the National Party obtaining 123 seats, the Conservative Party 22, the Progressive Federal Party 19, the New Republic Party one, and one independent. This naturally made the Conservative Party the official opposition. The results seem to indicate that the political scene was dominated by the rightist National Party and the far rightist Conservative Party. The more left-wing orientated Progressive Federal Party achieved no significant success with the elections. The last elections before the major change to full democracy actually witnessed the National Party amassing 52.9% of the votes, the Conservative Party 26.62%, the Progressive Federal Party 14.03%, the Herstigte Nasionale Party only 1.97%, and three Independent candidates 1.32%.[14]

The events following the 1986 elections witnessed a new movement in white politics. Some of the older parties faded from the public view with the New Republic Party's disbanding in 1988. The Progressive Federal Party suffered a series of defections and saw some of its members joining the National Democratic Movement[15] with the latter attracting three members. Thus in 1988 and therefore prior to the 1994 elections the strength of the parties was as follows: National Party 132, Conservative Party 23, Progressive Federal Party 17, New Republic Party 1, independent members 2, and the National Democratic Movement 3.[16]

The chapter on white political dominance came to an end with the National Party still in the majority. Although a number of efforts were made since 1948 to establish strong opposition groups, the electorate remained firmly behind the leadership of the National Party. Although the Conservative Party vociferously promoted a stricter form of segregation, it did not attract a large number of new members. This may partly be due to lack of a strong leader, but may also be as a result of a realization amongst the electorate that the policy of separate development was socially, economically, politically, and especially morally unacceptable.

This rather lengthy explanation is necessary to fully understand the party political scenario before the 1994 election. In the following paragraphs reference is made to party political development amongst the colored, Indian, and black population groups. Thereafter the events following the 1994 elections will be discussed in more detail.

## Colored Political Development

Coloreds as defined in the Population Registration Act, 1950 (Act 30 of 1950) did not succeed in developing strong political parties partly due to the restrictions on free elections for legislative institutions before 1983. The lack of political development could also be ascribed to the fact that the colored population as defined, in actual fact consisted of a variety of nonaligned groups of people (e.g., of mixed origin as well as Malay, San, Khoi, and Nama). It was only during the middle of the twentieth century that significant party political developments could be identified.

In 1968 the Labour Party was established and acted as the main contender for the tricameral parliamentary elections of 1983. The voting percentage of coloreds for this election was relatively low. The average was 68.2% with some areas only obtaining 25.2% of the electorate's votes. The main reason for this apparent lack of interest could be found in the fact that most of the coloreds opposed the tricameral system's racially based elections.

Of the colored political parties that participated in the 1983 elections the Labour Party obtained 74% of the votes and 76 of the 80 seats in the House of Representatives (chamber of Parliament reserved for the coloreds). The Progressive Coloured Party (PCP) succeeded in having only one member elected, while the Freedom Party failed to win a single seat. Two independent candidates, however, obtained seats. After a Supreme Court case, another Labour Party member was declared duly elected. In 1985 a Democratic Workers Party was formed as a breakaway from the PCP, but did not make any significant contributions to political developments.

As serious party political organization only commenced prior to the 1983 elections, the political allegiance was rather unstable. Members moved between parties and leaders struggled to establish clear power bases. Toward the end of the term of office of members of the House of Representatives, the representation of political parties were as follows: Labour Party 73, United Democratic Party 8, Freedom Party 1, and 1 independent member.[17]

It could be stated that the different so-called colored communities comprising "colored" as legally defined lacked a history of political participation. Therefore, their first encounter with party politics at the national level of government resulted in a rather fluid situation. Acrimonious allegations were made between political parties and thwarted efforts to achieve real success. This chapter in the history of South Africa's constitutional development could not be viewed as an attempt at restructuring the apartheid policy. It also did not allow people with political aspirations to be exposed to experienced leaders of other political denominations to gain experience in party political discourse.

*Indian Political Structures*

In 1884 Mahatma Gandhi established the first political movement amongst the Indian community in South Africa. This movement was called the Natal Indian Congress (Natal was one of the four areas that became provinces of the former Union of South Africa in 1910). It was later expanded to cover the rest of South Africa with the exception of one province that prohibited Indians from residing there. In 1920 the movement became known as the South African Indian Congress.

The South African Indian Congress (SAIC) remained a rather moderate organization until 1946 when it became more militant (in the context of the former South African political spectrum). In 1949 it formed an alliance with the African National Congress (ANC), to which reference will be made in the next section. As with the ANC the SAIC's efforts to achieve its political goals were countered by the former government's restriction on political organizations of population groups other than whites.

The adoption of the Constitution of the Republic of South Africa Act, 1983, for the first time allowed the Indian community to participate in the political activities of the central government. However, as in the case of the colored community it was not an acceptable way of giving effect to their political aspirations. Thus they did not participate fully in the elections that preceded the establishment of the House of Delegates as the chamber of Parliament responsible for Indian affairs. An average of only 20.29% of the Indian electorate turned out to vote, while in some areas it was a low as 6.9%.[19]

The main parties that obtained seats in the House of Delegates were the National People's Party (NPP) with 18 seats, the Solidarity Party with 17, the Progressive Independent Party succeeded in electing 1 representative while 4 members obtained seats as independents. The impasse between the NPP and Solidarity was resolved when two of the independents joined the NPP. Further developments during 1983 resulted in the NPP having 23 members against Solidarity's 21 with one independent member.

The period following the 1983 elections, experienced a variety of upheavals in party alliances, Supreme Court cases, allegations of misconduct, and internal dissent in parties. A new party, the Progressive Reform Party, was established in 1988, but disbanded to allow its members to join the Progressive Federal Party in the House of Assembly (the chamber dealing with the affairs of whites). A breakaway group formed the People's Party, only to disband and join the Solidarity Party.

At the end of 1988 the parties were represented as follows in the House of Delegates: National People's Party 16, Solidarity 11, People's Party 11, Independents 4, Progressive Federal Party 2, and Progressive Independent Party 1.[20]

It may be concluded that the fluidity in the Indian political scene could largely be ascribed to inexperience in party politics. A second reason could be found in different cultures in the Indian community dominated by religion, with Hinduism and Islam being the main divisive factor. During the period 1983 to 1993 (i.e., prior to the democratic elections of 1994), the Indian House of Delegates was hampered in its efforts to promote the political developments of Indians due to irreconcilable differences amongst the main political parties in the legislature.

## Black Political Developments

A starting point for a discussion of political aspirations in a contemporary sense could be traced back to the Black Representation Act (1936). This act removed black voters from the common voters roll in one of the four provinces (Cape of Good Hope) where they enjoyed full political rights. They were, however, entitled to elect only three white representatives to represent them in the House of Assembly (i.e., the directly elected chamber of Parliament). The partly elected Black Representative Council did not possess real powers and, therefore, failed to act in substantial issues on behalf of the black population.

A significant development in black political life was the establishment in 1912 of the South African Native National Congress, subsequently renamed to the African National Congress.[21] However, it should be noted that earlier efforts to elicit political support amongst blacks were undertaken, but had no perceivable effect.

During the 1950's the ruling National Party's apartheid policies estranged the black population to such an extent that the ANC and other politically motivated groups entered an era of political defiance. This resulted in various confrontations with government, forcing the black conscious and political movements underground. The ANC and a break-away group—the Pan Africanist Congress (PAC) engaged in different strategies to try and force the National Party government to change its policies. Some of these activities included lobbying to assure that South Africa is isolated in the economic, social, and political spheres.

In the so-called Bantustans (geographical areas established for different black ethnic groups) various political parties participated in the elections that were held to elect members of the different legislatures. In KwaZulu, for example, the Inkatha Party dominated the political scene. In the other areas the political parties were under severe threat of falling into disfavor with the South African government if they dared to openly criticize the government. Most of them consequently paid lip service to real political issues.

A concerted effort was launched toward the end of the 1960's to oppose any political initiatives of the former government. The latter responded by banning a number of organizations and jailing its leaders. (The latter included Mr. Nelson Mandela). It was only after the unbanning of the different political groups (e.g., ANC, PAC, and South African Communist Party) on February 2, 1990 and the release of its members that black communities could openly commence organizing to promote their political aspirations.

The unbanning of the political leaders brought to an end a policy of segregating the different population groups. It provided for the first time in the history of South Africa an opportunity for black leaders to openly engage in political activities and to recruit members across the board, throughout the country. Even political groups who had been limited to political participation in only one of the ten Bantustan areas could now become involved in party politics at the national level of government. Thus 1990 saw the end of centuries of political isolation for black communities and allowed them to campaign for political transformation and a nonracial legislature and executive institutions.

## A NEW POLITICAL ORDER

### Run-up to Change

On February 2, 1990 the State President of the Republic of South Africa under the 1983 Constitution announced in Parliament[22] during his opening speech that the following organizations were unbanned with immediate effect:

- African National Congress
- Pan Africanist Congress
- South African Communist Party
- Other restricted organizations including
  - Congress of South African Trade Unions (COSATU)
  - National Education Crisis Committee
  - South African National Students' Congress
  - White Liberation Movement of South Africa (Blanke Bevrydings-beweging van Suid-Afrika)

Furthermore, 374 persons jailed in accordance with the security emergency regulations were to be released. The latter implied that one of the ANC's most prominent leaders, Mr. Nelson Mandela, who had been imprisoned on Robben Island for twenty-seven years was to be released. His release as well as the release of other prominent leaders signalled a new era in South African politics. For the first time the scene was set for free political participation in parliamentary and governmental affairs on a nonracial basis.

As could probably be expected, the new policy options generated considerable interest. These political parties had to reconsider their terms of reference and manifestoes. Existing political parties, especially in the white community, had to decide whether to support or oppose this new political development.

From the existing political parties the National Party (NP) and Progressive Federal Party (PFP) as well as the Democratic Party (DP) decided to contest the elections scheduled for April 26–27 (later also 28), 1994. The Conservative Party (CP) decided not to participate in an effort to express their strongest possible opposition to the proposed nonracial elections. However, a new movement, the Freedom Front, under a former general from the South African National Defence Force (Gen. Constand Viljoen) decided to fill the hiatus on the right wing of the political spectrum by fielding candidates for the forthcoming general elections. Most of these parties still obtained the majority of their members from the white electorate.

The Inkatha Freedom Party, consisting mainly of members of the Zulu ethnic group, had its power base in one area (later known as KwaZulu/Natal). Although they represented the numerically dominant population group, their members consisted mainly of Zulu voters with a limited number of whites or other black ethnic and other individuals joining the party.

The African National Congress (ANC), since its unbanning in 1990, and with the support of foreign countries, played a major role in the run-up to the general elections of 1994. It was undoubtedly the most vociferous proponent of nonracialism and succeeded in obtaining the support of various black ethnic and other groups such as the Xhosa, Tswana, Sotho, Indian, colored, and various white members who opposed the former government's apartheid policies. The ANC could be considered as the major political party contesting the 1994 elections on a multiracial basis.

*First Democratic Elections*

The first fully democratic elections in the history of South Africa provided for proportional representation based on the party list system in accordance with the interim Constitution of the Republic of South Africa Act, 1993 (Act 200 of 1993).[23] This created a new political dispensation as all previous elections were conducted on a constituency basis on the principle of first-past-the-post, where the majority party commands sole power in government.

Before discussing the roles of the different political parties in the 1994 elections, one important issue that had a marked effect on the development of some parties has to be mentioned. This issue concerns the decision agreed to by the negotiating parties before the election that each party should be entitled to a fixed contribution by the state to enable it to muster support, establish organizational structures, and engage in election campaigns. This resulted in some opportunistic parties being formed without any proven support base. The results of the 1994 elections bear this out, through the fact that the ANC, the National Party, and the Inkatha Freedom Party (IFP) obtained 93.58% of the total number of votes (ANC 62.2%, National Party 22.4%, and IFP 8.3% of the total of 11,859,067 votes),[24] giving them access to 377 of the 400 seats in Parliament.

The Freedom Front, representing the rightist wing in the elections, obtained 2.8% of the vote with nine seats, the Democratic Party obtained 1.7% of the vote leaving them with seven seats, and the Pan Africanist Congress with its 1.3% was entitled to five seats. The party with the smallest representation in Parliament was the African Christian Democratic Party, which had the support of 0.45% of the electorate and thus two representatives in Parliament.[25] The following parties could not succeed in obtaining sufficient support to entitle them to any representatives:[26]

| | |
|---|---|
| African Muslim Party | 0.14% |
| African Moderates Congress Party | 0.14% |
| Dikwankwetla Party | 0.10% |

| | |
|---|---|
| Federal Party | 0.09% |
| Minority Front | 0.07% |
| SOCCER Party and the African Democratic Movement each | 0.05% |
| Women's Rights Peace Party and the Ximoko Progressive Party as well as the Keep it Straight and Simple Party each obtained | 0.03% |
| The Workers List Party and the Luso South African Party each obtained | 0.02% |

Most of the last-mentioned parties, without any support base in Parliament, disappeared from the political scene after the general elections. In limited cases some provincially constituted parties played a minor role in one of the nine provinces of South Africa, for example, the Minority Front in the province of KwaZulu/Natal.

*Composition of Government*

The interim Constitution of the Republic of South Africa Act, 1993 (Act 200 of 1993), provided for a Government of National Unity through

- The section 84(2) requirement that executive presidents be included from other political parties than the majority party
- Section 88(1), as amended by section 2 of the Republic of South Africa Constitution Amendment Act, 1994 (Act 13 of 1994), requiring that ministers be included in cabinet from the parties who have obtained at least twenty seats in the National Assembly (i.e., the directly elected chamber of Parliament).

These provisions allowed President Nelson Mandela as leader of the majority ANC party to appoint former President F. W. de Klerk as one deputy president and Mr. Thabo Mbeki from the ANC as his second deputy president. The cabinet thus consisted of 27 members, 21 from the ANC, 5 from the National Party, and the leader of the Inkatha Freedom Party, Mr. Mangusuthu Buthelezi.

The provisions for a Government of National Unity were not included in the final Constitution of the Republic of South Africa Act, 1996 (Act 108 of 1996). The comparable provisions simply authorizes the president to appoint ministers in his cabinet from amongst the members of the National Assembly. However, he may also appoint not more than two ministers from outside the National Assembly.[27]

The difference between the interim Constitution of 1993 and the final Constitution of 1996 regarding the composition of cabinet may partly be due to the withdrawal of the National Party from the Government of National Unity in 1996. The present provisions, however, still enabled the president to appoint Mr. Mangusuthu Buthelezi, leader of the Inkhata Freedom Party, as a minister.

## Party Political Allegiance

The system of proportional representation was introduced by section 40(1) of the interim Constitution of 1993. Section 46 of the final Constitution of 1996 expands the provisions regarding the electoral system. This latter section merely requires that members of the legislature are elected in terms of an electoral system that generally results *inter alia* in proportional representation.

An important provision included in the 1993 Constitution is section 43(b), which requires a member of the National Assembly to vacate his/her seat *inter alia* if he/she ceases to be a member of the party that nominated him/her as a member. The final Constitution of 1996 does not contain a comparable provision. Section 47(3) merely determines that a person loses membership of the National Assembly if such a person ceases to be eligible. However, in practical terms, members who are expelled from a party or resign, forfeit their seats (e.g., Mr. Clarence Makwethu, PAC; Mr. Bantu Holomisa, ANC; and Mr. Roelf Meyer, National Party).

The strong party allegiance resulting from the system of proportional representation has had the effect that little change occurred in the composition of the House of Assembly in the period April 1994 to June 1997. A number of significant changes have taken place since 1997 that had a marked effect on the image of some of the political parties represented in Parliament. This is discussed in the following section.

It should be pointed out that the electoral system of proportional representation seems to have had a major impact on the performance of representatives in Parliament. Numerous cases have been quoted of parliamentary committees and even sessions of the National Assembly that had to be cancelled due to the lack of a quorum to discuss issues. The consensus amongst political analysts is that the lack of constituents to call members to account for their performance or attendance of meetings may be the reason for their absence.

The system of proportional representation seems to strengthen party political allegiance at the center, but has a negative impact in the regions. A reason often quoted for the lack of interest in members' activities in Parliament is that the party leadership usually decides on the replacement of members if vacancies occur. This implies that regional offices have a limited say in who will be a member in Parliament. The usual arrangements of whips checking attendance also seem to fail in ensuring regular attendance. The nonattendance of members is highlighted, and branches in the regions become disillusioned, resulting in the breakdown of party structures.

*Party Political Developments after 1994*

The general elections of April 1994 introduced many South Africans for the first time to the real world of politics and especially party politics. The latter's codes of conduct imply that members should be loyal to the party, act in accordance with decisions taken at national conventions, and conduct themselves in such a manner that the party is in no way disgraced. It seems as though members of the emerging political parties, who only started operating as such in the run-up to the elections, sometimes viewed themselves in the same manner as liberation movements. Thus members sometimes failed to realize that political parties participating in government or in debates in Parliament have to adhere to strict party discipline and honor the party leadership's rulings.

As the current political dispensation is relatively new and no by-elections have been held, it is difficult to establish political party support. However, some prominent members of some major political parties have been expelled or have resigned. This partly indicates some dissent within party ranks. Although no extensive description is provided of all cases in this regard, some examples are quoted to illustrate the effects of changing policy perspectives within parties or divergent views on strategies to promote a particular party's goals.

**Developments in the ANC.** Constituting his cabinet, the president—Mr. Nelson Mandela—appointed amongst others Mrs. Winnie Mandela in accordance with section 94(2) of the interim Constitution of 1993 as a deputy minister representing the ANC. Mr. Bantu Holomisa, formerly a military ruler (after a coup d'état) of one of the former Bantustans, was also appointed as an ANC member under the same provisions as a deputy minister. Within a year after her appointment Mrs. Mandela fell into disfavor and was relieved of her duties as deputy minister. Although she struggled to retain her position, the decision was final and she relinquished her post. She is still a member of the ANC and active in the ANC's Women's League and other substructures, but is apparently not active in the ANC in general. This may also be attributed to the fact that the president instituted divorce proceedings against her that were finalized in 1996.

The next member to come under scrutiny was Mr. Bantu Holomisa. He was ultimately summoned before a disciplinary committee of the

ANC and suspended. He was also relieved of his duties. As he refused to leave the party, the process to expel him from the ANC was a long drawn-out process. He reluctantly conceded that the party's decision was final and that no recourse was available. After his expulsion he formed the National Consultative Forum and said that he would establish a new political party to contest the next general elections scheduled for 1999. From newspaper and other reports he seems to have a following in his former constituency of Transkei. Initially, no significant support could be identified in the rest of South Africa. Since 1997 its support has increased substantially.

A third government member to fall into disfavor with the ruling ANC was the premier of the Free State (one of South Africa's nine provinces). Steps were instituted by the ANC leadership to oust Mr. Patrick Lekota as premier. However, the ANC's regional branch immediately took steps to elect Mr. Lekota as the ANC's provincial leader. This could lead to an uncompromising situation as the premiership and the leadership of the party would not reside in a single person. To some extent the discontent of the provincial branch was alleviated by appointing Mr. Lekota as chairman of the Council of Provinces[28] (which replaced the Senate as the second chamber of Parliament). It remains to be seen what the effect of this move will be on the ANC's support at the next general elections in 1999.

**Developments in the PAC.** The Pan Africanist Congress participated in the 1994 general elections under the banner of a fully nonracial state and the continuation of the "struggle" until full liberation has been achieved. Its leader Mr. Clarence Makwethu's performance was apparently not acceptable to the party. Various allegations were made with Mr. Makwethu on the defense. Ultimately a national convention was convened and a vote by a majority of the members removed Mr. Makwethu as leader. Bishop Stanley Magoba was elected, but the followers of Mr. Makwethu held the view that the convention was not duly convened and challenged the decision. In some quarters Mr. Makwetu was still accepted as leader and he retained his seat in the National Assembly for months. Ultimately he was forced to vacate his office in May 1997.

Mr. Makwethu's reluctance to accept the decision of the party clearly illustrates the uncertainty of some members as to the status of the leadership as expressed at national conventions. It also indicates the absence of clear guidelines in some political parties regarding decisions and the requirement to abide by the decision of duly constituted bodies.

**Developments in the NP.** The National Party under the leadership of Mr. F. W. de Klerk, the former state president and deputy president under President Mandela, paved the way for full democratic elections in 1994. As part of the Government of National Unity since 1994 the party succeeded in retaining the support of the greater part of its traditional followers. The withdrawal of the National Party from the Government of National Unity immediately raised the question as to its future and its niche in the South African political scene. Of particular importance was whether the composition of the party would be able to reflect its ambition to be considered as a nonracial political party, free of its apartheid baggage of the past.

During 1996 a committee was appointed under Mr. Roelf Meyer, provincial leader of Gauteng (one of the provinces) and one of the party's most prominent members, to investigate ways and means to change the image of the party, propose guidelines to ensure its future and methods to attract members from all racial groups.

During May 1997 Mr. Meyer submitted his committee's proposals to the party's leadership. One of the proposals was that the National Party should be dissolved and that a new movement should be established. The proposed movement would then create the opportunity to involve new members and change the cultural image of the members. The movement could ultimately develop into a nonracial political party that could participate in the next general elections with a clean slate. The proposals were not, however, acceptable to Mr. de Klerk as leader and he disbanded Mr. Meyer's committee.[29]

During a meeting of the head council (hoofberaad) of the National Party on May 17, 1997,[30] Mr. Meyer tendered his resignation from the National Party. He immediately commenced with intensive negotiations to establish a support base for his proposed movement and established the New Movement (Proses vir 'n Nuwe Beweging). Various youth groups of the National Party resigned and joined the ranks of Mr. Meyer's movement. At the time of the writing only a limited number of senior members of the National Party have expressed support for Mr. Meyer openly and it seems that discontent is either limited or that members have adopted a wait-and-see attitude.

On June 7, 1997, Mr. Meyer as leader of the New Movement Process met Mr. Bantu Holomisa, an ousted member of the ANC and leader of the National Consultative Movement, with a view to possible cooperation. The political situation is presently very fluid but a new party has been established, namely the United Democratic Movement. However, it should be pointed out that the ANC has a clear policy framework with a relatively well-established organizational infrastructure. As such, the party is well positioned in South African politics. On the opposition side, the National Party is a well-experienced party albeit with some uncertainty as to its role, but with a clear mandate from its supporters and an identifiable niche in the political spectrum. Meyer and Holomisa's United Democratic Movement could position themselves between the ANC's and the National Party's policies. Especially if it is considered that this part of the spectrum is already occupied by, for example, the Progressive Federal Party or the Inkhata Freedom Party, it is clear that the Meyer/Holomisa party faces a daunting task in finding justification for its policy proposals.

*Party Political Support*

As has already been argued, it is rather risky to venture a guess as to party support at this stage. Without a wide spectrum of by-elections or related clear performance indicators, the only possible indicator is to be found in surveys. Reference is therefore made to two surveys conducted recently that could give some indication of the position of some prominent parties relative to their performance in the 1994 election (see table 10.1).

It is obvious that the ANC succeeds in maintaining its majority. In spite of discontent in the regional branches of the party, it still enjoys the support of its members and faces no serious threat from other parties at this stage. The National Party, the official opposition in Parliament, is apparently losing support steadily. The second survey was also conducted before the full effects of Mr. Meyer's resignation from the National Party had become effective. It could be expected that the NP may even lose more supporters if it does not succeed in attracting new members. The latter appears to be unlikely as it will have to attract black members, but its baggage from the past makes this highly unlikely. Simultaneously the surveys suggest that the Freedom Front as a rightist party seems set on at least retaining its support. Thus the NP does not appear to succeed in attract-

TABLE 10.1
Party Political Support in South Africa (%)

|  | *1994 Elections* | *Survey (1)* | *Survey (2)* |
|---|---|---|---|
| ANC | 62.6 | 62 | 61.1 |
| NP | 20.4 | 13.4 | 15 |
| Inkatha | 10.5 | 5.6 | 4 |
| Freedom Front | 2.2 | 2.1 | 2 |
| Democratic Party | 1.7 | 2.2 | 3 |
| PAC | 1.2 | 1.6 | 1 |

Sources: 1994 elections: SAPA, May 3, 1994; Survey 1: H. Kotze, *Culture, Ethnicity and Religion: South African Perceptions of Social Identity* (Johannesburg: The Stiftung, 1997); Survey 2: Markinor Survey as published in *Beeld*, June 4, 1997.

ing members from the right side of the political spectrum.

The Inkatha Party also appears to be losing support. This seems to be due to the lack of an efficient party political structure. Furthermore, the party relied heavily on the loyalty of the Zulu ethnic group for support. As a significant rift has developed between the Zulu monarch (King Goodwill Zweletini) as traditional leader and Mr. Buthelezi as political leader, Zulus seem to be divided as to who to support, thus resulting in a decrease in support of the political party.

A particular feature of the two surveys mentioned above is that surveys (1) and (2) indicate that 5% and 10% respectively of the respondents either don't know what party to support or support no party at all. This situation also seems to indicate that dissatisfied voters are seriously considering their position. This could have serious consequences for parties who are ill-prepared for the 1999 elections.

CONCLUDING REMARKS

South African party politics have to be evaluated within the context of the racially based policies that have been in operation for more than three centuries. The reign of the National Party from 1948 to 1994 has entrenched racial differences, deprived the majority of the South African people of the right to participate fully in party political activities, and has resulted in artificial political, economic, and social developments. Geographical isolation also contributed to the artificial development of parties that had to adopt policies within the National Party's framework or forfeit financial support for their Bantustans.

The democratic elections of April 1994 exposed more than 19 million voters to elections. It also introduced all South Africans to a totally new electoral system, that is, proportional representation. No previous experience could be relied on to establish the effects of this system on the electorate. Thus it is difficult to predict its effect on political parties. It appears at this stage as if supporters often find it difficult to establish whether they voted for a particular member and what the authority of the party leadership is. In this regard it also appears as though members far removed from the leadership become lackadaisical. This attitude renders the branch structures ineffective and therefore they do not succeed in calling errant members to account for failing in their duties.

The fully democratic system in South Africa is presently at the start of a new political era. It may be that only after the next general election, the first following the transformation introduced through the 1994 election will it be possible to establish whether the party political structures will survive the present turmoil.

## NOTES

1. A racial division is used based on the Population Registration Act (1950) to indicate the basis on which the South African society operated up to the fully democratic elections of April 26–28, 1994. The classification is not to be viewed in a derogatory sense.

2. *South Africa Year Book 1988/89* (Pretoria: Department of Information, 1989), p. 30.

3. Ibid., p. 31.

4. Ibid., p. 32.

5. Ibid., p. 33.

6. Ibid.

7. Ibid.

8. Ibid., p. 34.

9. Ibid., p. 35.

10. Ibid., p. 37.

11. Ibid., p. 40.

12. Ibid., p. 154.

13. Ibid., p. 155.

14. Ibid., p. 159.

15. Ibid., p. 160.

16. Ibid., p. 161.

17. Ibid., p. 166.

18. Ibid.

19. Ibid., p. 168.

20. Ibid., p. 169.

21. *South Africa Year Book 1996* (Pretoria: South African Information Services, 1996), p. 32.

22. Opening speech of State President F. W. de Klerk at the opening of the second session of the Ninth Parliament of the Republic of South Africa, February 2, 1990.

23. The nine provinces created by the Constitution also held their provincial elections simultaneously. However, these will not be discussed in this chapter.

24. *Africa Research Bulletin*, 1994, p. 11387.

25. Ibid.

26. SAPA, May 3, 1994.

27. Constitution of the Republic of South Africa, 1996, sections 91(3)(b) and (c).

28. Section 60 of the Constitution of the Republic of South Africa Act, 1996.

29. Newspaper reports in the *Sunday Times, Rapport, Beeld, Pretoria News, Sowetan.*

30. *Rapport*, May 19, 1997, p. 1.

# CHAPTER 11

# Russia:
## Party Formation and the
## Legacy of the One-Party State

## Edwin Bacon

The party system developing in Russia in the 1990s is built on the foundations left after the collapse of the old order of the Soviet Union. In the case of Russia, therefore, we are not dealing with a long-standing party system in crisis, but rather a post-authoritarian, even post-totalitarian, attempt to create a party system. At a time when political parties seem to be in decline, or at least in flux, the world over, Russia is ostensibly attempting to develop a polity based on the normative idea of a traditional party system. Some of the problems facing Russia in this attempt at party formation are situation-specific in that they are either difficulties peculiar to Russia as a great power in crisis, or they are difficulties common to postcommunist countries, but not encountered elsewhere in the world. Others have more in common with the difficulties facing established party systems elsewhere.

This chapter considers the interplay between the old order and the new in three areas central to our consideration of political parties in the 1990s. First, the institutional factors surrounding party formation in Russia. How have institutional arrangements—some designed to promote multiparty democracy, others surviving to varying degrees from the old order—affected the role of parties? Second, the "national idea." Russia, as a state, rejected the national idea of Soviet communism in 1991. This abrupt ideological vacuum has been filled by a combination of nationalism and regionalism that has blurred the ideological distinctives of the major parties and hindered their establishment as national organizations. Third, in conclusion to the discussion, the policy impact of political parties is assessed.

## INSTITUTIONAL FACTORS

*Institutional Collapse, 1989–1993*

The collapse of the old Soviet order in Russia in 1991 meant the presumption by the post-Soviet leadership that "parties" would take the place of "Party" in providing a link between the people and the national government. On one level this of course was no great jump for either government or people. The Leninist concept of party had held sway in the Soviet Union for some seventy-four years, with its distinctives being that a Party of activist members served as the guiding force of the masses. The concept of elections was not alien, although the idea of multiple candidates let alone multiple parties was a recent Gorbachevian construct. Throughout the Soviet period the people regularly and comprehensively turned out at the polls and cast their ballot in favor of the Party-approved candidate, who would form part of the chain of links that eventually reached Moscow.

In short, therefore, attempts in the post-Soviet period to introduce multiparty democracy have not been made on virgin democratic land. The shadow of things to come had long been in place in the form of electoral processes and the rhetoric of representation. The Brezhnev Constitution of 1977 had expressed as fact the aim of "catch-all" parties the world over, stating that "the Communist Party of the Soviet Union [CPSU] is the leading and guiding force of Soviet society and the nucleus of its political system." However, the existence of this shadow of a party system has thrown up as many problems as advantages when it has come to attempts to create the real thing.

First, the rejection of the Soviet shadow of a representative party structure meant that the very idea of party was tainted, carrying with it negative overtones of the Party, which had just been rejected. This appears to have been broadly so amongst the ruling post-Soviet elite and among the people at large. In the Soviet era, to varying degrees, support for the one party was compulsory. Party activists in the workplace or apartment block expected at least a show of support by attendance at the requisite meetings. The state required that support be expressed by voting correctly in the one-party elections. As a consequence, unlike in many other newly democratizing countries, the population of Russia can be said to have been thoroughly politicized. Such politicization, however, meant that one way of expressing dissent or disapproval of the regime was to refuse to participate in politics. The legacy of this is that the freedom *not* to participate in politics is an attractive gain of the post-Soviet era for many Russians and that there is a considerable degree of mistrust of political parties per se amongst the Russian population. The nationally representative New Russian Barometer III survey of 1994[1] found that given a list of some sixteen public institutions, political parties emerged as the least trusted bodies. This survey asked respondents to rank these institutions on a seven-point scale.[2] Political parties were given the highest distrust rating, with 82 percent marking them between 1 and 3.[3] If the flip-side of the decisive rejection of the old order was the acceptance of the new orthodoxy of Western-style multiparty democracy, then clearly the re-creation of a positive concept of party was required.

Second, a fundamental problem of postcommunist party formation facing a number of the would-be parties that attempted to invent themselves in Russia during the Soviet breakup was that power still lay with the old elite in Moscow. Two layers of power had existed in Russia in 1991, the Soviet All-Union layer and the Russian (RSFSR) layer. In practice these had been virtually the same thing for decades, and so both were dominated by CPSU members. In terms of party formation the Communist Party's role involved more than creating political space by means of its demise. Its various forms of fissure provided alternative routes to (the maintenance of) power. The CPSU itself by the end of the 1980s had strayed far from its Leninist principles of discipline and antifactionalism. Within the CPSU there existed from 1990 a Democratic Platform and a Marxist Platform, with the party structure acting as a sort of "umbrella of power," unifying groups whose only common feature was that they were members of the just-about-ruling party. These platforms were both critical of the CPSU itself, and, being the first factions to appear in the party since the 1920s, provided impetus toward elite party formation.[4] As politics in the Soviet Union began to be increasingly conducted at the national republican, rather than the All-Union, level, so the elite struggle took place in the developing structures of Russian politics. Boris Yeltsin was elected chair of the RSFSR Supreme Soviet in May 1990 and his hard-line opponents took control of the newly formed RSFSR Communist Party in June. These arenas served as fall-back positions from which the political struggle could be conducted as the All-Union party and structures collapsed. Consequently, they vitiated the need for the immediate creation of strong, disciplined parties. Yeltsin, especially after his resounding popular victory in 1991, saw himself as representing the Russian people as a whole, and therefore neither wanted to nor saw the need to create a party for himself. The Marxist platform, and their like within the RSFSR Communist Party, were engaged in a struggle *against* the introduction of multiparty democracy. In terms of the elite-level of struggle the urgency for party formation was not great.

This lack of urgency on the part of those in power continued through 1992 and much of 1993. The political buffer-zone to collapse that the RSFSR structures represented meant that a multiparty system, though lauded as the ultimate normative objective by the victorious reformers within both the legislature and the executive, did not constitute an immediate operative need. Both parliament and the president had recent popular mandates, and so, whilst transition policies concentrated on the economy rather than the polity, the electoral process so necessary to mobilize and consolidate parties failed to occur. Political debate was largely conducted within the cartel of the continuing elite and mass participation only manifested itself in the nonparty president versus parliament referendum of April 1993. Furthermore, many of the embryonic parties of the late Soviet period found themselves undergoing the common experience of postcommunist parties elsewhere. The common enemy that had temporarily united the most unlikely partners had been removed and so organizational and ideological shakedown began as new political schisms slowly became apparent.

As the nationalist "red-brown alliance" between communists and the extreme right grew in the early 1990s, within the democratic camp too there swiftly arose opposition to Yeltsin's perceived backtracking on democratic reform and also to his economic policies. Yeltsin's refusal, or inability, to build a party around the successful Democratic Russia coalition that backed his presidential bid contributed to a chaotic disintegration of broadly reformist/democratic forces. The debate over state building and the nature of a new constitution split the reformists, with the Yeltsin camp favoring a strongly presidential constitutional arrangement, whilst many of his erstwhile parliamentary allies, along with the large antireform bloc within the parliament, argued for a parliamentary system. The result was political deadlock. The extant constitution, dating from 1978, had been designed for a different political order, and had been amended over 350 times by 1993. Its authority as a fundamental law was therefore severely reduced; nonetheless it did clearly state that the parliament was the "supreme body of state power" and therefore enabled the parliament to annul presidential decrees.

In April of that year both parliament and president attempted to break the deadlock by means of a referendum. This four question referendum was a nonparty affair essentially seeking a vote of confidence in the president and his policies. The results were interpreted as a narrow vote for Yeltsin, with 58.7 percent of voters expressing their support for him (table 11.1). However, there were clear regional divides and limits to Yeltsin's support particularly in non-Russian areas and declining industrial towns, a factor that reflected the growing regionalism potentially undermining the formation of a settled national political order and of national political parties.

TABLE 11.1
Results of the April 25, 1993 Referendum in Russia

| Question | Yes (%) | No (%) |
|---|---|---|
| Do you have confidence in the President of the Russian Federation, Boris Yeltsin? | 58.7 | 39.2 |
| Do you approve of the socioeconomic policies carried out by the president and the government of the Russian Federation since 1992? | 53.0 | 44.6 |
| Do you consider it necessary to hold early elections to the presidency of the Russian Federation? | 49.5 | 47.1 |
| Do you consider it necessary to hold early elections for the people's deputies of the Russian Federation? | 67.2 | 30.1 |

The referendum failed to resolve the parliamentary-presidential impasse, and so in September 1993 Yeltsin took the strictly illegal step of declaring the parliament dissolved and calling new elections. Under the constitution he had no powers to dissolve parliament. The parliament refused to acquiesce and the dispute led to fighting on the streets of Moscow, ending with troops storming the parliament and arresting its leaders. It was against this background that the Russian Federation then embarked on its first multiparty election, the parliamentary election of December 1993.

Several features emerge, therefore, from an overview of Russian political parties between 1989 and 1993. Under the old Soviet order in Russia, the CPSU embodied the "national idea" of the USSR and mobilized the totality of its population in supposed support for this idea. The removal of the CPSU had a twofold impact in terms of party affiliation in the nascent multiparty system of the immediate post-Soviet era. First, it left a negative perception of the idea of party. Opinion polls seeking to assess the degree of trust that the populace had in public institutions gave the highest rating to the Russian Orthodox Church, a body seen as least tainted by the Soviet regime and the CPSU.[5] Second, it left no stable party alignment patterns. Under the old order everybody had voted for the CPSU. There had been no way of knowing whether a vote in a Soviet election was a genuine expression of support or a grudging nod of acquiescence given to avoid loss of privileges. Furthermore the recipient of these votes no longer existed and it was not until late 1993 that a clear "Successor party," the Communist Party of the Russian Federation (CPRF) led by Gennadii Zyuganov, began to emerge. This lack of esteem for parties in general and the lack of stable party alignment cleavages within society contributed to high levels of voter volatility and an equivalent volatility on the part of politicians when it came to party alignment.

The presidential-parliamentary conflict of 1992–93 served to hinder the growth of parties as a link between the government and the governed. It created a lack of institutional clarity and perpetuated the political divisions of the Soviet era, when both president and parliament had been elected. The lack of a timetable for general elections and a clear institutional arrangement of powers made it difficult for potential parties to organize. This weakness in the center of the state in turn encouraged the growth of regionalism, with ethnic divisions coming to the fore particularly in Russia's republics, where the more readily anti-Yeltsin stance demonstrated by the results of the April 1993 referendum could be interpreted not so much as a pro-parliament position but as an expression of the desire for greater regional autonomy.

*Institution Building, 1993–1996*

Between December 1993 and July 1996 there were three nationwide elections in the Russian Federation. On December 12, 1993, two years after the collapse of the Soviet Union, the Russian people went to the polls for their first post-Soviet election. As well as electing representatives to the upper and lower houses of parliament, they were also asked to vote in a referendum on a new constitution. If the constitution were not to be passed, then the election as a whole would be largely meaningless, as the parliamentary representatives elected would have no legally constituted parliament to attend. The parliament elected in 1993 served for only two years, being designated as a transitional parliament, after which the constitutionally designated term of a parliament would be four years. Consequently there was a second parliamentary election in December 1995.

From the point of view of party formation the foreshortened term of the first Duma arguably helped the formation of political parties and the development of a democratic political culture in Russia. In theory at least, with each set of elections, the mechanisms of multiparty democracy become more firmly established: both politicians and the electorate become more sophisticated in their understanding of the language and techniques of electioneering; the number of parties is reduced as rational party actors unite to maximize, for example, the reformist vote or the nationalist vote; and more stable party alignments develop as the leading parties provide links between different socioeconomic groups and the government. In practice, however, the number of parties contesting the elections in 1995 increased to 43 from the 13 on the ballot paper in 1993 and the volatility of the electorate remained at very high levels. For example, even the CPRF, which almost doubled its vote to 22.3 percent in 1995 compared with 12.4 percent in 1993, kept only two-thirds of its voters over the same period.[6]

There are various institutional factors that go some way to explaining the apparent failure of a stable party system to begin to consolidate after the 1993 parliamentary election in Russia. One of the primary reasons is that the third election to be held over the period 1993–96 was the presidential election of summer 1996. Under the new and heavily presidential 1993 constitution, this was the only election that could change the governing regime in Russia. The president appoints the government. He needs parliamentary approval for the appointment of a prime minister, but if the parliament rejects the presidential nominee three times then the parliament is dissolved. The president can, and does, issue decrees that have the force of law. In short the powers of the parliament in Russia today are severely limited. Consequently, the parliamentary elections of 1993 and 1995 never had the potential to change the regime. In 1993 the extreme nationalist Liberal Democratic Party of Russia (LDPR), led by Vladimir Zhirinovsky, gained almost a quarter of the popular vote on the party list section of the ballot. In 1995 a similar vote was received by the CPRF. In neither case was the successful party able to demand so much as a seat in the government.

The relative lack of importance of the parliamentary elections in comparison with the presidential contest served as a brake on the process of party consolidation in Russia. To any politician hoping to implement his policies in Russia, the presidency is the only prize ultimately worth seeking. The parliamentary elections of 1995, falling as they did six months before the presidential elections, served as much as a presidential primary as to elect a parliament, with the function of a party more often than not being to provide a platform for a presidential bid, rather than to provide a link between the electorate and the government.[7] In the presidential campaign itself the widespread denial of party was evident. The incumbent, Boris Yeltsin, remained resolutely "above party," refusing to tie himself to a potentially restricting organized mass body with an ideological commitment that might undermine his evident populism. His opponent in the second-round runoff—Gennadii Zyuganov, leader of Russia's largest and most popular party the CPRF—also ran as the candidate of a bloc of national patriotic forces, rather than solely on a party ticket. Although the CPRF had won the 1995 parliamentary elections with 23.5 percent on the party list ballot—double the votes of its nearest rival, the LDPR—under a quarter of the national vote would not be sufficient to win a majoritarian presidential

TABLE 11.2
Parties Passing the Five Percent Threshold in the Party-List Section
of Elections to Russia's State Duma, 1993 and 1995

| Party/Bloc | % of vote 1993 | % of vote 1995 |
|---|---|---|
| Agrarian Party | 8.0 | 3.8 |
| Communist Party of the Russian Federation | 12.4 | 22.3 |
| Democratic Party of Russia | 5.5 | — |
| Liberal Democratic Party of Russia | 22.9 | 11.2 |
| Party of Russian Unity and Accord | 6.8 | 0.4 |
| Russia's Choice | 15.5 | 3.9 |
| Russia Is Our Home | — | 10.1 |
| "Yabloko" | 7.9 | 6.9 |
| Women Of Russia | 8.1 | 4.6 |

election. Even Russia's most successful political party did not consider itself capable of mobilizing sufficient support for a presidential bid.

The second systemic factor that has had a decisive influence on the formation of political parties in Russia is the voting system used in parliamentary elections. The collapse of the old Soviet order, and its last vestiges in the parliament forcibly dissolved in 1993, provided a clean canvas on which a designer democracy could be created. With a politically literate population, an array of Western models to choose from, and an urgency born of the perceived need for stability after the upheavals of 1992 and 1993, the long evolutionary process of party creation in the West was neither a necessity nor an option. An electoral system was therefore designed ostensibly to foster the speedy creation of nationwide political parties.[8] The system adopted is a mixed proportional and majoritarian system. Half of the 450 deputies in the lower house are chosen by a single-round first-past-the-post contest in a constituency. The other 225 deputies are chosen under a party list system. To register a party for the ballot required, in 1995, the collection of 200,000 signatures, with no more than 7 percent being from any one of the Russian Federation eighty-nine regions.[9] To receive seats under the party list section of the ballot, a party must reach a 5 percent threshold. The intention therefore was that parties with a critical mass of geographically widespread support would prosper, and that consequently a limited number of parties with a national base would emerge.

After two elections under this system, in December 1993 and December 1995, it is too soon to judge the success of this attempt to encourage the growth of parties by systemic incentives. The marked failure of the growth of parties on the ballot paper from 13 to 43 from

1993 to 1995 may only be a short-term phenomenon, as the results of the 1995 election meant that only four parties (CPRF, LDPR, Our Home Is Russia, and Yabloko[10]) passed the 5 percent mark. Consequently, the election strengthened these parties at the expense of their thirty-nine rivals. However, there are a number of factors that have undermined and continue to undermine the effectiveness of the party list system as a tool for the creation of multiparty democracy with national parties.

First, for a supposedly proportional electoral system it has proved itself thoroughly unproportional, producing in 1995 "the most disproportional election result of any free and fair proportional election" with a proportionality some 49 percentage points away from perfect proportionality, compared with an average of 6 percent for Western proportional-representation systems and 21 percent for first-past-the-post systems.[11] A system that effectively disenfranchises half of the voters on the party list ballot can scarcely lay claim to creating a link between the electorate and the parliament. Second, the relative weakness of parliament, as noted above, means that the seemingly rational process of amalgamating small parties that draw votes from the same support base so as to maximize the chances of success under the list system gives way in the face of the larger goal of the presidency. A potential presidential candidate will have more to gain in terms of national publicity through heading up a separate party—each party on the ballot received political broadcasts—than through membership in a large party winning seats in an emasculated parliament. Third, even leading politicians without realistic presidential ambitions can still enhance their chances of election to the parliament as a party leader by using the system. If they set up their own party and themselves stand in a single-member constituency seat, then they are given national prominence through the party-list campaign and their local campaign is effectively financed by the state.[12]

## A NATIONAL IDEA

What was required in the normative ideal of postcommunist transition was the *rapid* creation of a multiparty system. Russia had to be governed, and there was both a commitment on the part of President Yeltsin and a consensus amongst the elite and populace alike that some form of multiparty democracy was the preferred form of government.[13] In practice this would mean the speedy elite-led creation of parties in Russia, rather than the lengthy evolutionary development of parties from the bottom up centered on socioeconomic cleavages. In a number of the post-Soviet states the nationalist protest against the control of Moscow had been taken up and assimilated by the republican Communist Party, thereby providing a measure of mass support for a transmuting party already holding power. These were states whose experience of the Soviet endgame was double-rejective:[14] a rejection of Soviet communism and of Russian imperialism. In Russia, however, there had not really been such a possibility. The party in power did not have the option of jettisoning a perceived occupying power and presenting itself as thereby made new. The revolution of 1991 could only be anti-Communist not anti-Russian. Therefore, the old single-party structure crumbled, and any mass support for an end to the Soviet era was dissipated across a range of opposition groups, rather than focused through the ruling party. Where mass support was brought to bear it was in support of individuals, and in particular support for Boris Yeltsin in the 1991 Russian presidential election, when he polled 57 percent of the vote securing a clear first-round majority over all the other candidates put together.

The oft-touted concept of embryonic civil society providing the seedbed for political parties was arguably never a serious option on the ground. The development of civil society in the USSR had been stifled by the dominance of the party-state until the late 1980s when the relative freedoms of Gorbachev's reforms allowed the emergence of "informal organisations." These groups, however, were ill-suited to serve a representative function as they had few resources, their structures were organizationally loose, access to official power was virtually nonexistent, and their policy agendas remained vague and poorly articulated.[15]

Opposition groups that might have been thought to constitute embryonic party formations can be broadly termed the *neformaly* or informals. These were groups, often single-issue based, who increasingly took advantage of the relative freedoms of the late 1980s to enter the arena of public debate. They were not all specifically political groupings in their causes, but were certainly political in their very action of being nonstate, therefore informal, organizations. There had long been a tradition of clubs and informal discussion circles in both prerevolutionary Russia, and, more secretively, in the Soviet era.[16] An important part of their raison d'être was that they were participating in independent activity, and as a generic grouping were less than willing to respond to Gorbachev's promptings that society should become more involved in the running of the state. The *neformaly* were as often focused on social issues as on political demands. However, from 1988 onwards, with the formation of the Democratic Union, more specifically political groups began to emerge. However, they were not parties *qua* parties, but rather relatively small coalitions taking the first steps toward articulating democratic demands. Democratic Union had its origins in two human rights monitoring groups. It was interested far more in protest politics than participatory politics. Whilst refusing to take part in the tentatively multicandidate elections of 1989 and 1990, it organized a series of mass rallies and protests, a similar tactic to that employed by opposition movements in the national republics of the Soviet Union. The difference was, however, that the Russian opposition lacked, as noted above, a real national idea to unite people across the vast territory of Russia. Other democratic forces took a more conciliatory line when it came to involvement in elections. The largest such group was Nikolai Travkin's Democratic Party of Russia (DPR), which formed in May 1990 and within a year had a membership of over 30,000.

The challenge of finding a national idea to replace the collapsing Soviet ideology led in two broad directions that presage the developing cleavages of the 1990s. A common concept amongst opposition groups on the collapse of the USSR was the belief that the Bolshevik revolution of 1917 had arrested the development of Russian democracy. Pointing to the period of the provisional government in Petrograd between February and October 1917 and the forcible dissolution by the Bolsheviks of the Constituent Assembly in 1918, the case was put that the end of the Communist Party's undemocratic domination of Russia meant that the development of Russian democracy could continue. Therefore, groups such as the Social Democrats and the Constitutional Democrats sought to present themselves as the successors of their prerevolutionary counterparts,[17] drawing on the idea of the development of Russian democracy. Other groups were more explicitly westward-looking in their search for identity, for example the Christian Democratic groups that emerged from 1989 onwards. They were not drawing on any Russian tradition of Christian Democracy, as no such tradition exists, but rather on the European tradition that was incidentally undergoing something of a resurgence at the end of the 1980s.[18] These groups though, whether seeking identity in Russian or Western traditions, were seeking to implant what had developed elsewhere (either temporally or spatially) into the specific circumstance of the Soviet collapse. They lacked the fundamental requirements of party building, having no social base, no mass support let alone membership, and limited elite involvement.

The new political cleavages that began to consolidate in 1992–93 reflected both the central ideological questions of Russia's post-Soviet existence and the pragmatic issues of state building. The grand questions concerned Russia's national idea, and manifested themselves in the coming together of nationalists and communists into a "red-brown alliance" protesting the Westernizing stance of Yeltsin and his government.[19] Reform efforts in the immediate post-Soviet period concentrated on the application of "shock therapy" in the economic sphere. Short-term economic results, not surprisingly, accelerated along the downward path of the late Soviet period. Living standards and output fell dramatically, thereby providing a ready base of support to those bemoaning the adoption of Western economic ideas. The other major rallying cry for nationalist and national-communists alike was the perceived plight of Russians who lived in the former Soviet republics bordering Russia. Over 25 million of the total Russian population of the Soviet Union found themselves living abroad after the collapse of the USSR.[20]

As noted above, in the Soviet era the CPSU did embody the national idea—communism—chosen by the rulers. With the collapse of communism as both a system and, for the majority of the Russian population, a desirable ideology, the national idea that has filled the vacuum created by the CPSU's demise has been broad Russian nationalism. Across the political spectrum, politicians have increasingly adopted nationalism, which in the Russian case is synonymous with "Great Powerism," at the level of both policy and symbol. Scarcely a serious contender in the 1996 presidential election did without the photo-opportunity of a meeting with leading figures of the Russian Orthodox Church, the clearest symbol of a commitment to Russian uniqueness. In terms of policy consensus, in December 1994 Boris Yeltsin met with the committee chairmen of both chambers of parliament. There was therefore a wide range of political opinion represented, much of it anti-Yeltsin in terms of domestic policy. However, consensus was reached on the question of "Great Powerism," and all participants agreed that this was an idea everyone could work for. A broad consensus exists within this place of agreement for the increased integration, and therefore Russian domination, of the Commonwealth of Independent States (CIS).

In tandem with this broad increase in nationalism, however, has been the emergence of regionalism with the separatist tendencies of the Soviet breakup continuing to be played out in the Russian Federation and particularly in the ethnic republics. The war in Chechnya between 1994 and 1996 brought this issue dramatically to the fore, but Chechnya was no isolated manifestation of ethnic and regional feeling. By the end of 1995, nine of Russia's twenty-one republics had signed a "bilateral treaty" with Moscow.[21]

The electoral arrangements outlined above were designed to avoid the promotion of separatist and regionalist policies on the national stage by means of the 5 percent threshold and the requirement for a broad geographical spread in terms of signature collection by parties seeking registration. Furthermore, the upper house of the Russian parliament, the Council of the Federation, was specifically created to represent the regions. Each region has two representatives regardless of its size or status. These representatives were directly elected to the upper house in

1993, but now a seat in the upper house comes with the posts of head of the executive and head of the legislature in each region. The Council of the Federation, representing local interests, has operated virtually as a nonparty body in the first four years of its existence. Although various parties put forward candidates at local level in gubernatorial and regional legislature elections in the latter half of 1996, there has been a marked tendency for victorious candidates to withdraw from ideological party stances and party discipline, and for factions in the upper house to form around economic issues.

As a result of these factors, regionalism has been reflected in party formation both in terms of the weakness of any regional or ethnically based parties on a national level, and the weakness of national parties at a regional level. In the 1995 parliamentary elections there were only two parties ("89 Regions of Russia" and "the All-Russian Muslim Social Movement") that could be considered to have a specifically regional or ethnic stance. They received 0.06 and 0.57 percent of the vote respectively. The Agrarian Party of Russia, which might arguably be placed in the category of having a specifically regional policy slate, has fared significantly better, receiving 8 percent of the party list vote in 1993 and nearly 4 percent in 1995. However, both the conservative policy stance and the voting returns of the Agrarians show that they could not lay claim to representing the rural community as a whole.[22]

If regional and ethnic parties failed to penetrate the national agenda significantly, what about national party penetration in the regions? The volatility of the electorate and the fact that the major parties are actively seeking to consolidate regional support in Russia combine to make a definitive conclusion difficult as the establishment and consolidation of a party system in Russia appears to be a center-outwards project, and therefore, if consolidation is to take place, then most of the regions will lag behind the urban areas of European Russia in appropriating a party system. Recent research, however, concludes that the parties in Russia during the State Duma elections of 1995 behaved as primarily urban formations and generally did not penetrate into the ethnic republics and regions, particularly in terms of recruiting ethnically non-Russian candidates.[23]

## CONCLUSION: POLICY IMPACT

What do the institutional and ideological specifics of Russian party formation following the collapse of the old Soviet order reveal concerning the role of "party" in the Russian polity? From the beginning of the post-Soviet state-building process, parties appear to have been marginalized by elite, electorate, and system. Take for example, the Democratic Party of Russia (DPR). The DPR accepted the importance of strong parties in order to develop a democratic state, its membership grew rapidly, and it had all the appearances of becoming the sort of party that might influence the Russian polity after the collapse of the USSR. The history of this party, however, models a number of the difficulties experienced in the post-Soviet period in Russia when it comes to party formation.

First, it was itself an amalgam of interests. The *neformaly* background of Russian opposition parties in the early 1990s meant that when parties did form up they often did so for tactical reasons, rather than for reasons of deep-rooted common cause. The DPR, for example, drew support from reformist writers, middle-ranking military officers, the anti-Stalinist *Memorial* group, and the Confederation of Labour.[24] The links between the various groups that came together to form parties—or more often, during the antiparty euphoria of 1989–92, blocs and associations—could easily be broken. Party discipline was rarely applied or accepted. Party identification was based on leaders rather than programs. Rivalry due to the personal ambitions of leaders led to factionalism and splits. In April 1991, for example, the DPR split as the program put forward by world chess champion Gary Kasparov was rejected.

Such splits have bedeviled the reformist parties in particular throughout the post-Soviet period in Russia. The party that won the most seats in the 1993 parliamentary election was Russia's Choice, led by former prime minister Yegor Gaidar. Although it had been beaten in the party-list ballot, its performance in the single-member constituencies meant that it beat the LDPR overall. However, between 1993 and 1995, out of the Gaidar-led Russia's Choice there emerged six parties to contest the 1995 election: Russia's Democratic Choice, Democratic Russia, "Forward Russia," the Pamfilova-Gurov-Lysenko bloc, Common Cause, and Our Home Is Russia.[25] The on/off negotiations on possible mergers between these and other reformist groups indicated repeatedly that presidential ambitions were more of a hindrance to cooperation than policy differences.

The extent to which political parties have managed to influence the policies and institutions of post-Soviet state building in Russia seems at first glance therefore to have been minimal. Their electoral activities have focused on the lower house of a two-tier parliament with few levers of control in relation to the executive. To a large extent the executive has been insulated from democratic party politics, with some institutional arrangements—and therefore political behavior—more redolent of the old Soviet order than of a new democratic regime.[26] There has never been a democratic regime change in Russia, and the current ruling executive relies on no party for its power. Nonetheless, it is possible to underplay the role of parties in the Russian polity since 1993. Although the success of the LDPR in 1993 and the CPRF in 1995 did not translate into direct access to decision-making power, their role in representing the views of disaffected voters seems to have influenced policy formation in the executive. Evidence for this is, by nature of the hypothesis, not straightforward. There are no reliable measurements of influence. Opinion polls, however, demonstrate that cleavage structures, albeit weak, do underlie support for these parties,[27] and these large groups of the population influence policymakers.

Considering the 1995 election, the CPRF vote is predominantly made up of older voters and workers with low levels of income and education. The LDPR electorate was similar in terms of income and education, but by and large younger and more likely to be male.[28] That so large an opposition vote exists in Russia has clearly impacted the policy agenda of Yeltsin, the populist *par excellence*, and his executive. After the surprising success of the LDPR in 1993, Russian foreign policy, Zhirinovsky's central campaign issue, moved firmly toward a more Eurasian, Russian nationalist stance.[29] Similarly, the ill-fated invasion of Chechnya in 1994 appears to have stemmed partly from the belief that a quick victory would boost Yeltsin's image as a man who would act as firmly and decisively as a Zhirinovsky to defend the territorial integrity of Russia.

The impact of the CPRF following their 1995 election success was complicated by the fact that the results clearly marked Zyuganov as Yeltsin's main rival in the 1996 presidential election, and to speak well of his opponent's policy stance might not have boosted Yeltsin's electoral chances. Since 1996, however, there has been a marked move toward co-opting some of the policies and personnel of the CPRF into the executive. Aman Tuleev, who ran on the presidential ballot as an "insurance policy" for Zyuganov and then withdrew shortly before the first round so that his potential voters would back Zyuganov, was appointed minister for CIS affairs in the Russian government shortly after the election. Zyuganov himself has regular meetings with the prime minister, and a number of observers see at least a section of the CPRF as becoming increasingly identified with the regime and playing the role of loyal opposition.

Despite the lack of *de jure* power achieved by the most successful political parties in Russia since 1993, therefore, they have clearly managed to have an impact of some significance on the policy process. However, this influence nonetheless relies on the degree to which the executive can be influenced. To build a party of power and not just influence in Russia today means the building of a presidential party. The question then arises, what comes first, the party or the leader? In the case of presidential "democracy from scratch," the leader comes first. In which case, the drawbacks of a large party organization, with the inflexibilities of organization and accountability, are clear. Yeltsin's success in the 1996 election, where media bias in his favor seriously undermined the fairness of the elections,[30] demonstrated the media fulfilling the role of link between electorate and candidate, though Yeltsin maintained significant organizational links through regional authorities and a number of parties and movements that backed his presidential bid.

Yeltsin's continued postelection reluctance to tie himself to any particular party—matched by the fact that two of the favorites to succeed him, Aleksandr Lebed and Yurii Luzhkov, also have no established party backing—suggests that the struggle for power in Russia will continue within a broad "regime coalition" not given to the perceived policy and organizational inflexibilities of parties. On the other hand, the disproportional results of the 1995 parliamentary election did create a distinctive group of four parties, whose leaders would all hope to use their parties as a basis not only to mobilize support for presidential bids, but also as a tool for organizing political action in the legislature and the regional polities. The only conclusion to be drawn with any certainty at this stage is that the party system in Russia is not yet firmly established.

## NOTES

1. Stephen White, Richard Rose, and Ian McAllister, *How Russia Votes* (Chatham, N.J.: Chatham House, 1997), p. 51.

2. The institutions in question were: courts, police, civil service, old trade unions, patriotic associations, new trade unions, foreign experts advising government, private enterprises, church, army, peasants' organizations, mass media, President Yeltsin, parliament, government, and political parties.

3. The New Russia Barometer is organized by the Centre for the Study of Public Policy, University of Strathclyde. See Richard Rose and Evgeny Tikhomirov, *Trends in the New Russian Barometer 1992–1995*, Studies in Public Policy, No. 256 (Glasgow: University of Strathclyde, 1995).

4. Arfon Rees (ed.), *The Soviet Communist Party in Disarray* (Basingstoke, U.K.: Macmillan, 1992).

5. White, Rose, and McAllister, *How Russia Votes*, p. 51.

6. Matthew Wyman, "Developments in Russian Voting Behaviour: 1993 and 1995 Compared," *Journal of Communist Studies and Transition Politics* 12.3 (September 1996): 277–92.

7. Edwin Bacon, "The Russian Presidential Election of 1996: Electoral Systems, Multipartism and the Depth of Democratisation," Annual Conference of the Centre for Russian and East European Studies, the University of Birmingham, Windsor, June 1996.

8. Richard Sakwa, *Russian Politics and Society* (London: Routledge, 1996), p. 105.

9. Our Home Is Russia is led by former Russian Prime Minister Viktor Chernomyrdin and is the "party of power," the nearest the Russian political system has come to a presidential party under Boris Yeltsin. Yabloko, led by reformist economist Grigorii Yavlinskii, styled itself as the "democratic opposition" to the Yeltsin regime.

10. In 1993 100,000 signatures were required to register a party, with no more than 15 percent being from any one of Russia's regions.

11. White, Rose, and McAllister, *How Russia Votes*, p. 227.

12. Wyman, "Developments in Russian Voting Behaviour."

13. Matthew Wyman, *Public Opinion in Postcommunist Russia* (Basingstoke, U.K.: Macmillan, 1997), p. 142.

14. Leslie Holmes, "Normalisation and Legitimation in Postcommunist Russia," in *Developments in Russian and Post-Soviet Politics*, ed. Stephen White, Alex Pravda, and Zvi Gitelman (Basingstoke, U.K.: Macmillan, 1994), p. 322.

15. M. Steven Fish, *Democracy from Scratch: Opposition and Regime in the New Russian Revolution* (Princeton, N.J.: Princeton University Press, 1995), p. 60.

16. Richard Sakwa, "The Development of the Russian Party System," in *Elections and Political Order in Russia*, ed. P. Lentini (Budapest: Central European University Press, 1995), p. 171.

17. John Keep, *Last of the Empires: A History of the Soviet Union, 1945–1991* (Oxford: Oxford University Press, 1995), p. 389.

18. Richard Sakwa, "Christian Democracy in Russia," *Religion, State and Society in Russia* 20.2 (1992): 136–68.

19. Walter Laqueur, *Black Hundred: The Rise of the Extreme Right in Russia* (New York: Harper Perennial, 1994).

20. Sakwa, *Russian Politics and Society*, p. 345.

21. Ibid., p. 189.

22. White, Rose, and McAllister, *How Russia Votes*, p. 146.

23. John T. Ishiyama, "The Russian Proto-Parties and the National Republics: Integrative Organizations in a Disintegrating World?" *Communist and Post-Communist Studies* 29.4 (December 1996): 395–411.

24. Sakwa, *Russian Politics and Society*, p. 147.

25. Michael McFaul and Nikolai Petrov, *Previewing Russia's 1995 Parliamentary Elections* (Moscow: Carnegie Endowment, 1995).

26. Edwin Bacon, "Russia's Security Council: Institutional Continuity During Transition," in J. Stanger and G. Stoker, eds., *Contemporary Political Studies, 1997* (Nottingham: Political Studies Association of the United Kingdom, 1997), pp. 761–71.

27. Wyman, "Developments in Russian Voting Behaviour."

28. Ibid.

29. Neil Malcolm, Alex Pravda, Margot Light, and Roy Allison, *Internal Factors in Russian Foreign Policy* (Oxford: Clarendon Press, 1996).

30. Bacon, "The Russian Presidential Election of 1996."

# CHAPTER 12

# Parties and the Millennium

## Susan J. Tolchin

The dinosaurs that once roamed the earth disappeared as soon as they failed to adapt. Do political parties face a similar fate? Will they become extinct as surely as the brontosaurus, whose brain was too small to figure out its changing environment?

The book's theme targets political parties as symbols of the old order, destined to be eclipsed as society lurches toward the millennium. On each continent, nations have endured massive upheavals that have resulted in historic shifts in power. Political parties play central roles in these dramas, often leveraging the forces of change, at other times reacting to them. Witness the transformation of the Communist Party in the former Soviet Union and its satellite countries; the eclipse of the Institutional Revolutionary Party (PRI) that dominated Mexico for most of the twentieth century; and the seizure of Congress by the Republican Party in the United States after forty years in the minority.

Does the "collapse of the old order" signal the disintegration of political parties? Do not failed political leaders take the party apparatus down with them? Or do the ongoing demises of the *ancien régimes* denote instead the collapse of the status quo, with political parties the willing ciphers of historic change?

Judging from the past, it is clear that parties are not dinosaurs; to the contrary, they seem to be infinitely adaptable to change. In fact, parties reflect society with a response rate far speedier than legislatures or public officials.

At their best, parties are a metaphor of society, reflecting all the confusion and ambivalence so characteristic of a changing world. Take the powerful trend in industrialized nations toward the *privatization* of the public sector: Celebrating Bastille Day in 1997 with dozens of fighter jets and military helicopters roaring overhead, French President Jacques

Chirac called for the state to reduce its role in commercial sector activities. Seeing no irony between his own words and the flamboyance of the government-supported military parade surrounding him, Chirac's message sounded a warning shot over the bow of France's new leftist government. If this uneasy coalition's leaders neglected to continue privatizing state-run companies, implied the conservative Chirac, the economy would falter and the loss of jobs would continue to plague the nation.[1] Indeed, even China is trying to sell off its numerous state-run industries, a policy that would send Mao spinning in his grave but an indication nonetheless of the strength of this trend.

Chirac's forceful statement also revealed another theme engulfing political parties in modern industrial states: the push toward *free markets in a global society*. This means tearing down trade barriers, opening up borders to goods and services, and allowing the global marketplace (as defined by multinational corporations, economists, key political leaders, and financial elites from the World Trade Organization, the World Bank, and other multilateral organizations) to determine prices. In other words, Chirac sought to convey in the strongest possible terms the threat that if his colleagues persisted in their refusal to winnow down the nation's top-heavy public sector (translation: too many bureaucrats) or neglected to sacrifice its agriculture and other home-grown products for the general good of the European Union (EU), France would be ostracized by members of the EU and would soon find its products excluded in the competition for global OMP markets in the United States and the Far East.

Countering the free market advocates in party councils are union leaders and their allies, who argue for the equally compelling but politically less powerful issue of jobs: how to create them; where to get them; how to grow them; and how to keep them. This appears to be more of an issue for European political parties, where citizens regard jobs as an obligation of the state, but after repeated downsizings have captured the public's attention in the United States and Canada, employment is slowly becoming a more important issue in those countries as well.[2]

Decentralization, or devolution, has also emerged as another important motif driving the behavior of parties. Depending on a nation's federal structure, an increasing number of political leaders seek ways to unload the power of national government down to the states. Viewed as a shrewd tactic, politicians know that by shifting the political burden to other government entities they are also removing themselves from much of the public blame and anger that has become the curse of modern elections.

The new Labour government in Great Britain has pledged to decentralize the United Kingdom, for example, with Prime Minister Tony

Blair in the peculiar stance of actually encouraging the Scots to elect their own parliament independent of Whitehall in the referendum of September 11, 1997. No British leader since 1707 has moved so swiftly to reduce national power, offering Scotland more local power, but leaving national economic policy and foreign relations to the Crown. The outcome of the referendum was curious, yet typical of nations approaching the millennium: a resounding "yes" vote for a parliament and an equally clear "no" vote for new taxes to pay for this new legislative independence![3]

*Corruption* also plans an important role in determining the direction of political parties, long viewed as the source of iniquity in politics. In Mexico, Italy, and the United States, accelerating charges of political corruption have contributed greatly to uprooting the electoral status quo. Indeed, the public is beginning to see corruption in political parties as the root of other evils, such as inefficiency in Italy and authoritarianism in Mexico.

At this time the United States finds itself embroiled in a fight over campaign financing that involves the question of how the two major political parties raise money for presidential elections. In fact, the root of most ethical problems affecting members of Congress as well as the president pertain to campaign finance, with a singular lack of clarity as to what is illegal, immoral, or simply unethical. The real conundrum in the United States is how to raise money without violating the law, since the key to success for high-level party officials is learning the loopholes, some large enough to accommodate a Mack truck.[4]

John Huang, the Commerce Department employee who raised a great deal of "soft money" for the Clinton reelection campaign, received "extended training" before assuming his post with the Democratic National Committee (DNC). He learned what was "right, what's wrong, what's legal, [and] what's illegal," testified Richard Sullivan, former finance director of the DNC between 1995 and 1996 at hearings before the Senate Government Affairs Committee on July 9, 1997.[5] What the hearings, chaired by Senator Fred Thompson, a Republican of Tennessee, have revealed is that no one from either party has mastered the Byzantine intricacies of the electoral laws; that officials and candidates from both parties have ignored the laws with impunity; and that the desire for change will continue to be stifled by incumbents who fear changing the status quo. Campaign finance reform was pronounced dead in the water by both houses of Congress in late September 1997.

The problem for both parties is that voters are becoming increasingly sophisticated about issues involving political corruption. They are demanding more *transparency*, meaning more visibility, in order to decide what is right and wrong with the system. As media scrutiny over party activities increases, the flaws in the system inevitably get exposed; voters grow angrier; and parties find they can no longer count on a stable electoral base.[6] How else can the Ross Perot phenomenon be explained? When a third party and its candidate take nearly 20 percent of the vote in a presidential election, as they did in 1992, unseating a sitting president and throwing the entire election up for grabs.

The big question involves the future of parties in a post–Cold War world. Are these issues of *corruption, transparency, privatization, less government,* and *free markets* merely a sign of "millennial fever," the mass hysteria that tends to affect nations as the new century approaches? Or are they signs of a more substantive dilemma: the question of whether parties are adequate to the task of governance in the post-Cold War era?

Some of the questions that relate to the larger issues have moved to the front burner, namely:

- Are parties obsolete? Are they being replaced by single-issue advocates, who reflect small but determined constituencies? Or by large, but equally determined constituencies, such as the Christian Coalition? Or by political consultants, like Richard Morris, the mastermind of President Clinton's reelection, who represent whoever can afford to pay them?

- Do parties address major issues of our times, such as *jobs* or *globalization*? Or are they solely pragmatic, absorbing issues only after they have proven their merit in outside arenas?

- How do the parties deal with today's bipolar issues? Have they retained their traditional roles as vehicles for compromise? Or are they buffeted by the ideological pressures that are fragmenting the nation and preventing consensus? This dilemma has confronted the U.S. Republican Party for the better part of the 1990s: 40% of the party identifies with the philosophy of the Christian right, while only 10% of the electorate finds these views acceptable. How can a party win a national presidential election faced with that disparity? More specifically: How can Republicans field candidates who can win acceptance by the mainstays of the party, yet appeal to a broader national constituency at the same time?[7]

- Can parties retain their historic role as links between citizens and the state, in effect, making government more accessible to the public? Paradoxically, as parties become more "professional" and less inclined toward traditional practices like patronage for party workers, they inevitably become more elitist: indeed, the image of wealthy donors sleeping in the Lincoln Bedroom and sipping coffee with the president tarnishes the party as well as the chief executive. Meanwhile, the clubhouse, once the neighborhood unit that humanized government, recedes into the distant past as the parties "internationalize," professionalize, and serve difference masters.

Whatever their incarnation, it appears that parties are here to stay; that instead of heading for extinction, they are jumping on bandwagons that sound themes fully congruent with modern society. In this way, they can easily adapt to their new environments, rarely leading but determined to cling to power in the only way possible: by modifying, adjusting, and tailoring their philosophies to the fashion of the times.

## PARTY UPHEAVALS AND RESPONSES

### The United States

Miraculously, Americans live with deep divisions in their ideology, ethnicity, religion, and racial background, yet sustain a relatively high level of consensus in their politics. What keeps them together are two beliefs that transcend their differences, (1) that hard work leads to rewards; and (2) that "government does more to hinder the American dream than enhance it," according to pollsters Peter Hart, a Democrat, and Robert Teeter, a Republican.

John Kenneth White and Philip John Davies relate this conundrum to current problems in party politics in their essay on "The American Experience." Their analysis draws together all the factors that have worked to divide Americans and render the political system "antiparty and expensive."[8]

Americans need not look far for examples of dissatisfaction with government:

- The role of the media has exploded, with technology and new attitudes forming a new crucible of discontent. "Virtual reality" in voters' living rooms has brought a new level of exposure of events heretofore relegated to the pages of daily newspapers, television clips, or back-room discussions. The process of witnessing the Watergate hearings first-hand through their televisions screens, and watching the burning villages in Vietnam created a now level of disgust on the part of Americans for their political leadership.[9]

- The role of politicians in exacerbating the public discontent has also accelerated. President Jimmy Carter talked about a "public malaise," a frustration and crisis of confidence about government that he believed he could cure through preaching about it. His successor, Ronald Reagan, addressed the "malaise" by acting confident, "walking tall," and linking himself and his party with the anti-government sentiments so prevalent today among American voters.

- The Perot phenomenon. Also known as when voters would rather vote for an unknown than for candidates representing the two political parties. "In 1995," write the authors, "60 percent told the Gallup Organization that they would like to see a third major party take root." In 1996, the two major parties were so frightened of Perot and what he represented that they refused to allow him, and his highly articulate vice presidential, candidate, Dr. Pat Choate, to enter the televised pre-election debate.

- The decline of the middle class. This includes fears of further downsizings; the inability of those who were downsized to adjust; the increasing wage gap—the United States is the only industrialized country in which the wage gap between rich and poor is widening; and the eroding earning power of wages.

- Divided government. For the last two election cycles Americans have grappled with a Republican Congress and a Democratic president. As indicated by the polls, many citizens are content with this state of affairs; after all, that is what the separation of powers, and checks and balances is all about, isn't it? It wasn't until voters experienced the full consequences of divided government, which meant two full government shutdowns from 1995 to 1996, and "gridlock" between the White House and Congress on practically every significant public policy issue, that people sat up and took notice. The sight of their nation's inept political leadership as it confronted the shutdowns only accelerated the public's cynicism toward government.[10]

- Last but not least is the country's sorry state of financing elections. The Thompson hearings have only hastened the sense of "virtual reality," as the actual realities of political funding keep emerging under the harsh glare of the klieg lights. The Democratic National Committee spent $85 million from July 1995 until election day *on television ads alone*, according to White and Davies. What is regarded today as excessive spending in the realm of "soft money" was necessary then, argue party leaders, in order to compete with Republicans, who have traditionally been more successful in fund-raising. Success speaks for itself: the brainchild of Richard Morris, who argued that the only way to get out the president's message and attack the Contract with America was through television advertising. But the success was short-lived. Clinton won, but he was saddled with a Republican Congress, very reminiscent of the

1980 election, when Jimmy Carter and the DNC hogged their soft money for the presidential campaign, then lost not only the election but many of the congressional seats as well. Clinton was also forced to endure months of congressional hearings, choreographed by angry Republicans, on the subject of how he raised so much "soft money" for his presidential campaign.

Tens of millions of dollars in television advertising, most of it negative, won the election—as it did for Republicans in Congress—but it also spun a web of distrust between the public and the parties. Even though presidential campaigns have traditionally skirted election financing laws by allowing the parties to fund their own elections with "soft money," the public disgust reached elevated levels in the 1996 campaign, and led to the Thompson hearings and other attempts to rein in election activities that in the minds of the voters had spun way out of control.[11]

No wonder Americans are suddenly so suspicious of parties and politics? So skeptical, in fact, that their confidence in government has steadily declined from a rate of 77% in the 1960s, to less than 12% in the 1990s. That level of negativity has created a very serious state of affairs for political leaders, leaving them mystified as well as hostile toward the electorate. Between 1994 and 1996, for example, dozens of senators and members of Congress who were considered "moderate" left office, rather than confront the animosity of the voters. Sen. James Exon, Democrat of Nebraska, attributed his decision not to seek reelection in 1996 to the "vicious polarization of the electorate . . . that has all but swept aside the former preponderance of reasonable discussion. . . . The 'hate level' fed by attack ads has . . . become the measurement of a successful campaign."[12]

Yet political "parties have historically provoked an ambivalent response from the leaders who are supposed to like them and from the public they are supposed to serve," wrote White and Davis. It is just getting much worse today, when the "traditional Democrat and Republican duopoly has come under suspicion." So much so that party organizations have suffered; there are ever lower levels of party activity; and membership has declined to under 5 percent of the population. Pride in personal independence has grown as party loyalty has dwindled; more people than ever vote for the "person," and not the "party." Voters today do not realize the damage this has done; even the worst outcomes of divided government have not convinced the public to vote for candidates from the same party for the executive and legislative branches.

The authors blame the Federal Election Campaign Act for weakening the parties, an "unintended consequence" that diminished the parties and substituted them with issue-based advocacy groups. In other words, voters get faster results by directly targeting politicians than by working through the party. Issue orientation has not helped the party system: On the contrary, it has led to more disillusionment on the part of the voters; as well as the encouragement of political aspirants who tend to be charismatic, wealthy, or manipulative—for example, Ross Perot, Steve Forbes, Pat Buchanan, and Newt Gingrich.

## Upheaval in the United Kingdom

Britain quickly followed the international trend toward party upheaval. In power for eighteen years, the Conservative Party took a beating in 1997 that left it without representation in Scotland, Wales, or most of England's most populated cities.

The Labour Party, led by the young, charismatic Tony Blair, out-performed any of the great twentieth-century victories, including the "achievements of Clement Atlee and the Labour Party in 1945 or Margaret Thatcher and the Conservatives in 1983," according to Tim Hames, a reporter for the *Times of London*, and a lecturer at Oxford University.[13] The Conservatives, on the other hand, continued to feed off the reputation of the colorful and eloquent Margaret Thatcher, replacing her with the drab and rather tired-looking John Major. Meanwhile, the party leadership neglected to address the decline in party membership, as well as its own rigid, hierarchical power structure.

Commentators had been predicting Labour's demise for many years, but the party survived by vigorously reforming itself. Motivated by the loss of four general elections, it recognized the "mismatch between its traditional party structure and the society and electorate it faced." In Labour's case, it meant moving more toward the middle of the political spectrum, and "firmly" crushing the left wing of the party. Although Labour remained allied with the trades union movement, it also decreased its influence at the same time. Most important, the party modernized its management system by:

- computerizing membership lists,
- personalizing an appeal for ideas and new members,
- increasing the sources of funding beyond the trades unions (in 1980, 90% of all funds came from trades unions; by 1996, the figure was less than half),
- mastering the media and streamlining its message, and
- "Americanising," modeling itself after the Clinton administration and the Democratic Party.

Events also conspired to help Labour. As the British public's strong reaction to the death of Princess Diana revealed, the cold, hidebound, royalist traditions no longer held much appeal. At the same time, Great Britain, had already witnessed a decline in traditional institutions—a theme prevalent all over the world—such as "mainstream churches [and] sectional interests." A "plethora of new alternative institutions mushroomed," with everything threatened by "individualism, antipathy [to many traditional symbols] and fresh alternatives." Labour also presented a united front when it came to matters involving Britain's role in the European Union, a very controversial issue for voters. The Conservatives, on the other hand, sat by and allowed the single-currency issue to tear the party apart.

Changes in the economy were also critical to Labour's success. An embourgeoisment of the working class was taking place, with the "middle and skilled working class" claiming ever larger shares of the electorate. The jobs issue and the rise in unemployment in the 1980s also helped Labour, as did the manufacturing slump and two recessions. More consumerist voting, along the lines of "what is the party doing for me," also took hold at the time, with increasing public anger focused on the Conservative Party, which was held responsible for current economic woes.

The victory for "New Labour" represented a landslide victory at the time, with the Tories 21-seat majority wiped away. Labour emerged with 419 seats, and a majority of 170, the largest in history, while Conservatives were left with only 165 Members of Parliament, their lowest number since 1906.

The big question in Great Britain today is whether the Conservative Party will regenerate itself along the lines of the Labour Party's efforts. Labour refused to become obsolete. Are the Conservatives able to follow suit?

### Corruption and Blocked Democracy: Italy

Democracies provide their public with the best outlet of all for expressing outrage: the ballot box. In Italy, one reason that patterns of political corruption persisted for the last half century was that political parties had settled into a state of inertia, unwilling to reform or change. And why should they? A joint electoral coalition of Christian Democrats and Communists together consistently polled 60 percent of the vote, leading to an uneasy alliance; between them, they controlled government by pooling their power and their patronage.

It was an uneasy but complacent coalition. By pooling government jobs, the public sector became a joke, synonymous in fact with inefficiency and corruption. Slowly, the very legitimacy of the state began to erode, a situation all the more potent as economic problems grew worse and as the government's inability to control organized crime in the South became more apparent.

Finally, in the 1990s public disgust with government began to emerge in electoral terms. Why did it take so long? Because so many Italians were coopted by so much patronage, and *clientelismo*, a system of doing favors for preferred constituents. The public also reacted to the lack of *transparency*, favoring a more open system.

The "fatal embrace" between the two parties led to party-weakening fights, and to the temptation to continually increase the size of the public sector. By the late 1980s, Italy was known as the economic basket case of Europe, and the old order began to unravel. The collapse of the Soviet Union and the end of the Cold War also hastened the demise of the Communist Party, which reconstituted itself as Social Democrats.

By 1994, the collapse of the old system was complete: new electoral laws created new parties, and the "virgin political class" revealed that more than 71 percent of the deputies had no experience. Although there were still too many parties, at least there was some evidence that voters were occasionally voting for candidates from a party, actually a right-wing three-party coalition (The Forza Italia Party) headed by Silvio Berlusconi, a media tycoon who was soon disgraced and deposed by yet another series of scandals.

A short two years later, the fifty-fourth government since World War II resigned and a new one—a center-left coalition—came to power. The reason: the government's failure to implement the political changes brought about by the "*Tangentopoli*" scandal.[15]

## Economic Reform, Corruption, and Changes in Western Europe

The scandal, which revealed kickbacks amounting to over two-thirds of Italy's public debt to hundreds of local officials and 300 deputies, would probably never have come to light were it not for pressures from the European Union. The EU'S demands for transparency and economic reform affected many nations, and provided the impetus for party reform that had been stalled for so long.

Responding to pressures from the EU, French President Jacques Chirac held elections in France ten months early—a calculated risk that the French public would be as anxious as he was to tighten their belts in the interest of regional unity. His calculated risk did not pay off: French voters instead voiced their discontent about high unemployment and austerity measures designed to get France in line to participate in the conversion to the Euro—the planned uniform currency for the EU.

As a result of the election, the unpopular Prime Minister Alain Juppé resigned, and Socialist leader Lionel Jospin took over, leaving France governed by a left-wing coalition (including the Communist Party) in the legislature, and a Conservative president, Chirac. In other words, a divided government rules France, very similar to the situation in the United States, where people also lack trust in their political parties.

Similar to the United States, Mexico, Italy, and other countries, France also experienced a high level of intraparty fighting, corruption, patronage exposure, unemployment, and increased crime and violence. Following the United States, France also witnessed a surge in anti-immigrant fervor—the National Front Party drew 15.2% of the vote in the 1997 election, from less than 1% of the vote in 1972. The parties in France also moved further from the voters' "demands and preoccupations," according to Colette Ysmal; the gap reflecting even more dramatically their inability to "act as links between the citizen and the State" more focussed on their own interests and ever more remote from the voters' interests.[16]

In Germany, the Christian Democrats have ruled since World War II, but many analysts wonder if that nation will follow Great Britain and France in turning toward the left and jettisoning the party that has held power for the last four governments.[17] Unemployment reached record levels in Germany in 1997, with 4.6 million Germans, or 12 percent of the workforce out of work. Unemployment has become a particularly troubling issue for young people and the former citizens of East Germany, whose expectations of the benefits of unification have long been dashed. Costs of unification have surpassed even the most pessimistic estimates; now Germans worry that their deutsche mark will carry the weaker currencies in the new Euro, which can only further damage their economy. Conversely, the other nations fret that the Germans will dominate the Euro—to the ultimate disadvantage of other countries.[18]

*Corruption, Free Trade, and the*
*NAFTA Nations: Mexico and Canada*

Except for the former Soviet Union, Mexico experienced the greatest upheaval in party government. After sixty-eight years, the longest rule of any party in the world was finally ended when the PRI of Mexico lost control of the lower house, and handed over the reins of power to the left-of-center Democratic Revolution (PRD) candidate, Cuauhtémoc Cardenas, who became mayor of Mexico City.

On August 30, 1997, four opposition parties formed an alliance that gave them 261 seats of the 500 seats in the lower house of Congress. This event, tantamount to a political earthquake, marked the first time in history that the PRI was forced into the minority.

Change is the buzzword now in Mexico, marking the end of what Michael Foley calls "one-party pluralism." What led to the trajectory that brought a "hegemonic party" to the status of "political dinosaur."[19] Many of the same reasons, actually, that led to changes all over the world; only in Mexico, the party held responsibility for monumental excesses in the exercise of power, namely:

- Authoritarianism
- Structural weakness
- Violent repression of student revolts
- Election fraud (documented in Chiapas)
- Constitutional measures that precluded land reform
- Privatization for purposes of rewarding political allies
- Failure of the presidential system
- Corruption
- Unstable currency
- Political scandals, such as the arrest of former President Carlos Salinas's brother Raul, with the revelation that he had hidden between $120 and $300 million in foreign banks.

The big question in Mexico is whether the nation—or the center— can hold without the stability of one-party pluralism. Even with its reputation for corruption, which was known for decades before its demise, the PRI was long credited with holding Mexico together; indeed, Mexico was the only Latin American country "not to have experienced a military coup in the years since the Mexican Revolution (1910–1919)." Can this continue today, with new parties in power, and with the pressures (not unlike the EU and the European nations) on Mexico from Canada and the United States to adhere to the free trade rules of NAFTA, the North American Free Trade Agreement.[20]

Canada has also experienced enormous changes in political power, with NAFTA and regional identities tearing that country apart. The June 1997 elections brought the Liberals back to power, but with only 38 percent of the popular vote, and a bare majority in the legislature. The Conservatives lost the last election because they lacked the flexibility to make policy decisions on the two most important issues to Canadians: NAFTA and the independence of Quebec. Interestingly, trade is a much more important issue to Canadians and Mexicans than it is to

American voters, whose leaders have ironically led Canada and Mexico into the trade wars.

Like Mexico and the United States, transparency was a significant issue in Canada, where myriad scandals tore apart the parties. Neither the Liberals nor the Conservatives were able to stem the inevitable secession of Quebec, nor were they able to deal with any of the bigger issues. According to Arthur Johnson, polls reveal a "growing lack of faith in the ability of parties to grapple with the big problems."[21]

### A Clean Sweep: Out with the Old

Although different in name, the Soviet Union also experienced an era of one-party rule in much the same time period as Mexico. In an important sense, the Communist Party performed one of the most important functions of a political party, according to Edwin Bacon, that of broker between the individual and the state, although the CP was tainted with "negative overtones." The negativity associated with the only political party allowed to exist does not bode well for the future flourishing of political parties; in fact, in a poll where voters were given a list of sixteen institutions, "political parties emerged as the least trusted institution."[22]

The most trusted institution was the Russian Orthodox Church, long suppressed by the party, but the least tainted by communism. No wonder leaders today steer clear of parties; President Boris Yeltsin recently ignored pleas from U.S. political leaders, and endorsed the emergence of the church as a *de facto* established religion in Russia.

Today, the Russians and the nations that used to form the Soviet Union struggle with developing a party system despite their lack of tradition of democratic party government. Yeltsin continues to avoid committing himself to a political party, preferring to concentrate on the economy and develop a presidency not dependent on party organization. Yeltsin saw himself "as representing the Russian people as a whole, and therefore neither wanted to nor saw the need to create a party for himself" or a multiparty structure for the nation.

With no compelling need to build a party structure, Yeltsin commanded an enormous mandate; in the 1991 election he drew 57 percent of the vote, but in the 1996 election, he was forced into a runoff with a Communist rival. Unfortunately, the old Communist Party has begun to reemerge, with many of the same apparatchiks taking the reins; Yeltsin only won 35 percent of the vote, compared to 32 percent for his Communist opponent, Zyuganov. By the summer of 1998, Yeltsin found himself in deep trouble. Blamed for the downward spiral of the Russian economy and faced with a Communist-dominated legislature (Duma),

Yeltsin fought pressures from all sides that demanded his resignation. The real challenge for Russia is finding a sufficiently compelling idea to replace the prevailing Soviet ideology.

Indeed, that remains the challenge for political parties the world over: meeting the needs of the voters; achieving the flexibility to change their views when they prove outdated; and revitalizing their leadership.

## NOTES

The author wishes to thank her research assistant, Andrew Sisk, of the Public Administration Department of George Washington University, for his help.

1. *The New York Times,* July 15, 1997, p. A3.

2. For incisive, comparative analyses of job policies in industrialized countries, see Richard B. Freeman (ed.), Working Under Different Rules (New York: Russell Sage Foundation, 1994).

3. *The New York Times,* September 21, 1997, sec. 4, "The Week in Review," p. 4.

4. For a historical overview of party patronage and political corruption, see Martin and Susan Tolchin, *To the Victor: Political, Patronage from the Clubhouse to the White House* (New York: Random House, 1971).

5. *The News & Observer,* Raleigh, North Carolina, from *The Washington Post News Service,* July 10, 1997, p. 9A.

6. An excellent discussion of the usage of the term "transparency" as well as the concept occurs in the "On Language" column of William Safire, titled "Transparency Totally," in *The New York Times Magazine,* January 4, 1998, p. 4.

7. Clyde Wilcox, *Onward Christian Soldiers? The Religious Right in American Politics* (Boulder, Colo.: Westview Press/HarperCollins, 1996).

8. John Kenneth White and Philip John Davies, "The American Experience: Public Skepticism, Economic Dislocation, and Partisan Decay," in this volume.

9. For additional material on the roles of the media in politics, see Matthew Kerbel, *Remote and Controlled: Media Politics in a Cynical Age* (Boulder, Colo.: Westview Press, 1995).

10. Susan J. Tolchin, *The Angry American: How Voter Rage is Changing the Nation* (Boulder, Colo.: Westview Press/HarperCollins, 1996).

11. Guy Gugliotta, "Campaign Finance Examiners Know Pressures of Money Chase," *Washington Post,* July 8, 1997, p. A13; and "Excerpts From Remarks on First Day of Campaign Finance Hearings," *The New York Times,* July 9, 1997, p. A11.

12. Susan J. Tolchin, *The Angry American,* p. 4.

13. Tim Hames, "The United Kingdom—Change within Continuity," in *The Collapse of the Old Order, op. cit.* Seymour Martin Lipset offers a similarly interesting perspective on the Labour Party's embrace of capitalism, in "The Left Moves Right," *Washington Post,* April 21, 1997, p. A17.

14. Nick carter, "Italy," in this volume.

15. "Right Wing Routed in Italian Elections," *Labor Militant*, International Reports, Summer 1996; and William D. Montalbano, "Right-Wing Billionaire Wins Italian Election," *Los Angeles Times*, March 29, 1994.

16. Colette Ysmal, "French Political Parties: A State within a State," in this volume.

17. Charlie Jeffrey and Charles Lees, "Whither the Old Order?" in this volume.

18. David P. Conradt (ed.), *Germany's New Politics: Parties and Issues in the 1990s* (Tempe, Ariz.: German Studies Review, Arizona State University, 1995).

19. Michael Foley, "Mexico: The End of One-Party Pluralism?" in this volume.

20. See, also: "Mexico Becomes a Competitive Party System," *Party Developments* 32 (September 1997): 1, 23; Molly Ivins, "Viva Mexico's Election," *The News & Observer*, Raleigh, North Carolina, July 9, 1997, p. 15A; and Anthony DePalma, "First Battle in Mexico's New Congress: Tax Cuts," *The New York Times*, August 9, 1997, pp. 1, 4.

21. Arthur Johnson, "Canadian Political Parties: Contemporary Change," in this volume. See also Jeff Kerr and Bryan Thomas, "Campaigns and Elections," 18.7 (August 1997): 32–34.

22. Edwin Bacon, "Russia," in this volume.

# ABOUT THE AUTHORS

*Asher Arian* is Distinguished Professor of Political Science at the Graduate Center of the City University of New York, and Professor at the University of Haifa, Israel. Among his recent publications are *The Second Republic: Politics in Israel*, and *Security Threatened: Surveying Israeli Opinion on Peace and War*.

*Edward Bacon* lectures in Russian politics at the Centre for Russian and East European Studies, the University of Birmingham, England. He was previously a Senior Research Officer in the Foreign and Commonwealth Office, and is the author of *The Gulag at War: Stalin's Forced Labour System in the Light of the Archives* as well as a number of articles on Russian security and politics.

*Nick Carter* is Lecturer in Modern European History at De Montfort University, Leicester, U.K. A specialist in nineteenth- and twentieth-century Italy, he has written on a wide range of subjects from Anglo-Italian relations at the time of Italian unification, to contemporary political corruption in Italy.

*Philip John Davies* is Professor of American Studies at De Montfort University, Leicester, U.K. His most recent work has included *Representing and Imagining America, Political Issues in America: The 1990s Revisited*, and *An American Quarter-Century: U.S. Politics from Vietnam to Clinton*. He has published widely on aspects of U.S. domestic politics and culture. He is Chair of the British Association for American Studies and General Editor of the BAAS Paperback series.

*Michael W. Foley* is Associate Professor of Politics at the Catholic University of America. He has published widely on contemporary Mexican politics, post–civil war El Salvador, and civil society and the "social capital" debate in the United States. A Jennings Randolph Fellow at the United States Institute of Peace for 1997–1998, Professor Foley is working on a book entitled *The Betrayal of Rural Mexico: Failed Development, Peasant Organization, and Insurgency*.

239

*Tim Hames* is a political writer for the *London Times* newspaper. Until 1996, he was a Lecturer in Politics at Oxford University specializing in modern British and American politics.

*Charlie Jeffery* is Reader in German Politics and Deputy Director of the Institute for German Studies, University of Birmingham. He has written extensively on all aspects of European politics and policy, including regional governance and multilevel governance in the EU, German federalism and the adaptation of federal structures to European integration, German party politics, and Austrian political history. He is co-editor of *Regional and Federal Studies*.

*Arthur L. Johnson* is a Professor of American and Canadian History at the State University of New York College at Potsdam. He holds a Ph.D. from the University of Maine. His articles and reviews have appeared in *American Neptune, The American Review of Canadian Studies, Ontario History, Railroad History,* and the *Quarterly* (St. Lawrence County Historical Association).

*Charles Lees* is Lecturer in Politics at the University of Sussex, having completed his Ph.D. researching the processes of coalition formation and maintenance in the German *Lander* at the Institute for German Studies, University of Birmingham. He has recently written on coalition theory, the PDS, the 1994 European elections, German *Land* elections, and environmental politics and policy.

*Rodney Smith* is a Senior Lecturer in Political Science at the University of New South Wales, Australia. He specializes in Australian and comparative politics. He is the editor of *Politics in Australia* and author of a number of articles and chapters on Australian parties, parliaments, and political culture.

*Christopher J. Thornhill* is Dean of the Faculty of Economic and Management Sciences at the University of Pretoria. He is the author of eleven books and numerous articles in professional journals. From 1987–1992, Professor Thornhill was inter alia chairman of the Committee of Investigation into a new system of local government for South Africa, as well as chairman of the Committee of Investigation into Metropolitanization in South Africa. He was also a member of the Local Government Loans Fund Board, the Permanent Finance Liaison Committee, Committee of Investigation into Inter-fiscal Relations and Chairman of the Functions Committee regarding housing budgets in South Africa and the self-governing territories. Professor Thornhill was awarded the Stals prize for Political Sciences and Development Administration in 1995.

*Susan J. Tolchin* is Professor of Public Policy at George Mason University. She has authored or co-authored six books, including *The Angry American: How Voter Rage is Changing the Nation* (Westview/Harper-Collins, 1996); *Selling Our Security: The Erosion of America's Assets* (Knopf, 1992); *Buying Into America: How Foreign Money is Changing the Face of Our Nation* (Times Books/Random House, 1988); *Dismantling America: The Rush to Deregulate* (Houghton Mifflin, 1983); *Clout: Womanpower and Politics* (Coward, McCann & Geoghegan, 1974); and *Toe the Victor: Political Patronage from the Clubhouse to the White House* (Random House, 1971). In 1997, Dr. Tolchin won the Marshall Dimock award for the best lead article in the *Public Administration Review* for 1996, entitled "The Globalist from Nowhere: Making Governance Competitive in the Global Environment." She is also a Fellow of the National Academy of Public Administration, and a national board member of the Cystic Fibrosis Foundation.

*John Kenneth White* is a Professor of Politics at the Catholic University of America. His most recent book, *Still Seeing Red: How the Cold War Shapes the New American Politics*, was published by Westview/Harper-Collins in 1997. He is also the author of *The New Politics of Old Values* (1990) and *The Fractured Electorate* (1983). He is the editor of numerous books including *New York State Today* (1989), *Governing New York State* (1994), *The Politics of Ideas* (1996), and *Challenges to Party Government* (1992). He serves as Vice President of the Center for Party Development, co-chair of the Committee for Party Renewal, and editor of the SUNY Press series on the American presidency.

*Colette Ysmal* is Director of Research in the Centre d'Étude de la Vie politique française (Center for the Study of French Political Life), a research institute of the Fondation nationale de Sciences politiques in Paris. She is particularly interested in political parties in France and in Europe. She is a member of the Editorial Board of the journal *Party Politics*. She has published widely on political parties and party system change and elections and electoral behavior, including *Les Partis politiques sous la Cinquième Republique* (1989) and has recently co-edited, with Piero Ignazi, *The Organization of Political Parties in Southern Europe*.

# INDEX